Realism and 'Reality' in Film and Media

Northern Lights

Film and Media Studies Yearbook 2002

Northern Lights is an annual publication dedicated to studies of film and media. Each yearbook is devoted to a specific theme. In addition, every volume may include articles on other topics as well as review articles.

Northern Lights covers the full range of media – from film and television, the press and radio, to the Internet and other computer media. The editors welcome contributions from all traditions of inquiry within the interdisciplinary field of film and media studies.

Northern Lights reflects the research activities of the Department of Film and Media Studies at the University of Copenhagen, Denmark (www.ifm.ku.dk), and simultaneously serves a forum of interchange for the international community of media and communication researchers.
The yearbook invites scholars from across the field to submit their work to Northern Lights.

Realism and 'Reality' in Film and Media

Edited by
Anne Jerslev

Northern Lights
Film and Media Studies Yearbook 2002

MUSEUM TUSCULANUM PRESS
UNIVERSITY OF COPENHAGEN
2002

Realism and 'Reality' in Film and Media
Northern Lights
Film and Media Studies Yearbook 2002

Series editor: Ib Bondebjerg
Volume editor: Anne Jerslev

Front cover by Veronique van der Neut
Set and printed in Denmark by Narayana Press, Gylling

ISBN: 87 7289 716 3
ISSN: 1601 829X

Published with support from:
The Faculty for the Humanities, University of Copenhagen

The photo on the front cover is
from the Danish film "Idioterne"
by Lars von Trier and shows the
actors Bodil Jørgensen and Anne
Louise Hassing. Photo by Jesper
Jargil. Reproduced with
permission from Zentropa.

Museum Tusculanum Press
University of Copenhagen
Njalsgade 92
DK-2300 Copenhagen S
www.mtp.dk

Contents

Anne Jerslev

Introduction

The theme of the 2002 Yearbook from The Department of Film and Media Studies, University of Copenhagen is "Realism and 'reality' in film and media." It addresses and contributes to the increased interest, both inside and outside academia, in questions of reality and the media in the broadest sense. This interest is found within the institution of television where recent years have witnessed a proliferation of documentary formats, first and foremost so-called 'reality' programs, which have attracted large audiences both in the US and in Europe. It thus seems no coincidence that the hyped 150th anniversary episode of *X-Files,* shown in February 2000 on the Fox network, borrowed its form and style from the famous reality TV magazine *Cops.* The interest in reality is also seen within the institution of film – in the growing audience interest in documentary films. At least in the Scandinavian countries, a number of feature-length documentaries have opened in cinemas in the last few years, meeting great success. The same interest is seen in genre hybrids mixing fictional with documentary codes, such as *The Blair Witch Project,* and it is seen in the great activity generated by the *Dogma 95* project that was created by Danish director Lars von Trier and colleagues, a project that might be regarded as an effort to reduce the distance between the act of filming and the reality being filmed and thus to contribute to an increased feeling of reality in the cinematic experience. The interest is also seen in a slight, but significant shift within fictional TV programs and films, away from irony and intertextuality and towards a variety of realist styles which may, simultaneously, incorporate intertextuality as well as irony as part of their overall realism. And the interest in 'reality' is seen in the growing theoretical focus on issues of 'realism' within film and media studies as well as in interdisciplinary studies and research projects. The contributions to this year's issue of *Northern Lights* join these discussions from both a theoretical and an analytical point of view.

The growing theoretical debate might be regarded as part of an effort to both problematize and move beyond the often radical contestation within postmodernism of any notion of reality in a mediated culture and the theoretical claim of postmodernist positions to a dissolution of epistemological differences between media representations and the world. 'Representation rules,' has been one of the vulgarized, though not completely inaccurate ways of condensing postmodernist thought into two words. However, the renewed interest in 'realism' and 'reality' might also be regarded exactly as a debate 'post *postmodernism*,' in the sense that 'postmodernism' has shed light on the way in which the contemporary media environment is a producer of reality in line with other social systems, and is not just offering pseudo-realities. In a similar vein, contemporary discussions of reality and the media seek to problematize any understanding of a relationship between the two concepts that is based on absolute ontological differences. This is demonstrated clearly by the articles in this issue, although from different points of view than those of postmodernism.

Aesthetic discussions have sought a more elaborated notion of the visual sign, and have turned toward Charles Sanders Peirce's idea of the indexical aspect of the sign and the notion of 'closeness' between sign and referent.

The rise of reality formats such as *Big Brother* and *Survivor* have further radicalized the questioning in recent years of the traditional differentiation between subject and object in documentary discourses, since the subject – the program producer – is at the same time an object in the sense that he is co-organizing the recorded reality. This discussion is also pertinent to contemporary documentary films where 'blurred boundaries' seem to be the general structuring principle. Specifically, the blurring of boundaries occurs between, for example, traditional documentary modes and fictional stagings in performative documentaries, and a further dissolution of boundaries can be witnessed between subject and object and between inner and outer reality in documentaries which place the director himself center stage, such as video diaries and other intimate performances of the directorial self. Finally, different film-theoretical positions argue in a wide variety of ways that 'realism' is not merely a question of aesthetic norms or of a certain view upon a specific area of the social world, but also arises from an experience of visual representations as 'real.' Thus, realism might be understood, first and foremost, as a specific relationship between media texts and their viewers. Therefore, realism is today a very wide theoretical category, since the effort to understand what is experienced to be real raises question in relation to the field of aesthetics, the field of cognition and emotion, and, of course, in relation to the whole field of genres, which are, in contemporary genre studies, theorized as more local than global and more disparate than coherent systems 'crossing boundaries' in complicated ways.

The contributions to the 2002 yearbook approach the overall theme from a diversity of analytical and theoretical angles, covering aspects of discussions related to both fiction and nonfiction and different media. The volume opens with two articles about Danish films and realism. In his article "Realism and Danish Cinema," Birger Langkjær discusses the specificities of a Danish postwar realism, taking as his point of departure that it might be a worthwhile undertaking, when discussing the concept of realism, to look at films traditionally labeled realist by both reviewers and scholars, and next to try to figure out why this is so. Langkjær takes a closer look at three canonical realist films from different periods in the Danish postwar film history, discussing historical differences but also substantial narrative continuities. This approach suggests the relevance of talking about 'Danish film realism' and thus about the specificities of realism within the context of national film histories.

Lars von Trier's film *The Idiots* and the different media texts surrounding this second Dogma film is the subject of Anne Jerslev's article "Dogma 95, Lars von Trier's *The Idiots* and the 'Idiot Project'." The article argues that the claim of the Dogma 95 Manifesto to realism may be regarded as a formal and technical strategy in order to enhance visual presence and immediacy in fiction films and thus to accentuate the indexical aspect of the photographic image. The article suggests that both the pornographic scenes and the inserted interviews in *The Idiots* may be part of this indexicality, and the article, further, discusses how the film establishes a tension between fiction and reality and between performing and 'being' as part of the realism of the film.

The following section of the yearbook deals in more general terms with theoretical discussions pertaining to 'realism' and 'reality.' Torben Grodal suggests, in his article "The Experience of Realism in Audiovisual Representation," that realism is an evaluative feeling. Grodal distinguishes between 'realistic' and 'real,' arguing that the 'realistic' is not necessarily 'real' but that it must be experienced as 'real.' The article describes basic forms of feelings of realism such as 'perceptual realism' and 'categorical realism,' and it discusses a range of processes and textual strategies which cause viewers to experience audiovisual representations as realistic, some of which may for example be regarded as compensations for lack of perceptual realism.

Along the same theoretical line of thought, scrutinizing the relationship between 'fiction' and 'reality,' Johannes Riis discusses in what ways the experience of realism may be conceptualized when considered in relation to analyses of style. The article "Is a Realist Film Style Aimed at Providing an Illusion" suggests that an understanding of the paradox relating to fiction films – that we at once feel a story to be 'real' and know that it is not – may be covered by the term 'illusion,' which Johannes Riis regards as being of both of a cognitive, an emotional, and a perceptual nature. Riis then compares 'illusion' with concepts such as 'imagination,' 'simulation,' and 'fiction' in order to argue that 'illusion' may provide the best tool for understanding the involuntary nature of the experience of realism in cinema.

Finally, from a sociological and system-theoretical point of view, Mikkel Eskjær questions the reality status of cinema in his article "Observing Movement and Time – Film Art and Observation," noting that earlier discussions have produced a variety of often contradictory positions. Eskjær offers a different angle by taking the concept of observation as his basic tool for understanding cinema as a communicative medium, thus focusing instead on how the reality of cinema is produced. The article argues that such an approach might be a step toward an understanding of the social role and functioning of cinema as a communicative medium, in and of the social world.

Introduced by John Corner's article "Documentary Values," the next section of the yearbook deals with questions regarding documentary and journalistic genres and mass-mediated uses of the photographic image of the real. Corner begins his article by claiming that the heightened interest in the documentary genre is related to the growth of reality television. Correspondingly, reality television has proffered important reconsiderations of what is meant by 'documenting.' The article argues that these shifts may prompt us to reconsider the term documentary, which mobilizes notions of 'public' and 'social.' By means of the term 'post-documentary,' we may avoid dismissing classic ideals of the documentary project or nostalgically regretting that it no longer exists, and we may instead take into consideration how this new range of popular images of the real may invite continuous debates about the ideas and values of different documentary projects.

In his article "The Mediation of Everyday Life. Genre, Discourse, and Spectacle in Reality TV," Ib Bondebjerg then outlines the globalized reality television genre which John Corner takes as an example of a new function for documentaries, namely documentary as diversion. Ib Bondebjerg regards reality television as a result of profound social and institutional changes, including globalization, the dissolution of traditional definitions of media and social institutions, the public and the private, among other things. One aim of the article is to discuss the genre from a variety of theoretical angles, as well as in a historical perspective, thus shedding light on a television genre that is much more than television. Another aim is to define and further analyze three basic sub-types within the genre of reality television, what Bondebjerg labels the docu-soap, the reality magazine, and the reality show. An example of the last sub-genre is *Big Brother*, which the last part of the article analyzes in greater detail.

Ib Bondebjerg underlines that *Big Brother* was launched as an interactive multimedia event, covering many different genre formats, as well. John Ellis' article, "A Minister is About to Resign: On the Interpretation of Television Footage," discusses the blurring of boundaries between genres and media from a different perspective. Taking as his point of departure the immediate and involuntary sliding between an indexical and iconical level, between the concrete and the general, in, for example, a press photograph, Ellis goes on to discuss meaning making as a process that is always founded within communities of understanding and consequently within concrete organizations. The article suggests that genre might be regarded as just such an institution of meaning, a shared and dynamic relationship of expectations and appropriatenesses, and the author further suggests that genre might be an appropriate term at many different levels of analysis when dealing with audiovisual culture.

Arine Kirstein delineates the blurring of boundaries and the suspension of traditional documentary discourses in two 1980s documentaries in her article "Decentering the Subject: The Current Documentary Critique of Realism." The article discusses the performative mode as a radical means of questioning our knowledge of reality and accustomed spectatorial positions *vis-à-vis* representations of reality. The article thus ultimately claims that the performative mode of defamiliarizing reality in particular documentaries function both diegetically as specific aesthetic operations and extra-diegetically, creating a specific relation of the documentary to the audience.

In the final article in this section, entitled "Simulated Conversations. The Simulation of Interpersonal Communication in Electronic Media," Stig Hjarvard discusses processes of interchange between interpersonal communication and mediated communication. Hjarvard's point is that the two forms of communication are different, but not radically different. They are mutually dependent in the sense that the development of media technologies and media contents increasingly draws on forms of interpersonel communication, while forms of expression from interpersonal communication are transferred to mediated communication by means of different discursive procedures. Thus, paradoxically, mediated communication tries to overcome the limits of interpersonal communication at the same time as new media seek to re-establish characteristics of interpersonal communication.

The yearbook ends with John Caldwell outlining recent activities in the technological realm of media convergence and the industrial realm of mergers between digital and interactive media by television networks and Hollywood studios. The article, "New Media/Old Augmentations: Television, the Internet, and Interactivity" provides descriptions and analytical insights into actual textual and interactive forms in TV web sites that seek to expand and prolong viewer interest; gives examples of different strategies for succeeding in the interactive entertainment business; and discusses the forms of capital, labor, and consumption in the new media production culture.

Although John Caldwell discusses neither 'realism' nor 'reality,' his article provides the technological background to the interest in the relationship between visual media and the social world at large. Indeed, the various articles within the covers of the yearbook may all be regarded as discussions of realism and 'reality' in the era merging old media and new, digital media.

Birger Langkjær

Realism and Danish Cinema

In a Danish and Scandinavian context (and a British one too, I suspect), realism has had a special status and has been considered a kind of mainstream film practice. Since the postwar years, the most common roads taken by Danish films have been those of realism, comedy and, on a much smaller scale, crime, although there have also been some cases of art films, especially films by Carl Theodor Dreyer, and in recent times by Lars von Trier (to name only the most well known). Realism is usually not defined as a genre (too broad and varied), and it ought not to be considered an art film (too accessible). Furthermore, as a category of fiction, it has little to do with documentary films or reality-shows on TV.

In what follows, I will consider some notions of realism, and make three brief analyses of Danish films now considered major realist landmarks in national film history. In conclusion, I will show that these films share some significant characteristics that might specify what realism is all about.

Realism as a concept

In his essay, "On realism in Art", Roman Jakobson notes "the extreme relativity of the concept of realism" (Jakobson 1971: 42). He stresses that realism is not just considered to be part of a given work of art. Realism has often been manifest as an artistic intention among artists in the production of works not normally considered part of any realism:

Classicists, sentimentalists, the romanticists to a certain extent, even the "realists" of the nineteenth century, the modernists to a large degree, and, finally, the futurists, expressionists, and their like have more than once steadfastly proclaimed faithfulness to reality, maximum verisimilitude – in other words, realism – as the guiding motto of their artistic program (Jakobson 1971: 39).

This might appear confusing at first. But taking into consideration that these different movements might be seen as representing different levels of reality, it makes more sense: expressionism intends to give shape to some inner or psychic experience; and futurism expresses a technologically inflected sensibility having many affinities to the contemporary life of the early 20th century. The basic project of any modernism or avantgarde is to reinvent reality giving it artistic form and a convincing freshness: in the jargon of neoformalism, realism is defamiliarization, that is, an aesthetic technique that makes something appear as if it is seen for the very first time (Shklovsky 1965; Thompson 1988).

Jakobson discusses five ways to make sense of realism, that can be summarized as follows:

a. Realism can be an artistic intention, e.g. some kind of quality the artist considers his own work to inhabit.
b. Realism can be something perceived (by others than the artist himself, I suspect) as realistic.
c. Realism can refer to specific periods in art history defined by critics and art historians.
d. Realism is defined by certain narrative techniques (e.g. the habit of spending time on actions and events of no central importance to the narrative).
e. Realism is defined by the way it motivates style or narrative, like if some stylized technique can be explained as expressive of some abnormal psychic condition.

Thus expressionism can be seen as a representative of a. and sometimes d. but usually not as a representative of b., c. or d. Furthermore, a given work might be considered realistic even though it is not part of a period characterized by realism (c.). And certainly, d. and e. can play a determining role in whether or not we recognize something as a realism.

Even though Jakobson's defining characteristics can be very useful, they are also formalistic. They appear to downplay the importance of subject matter, which seems to be an important aspect of what makes most viewers recognize something as realism. Realism often exhibit a catalogue of events considered of major importance in developmental psychology or themes heavily burdened with social implications. In the words of Raymond Williams, realism is often "socially extended" (Williams 1977). But even though this is true, it is not a defining characteristic in and of itself. Many films considered to be realistic are not greatly socially extended (even though social matters do play a role, but this is almost always the case), such as *Der var engang en krig* (Once There Was a War, 1966*)*, *Drenge* (Boys, 1977) or *Tro, håb og kærlighed* (Twist and Shout, 1984). And furthermore, such a definition would have to include many genres such as crime, to some extent action, and even science fiction, to mention but a few genres which are occasionally socially extended.

Noël Carroll has some brief but suggestive remarks on realism in his article, "From Real to Reel: Entangled in Nonfiction Film". He refutes two notions: first, that realism consists of some kind of mimetic relationship between representation and what is represented. Second, he refutes the notion that there can be any trans-historical realism that can be defined for all times:

A film or film style is realistic when it deviates from other specified films or styles in such a way that the deviation can be construed as like some aspect of reality that was hitherto repressed or merely absent in previous films or film styles [...] Given this, it is easy to see that there is no single Film Realism – no trans-historical style of realism in film. Rather there are several types of realism (Carroll 1996: 243-244).

Thus, Carroll considers realism always to be *aspectual*, that is, realistic in some sense but not necessarily in another. This seems to be a real catch saving academic embarrassment for other topics. We could evade an all-in-one definition and go straight to the specifics of a historical realism. But, like in the case of Jakobsen, Carroll's notion seems to ignore aspects of content that might not be trans-historical (*and* transnational) but nevertheless exhibit some recurring features of central importance to our sense of realism.

In film studies, the concept of realism has suffered from quite a turbulent history. Cinema has often been acknowledged for its convincing likeness to reality (Bazin 1967; Balazs 1970; Kracauer 1961), and some have emphasized specific cinematic styles as being more realistic than others, as noted by Bazin (1971) in his writings on deep focus photography. In the late '70s and early '80s, classical narration and a so-called invisible style, that is, a mode of film practice designed to disguise itself as a man made artifact, was considered realism (McCabe 1981 among others). Thus, film studies tends to somehow overrate the specificities of the medium in its changing definitions of realism, as when the baffled reader of Julia Hallam and Margaret Marshment's book *Realism and popular cinema* suddenly finds himself in an extensive treatment of realistic elements in Jean Pierre Jeunet's *Alien: Resurrection* (1997). Ib Bondebjerg (2000: 124) as well cannot resist mentioning that even the *Star War* films contain elements of realism. It is as if such theorists presuppose the following: whenever we recognize something for their perceptual likeness with something we know from our non-mediated experiences, it is realism. But it is a serious non-starter to equalize perceptual realism and realism as an aesthetic and fictional form.

In the following I will propose four different levels of realism:

a. Perceptual realism (media specific),
b. Realism of style (for example visual style, acting style, musical style, mise-en-scène),
c. Narrative realism, and
d. Recognition, whether social, psychological, cultural or otherwise.

ad. a: Acknowledging perceptual realism as something specific for the media in question is a notion that can be accounted for in different forms, some more attractive than others. One recent argument is the cognitive notion that perceiving film is very much like perception in everyday environments: both situations suggest the use of similar perceptual skills. Thus, we can actually recognize people in reality we have hitherto only seen in magazines, on TV, or in the movies. But in and of itself, this does not have much to do with realism as this is also true for other genres, such as adventure, action, and science fiction. No one would accuse a film like *Far til fire* (Father of Four, 1953) of being realistic, even though it does make use of a perceptual specificity for humor and fascination, as when both Søs and the film audience recognize Poul

Reichardt, a great Danish movie (and theatre) star in the 1950s, not as a fictional character, but as himself. If perceptual realism is of any importance to the question of realism as an aesthetic category, it lies in whether the specific film makes us recognize something as more or less familiar, more or less related to our (immediate and/or mediated) experience with reality.

ad. b. Realism has often been considered equivalent to a zero degree style (Bondebjerg 2000), or a part of the classical style of Hollywood as described by Bordwell, Staiger, and Thompson (1985). The classical style is an invisible style that goes unnoticed, always appearing to be motivated by events and actions in the narrative. It conveys itself as natural, as something that could not be otherwise. Bazin (1971) considered deep focus photography to be more realistic than other photographic choices, and Gregory Currie (1995) argues almost along the same lines. But it seems to be problematic in any context to isolate one technical device as being more realistic than any other. We might consider other more excessive styles that have the psychological effect of providing a realistic credibility to a narrative event, like the kind of documentary realism used in a film like *Balladen om Carl-Henning* (The Ballad of Carl-Henning, 1969), or by many Dogma 95 films. The visibility (and audibility) of the technical apparatus seems to guarantee the diegesis a pre-cinematic status, as the camera (often a little to late) catches a glimpse of reality here and there but never quite seems to be on top of the events, continuously unable to foresee the action. It might be added that non-technical aspects of style such as mise-en-scène and acting style are very important stylistic elements. Far to often are they ignored at the expense of "apparatus-style" but they must not be forgotten here, or when taking realism into consideration.

ad. c. Realism can also be considered a narrative technique or narrative form. One candidate for this type of realism is the narrative form of some nineteenth century novels. Another is the more condensed dramatic form of classical Hollywood narration where everything seems to happen by necessity, as if it could not be otherwise. Films by Bille August, especially *Zappa*, exhibit an extremely tight narrative structure. On the other hand, Bordwell (1993) has made clear, that art films can motivate their events as realism through the use of loose narratives, unexplained accidental happenings and open endings. By leaving things undone and unexplained, they somehow imitate life. Films by Nils Malmros, like *Drenge* and *Kundskabens træ* (The Tree of Knowledge, 1981), appear to be closer to this sort of narrative form. To be sure there is no single narrative form that in and of itself implies realism more than another.

ad. d. Realism as recognition: Recognition is a broad term including recognition of social, psychological, cultural and even emotional elements. Social and psychological conflicts and depictions of specific cultural and social environments have often been considered (understandably) a hallmark of realism. But in Scandinavian realism, the lower middle-class might be more commonly depicted than the working class. Even though realism is "socially extended" it is not specified by one social strata. And we might add that even films and TV-series, that by most standards seem far from realism, can be experienced as being true to life emotionally as was seemingly the case with the TV-series *Dallas* (Ang 1985). Fashion, manners and social setting will not constitute any realism in and of itself. Thus, recognition of some specific aspect as realistic might or might not add up to an overall impression of realism.

I believe that to consider film realism a conceptual problem to be solved by philosophical arguments, gives rise to many fruitless discussions. Defining realism by specific details out of a larger context, or by its likeness to reality, or by likeness to cognitive operations deployed in order to understand both film and real life, are all conceptual means by which to address realism. But there is another option. We might take a closer look at those films normally considered representatives of realism and try to figure out why this is so, that is, being specific as well as systematic in intention. What are their specific characteristics, and what characteristics do they share? How do we recognize realism?

In what follows, I intend to be specific and systematic on a small scale by analyzing three films normally considered hallmarks of Danish film realism, all from different historical periods in Danish cinema: *Soldaten og Jenny* ("The Soldier and Jenny", 1947), *Balladen om Carl-Henning* (1969) and *Drenge* (1977).

Ordinary people: Soldaten og Jenny ("The Soldier and Jenny", 1947)

A young couple, Robert (the soldier) and Jenny, meet accidentally in a cheap café and fall in love. But unbeknownst to Robert she is taken to court for an abortion she had some years ago. As a result, she is banished from her home by her father, she loses her job as a saleswoman and persuades Robert that they commit suicide together. At the last moment a lawyer intervenes. The lawsuit against her has been dropped. The trial was retarded because the main prosecutor was involved in a car accident, thereby causing the charges to become obsolete.

Soldaten og Jenny is part of a new realism which appeared, as in many other European countries, after the second world war. The film is originally based on a play staged at Folketeatret in 1940 and written by Danish dramatist Soya. The film is directed by Johan Jakobsen and follows the play almost word for word but some outdoor scenes have been added.

The film received enthusiastic reviews. It was praised for its overall authenticity, for its social indignation (even though some reviewers found it too harsh), for its recognizable physical and social environments and foremost, for acting and dialogue.

Two reviewers did have some interesting objections to the casting of the female protagonist played by the popular star of Danish theatre and film at the time, Bodil Kjer:

Naturally, she plays her role excellently. But she is simply too beautiful, too wonderful – to say it straight out – to be that common girl Soya had in mind. If Jenny has glamour like Bodil Kjer, her fate would have been different. (Frederik Schyberg, *Politiken*).

It might seem an odd objection to make as the new realism of Danish cinema only occasionally used non-actors (even then it was most often kids), despite the well known practice of a contemporary Italian neorealism. All the actors in *Soldaten og Jenny* were well known as actors from the Danish Royal Theatre and from many popular films. Furthermore, the male protagonist's role was performed by another young film star, Poul Reichardt, who was highly praised by the same Schyberg for creating an illusion evenly "strong and touching" to that given by Bodil Kjer. But even though Kjer's star personae cannot be said to spoil the realism, it somehow seems to counteract the film's intention of authenticity.

I might suspect Johan Jakobsen as having had more than a vague concern here. Especially the beginning of the film seems to reflect this. Despite Kjer's outstanding performance and boxoffice appeal, the films goes to great length in order to downplay her star-appearance. At first we see a backyard with linen hanging on line accompanied by a small segment of "amusing" music. This is followed by a sweet little tune played on muted trumpet accompanied by brushes and a walking bass, giving it a forward drive. Another amusing tune is heard and we now see a corner (at Dronningens Tværgade) and behind it a big square bathed in daylight. A streetcar enters the frame, and stops to let people off. Just as the driver rings the bell, the music goes ding-ding, a small but comic detail that gives the goings on a lighter quality. We see more people and from behind the credits, a young well dressed and beautiful woman recognized by Danish viewers as Bodil Kjer. But before she comes to the foreground, the scene changes again. Kjer is now seen crossing a street from a distance, as she stops outside a cheap café. As she moves on again, the film cuts to inside the café and we will not see Kjer again before halfway through the following scene (and it's a long one). In other words, the film presents its major star in a very low key fashion as if she was someone you might meet on the street. She is not allowed to be framed as a star.

Bodil Kjer and Poul Reichardt both make use of common techniques to appear authentic, like unfinished sentences, low voices and downward glances. They seem less articulated and more downplayed in their gestures and diction than most other actors in the film, having a more Danish Royal Theatre-esque performance style. The performance of both Kjer and Reichardt thus appeals to a sense of realism that is experienced as being stronger by differentiating it from the other actors who play in a tradition of comedy and naturalistic theatre. But both Kjer and Reichardt display some surprisingly exaggerated acting at certain dramatic points. When Robert tells Jenny that he once killed a human being, he begins to stare, moving his hands in repetitive half circles speaking monotonously. This acted mannerism dissolves into a flashback, that is done as a single moving p.o.v. shot showing the events that lead up to the killing. Thus, his sudden change in acting style seems to be justified by the sombre tone of the story he is about to tell. The other instance of mannered acting occurs in the closing scene as Jenny grasps Robert and, in despair, asks that they kill themselves together. Most of the indoor scenes in the film are done without music but at this particular moment, Kai Møller's music enters to reinforce the already exaggerated forcefulness of Kjer's gesture with a full blown tutti immediately followed by a gypsy-like melody played solo on a violin. But even though it seems somehow overblown, it certainly does the trick as all the emotional power of the film seems to be condensed into what can only be described as a melodramatic moment.

The technical style of the film appears to be classical. Framings give access to significant objects, people and events in diegetic space, while reframings and cuts are usually motivated by character-movement or by the entrance of new characters. But the film does vary in style and emotional range. It is filmed in indoor studio-sets with almost expressionistic lighting at times, as well as outdoors, on location in the streets of Copenhagen where the images sometimes seem overexposed. Furthermore, its "tone" shifts between poetic moments, pathos, the psychologically intense, low key humor and excellent tragic comedy.

Many post-war films such as *Ditte Menneskebarn* (Ditte – Child of Man, 1946), *De pokkers Unger* (Those Damned Kids, 1947), *Ta' hvad du vil ha'* ("Take Whatever You Want", 1947) and *Soldaten og Jenny* were considered part of a new realism, a realism I will refer to as "postwar realism." The characters are usually played by well known theatre actors and they were often shot in studio-sets. Even *De pokkers Unger* that is set almost entirely in a courtyard is filmed in a studio. The technical style of these films was quite "classical" whereas acting style involved Royal Theatre character-acting, downplayed realism and even amateurism, like the kids in both *Ditte Menneskebarn* and *De pokkers Unger*, both of which were highly praised by most reviewers (especially *Ditte Menneskebarn*). In terms of narrative structure, there seems to be allowed some differences. *Ditte Menneskebarn* is about a girl with a heart of gold beyond the reach of corruption despite whatever horrible fate coming her way. The film exhibits a melodramatic form and an epic structure that *Soldaten og Jenny* only partly shares. *Ta' hva du vil ha'* takes place in a bourgeois milieu and has an episodic structure connected by the events surrounding a dying grandmother whose grandson turns out to be illegitimate. The grandson is involved with his young "cousin" as well as with her mother, and he is blackmailing a homosexual schoolteacher. He forces an old alcoholic couple to commit suicide and the grandmother to die by giving her a shock. Finally, he drives himself to death in a car accident. The disturbing thing about *Ta' hva du vil ha'*, apart from the overwhelming amount of tragedy, is that there seems to be no character for the spectator to sympathize with for more than but a moment.

In postwar realism, the characters' goals are usually not that clear-cut (with the possible exception of *De pokkers Unger* which involves a common goal for the kids, a crime and its final solution). The films exhibit great variety by including positive open endings, open but fatalistic endings and a few (almost) happy endings implying more or less narrative closure. Despite different narrative structures, different social set-ups and time periods, the common denominator for these films is their socially implicated themes, that is, the ability or lack of ability of the protagonist to react properly to or to manage his or her social situation. Thus, simple closure is not a goal in and of itself as the kind of social ability required by the protagonist cannot be shown by some conclusive action. Instead, the spectator has to be provided the impression that the protagonist *will* be, *might* be or might *not* be able to handle his or her life in the future, ahead of what plot-time reveals.

A miracle in Danish film: Balladen om Carl-Henning
(The Ballad of Carl-Henning, 1969)

Carl-Henning is a not too bright young man living in Ballum, a small village in southern Jutland. He works at the local dairy farm and acts in an amateur theatre. When his best friend, Paul, leaves for the bigger city, Aalborg, everything goes wrong. Having gotten drunk at a local ball, he steals into the night to get a small "loan" from his employer. But he is caught in action and gets into a fight. Believing that he has killed the dairy-farmer, he takes flight for Paul in Aalborg where he is allotted a room at Fede-Kai [Fat-Kai] who is involved in smuggling cigarettes. One evening, he brings Carl-Henning and, by accident, Carl-Henning drowns in the harbor. He is buried in his home village.

The reviews were extraordinary by any standard. There was an overwhelmingly positive response to the film and everyone could relate to the strong sense of social (and national) sentiment, as expressed in the following statement from newspaper critic Jørgen Stegelmann:

He, who for years has been complaining about Danish film, that it never would come around something like Danish everyday life, will come to believe that Balladen om Carl-Henning is what he has been waiting for. This film is a typically Danish film as a typically Danish film always should look like (Stegelmann, *Berlingske Tidende*, April 8, 1969).

Thus, Stegelman considered *Balladen om Carl-Henning* to be prototypical of a kind of Danish film that did not exist, that is, the ideal for a national film to come. The reviews showed great enthusiasm for the actors, especially the main actor, Jesper Klein: "He does not play this "part," he lives it" (Stangerup, Politiken). Furthermore, the use of many local amateurs was praised for its authenticity. What was less praised was its technical style: the hand-held, jerky camera and sudden cuts; the sudden changes between over-exposed, under-exposed and heavily backlighted images; the less than exact and sometimes indistinct dubbing of dialogue. What the reviewers failed to mention is the documentary effect that resulted; the camera always seems to be to late to catch the action as it happens. It gives the impression of a reality already there for the camera to catch, sometimes more successfully than others.

The authentic acting style and the documentary technique is combined with what might be termed a syncopated narrative structure characterized as follows:

a. Most scenes focus on Carl-Henning in a specific relation to another person and usually imply a thematic characterization, like Poul and Carl-Henning together (friendship); Carl-Henning and his father (paternal authority); Carl-Henning and his mother (maternal care); or Carl-Henning and the sports girl (clumsy flirtation). But those relations and themes focused upon in each scene, are not what cause the next thing to happen. If there be elements of dramatic importance to the following scene, they will appear in the periphery of what immediately catch our attention, that is, causality between scenes appears unfocused;
b. Many scenes are even without dramatic focus. We might see one person and get a snip of dialogue making that person stand out for a moment, but this kind of momentary characterization is most often without any direct dramatic implications;
c. Further, the characters do not exhibit any need to reflect. There might be minor conflicts but the most important conflicts are never discussed or acknowledged as such by any character in the film. Our concern for characters and their problems is to be sustained despite that the characters themselves seem to ignore the existence of any substantial problems.

Important facts, like when Paul is about to leave (despite that he is Carl-Henning's best friend and protector, and he has a girl friend) are only given, in a very subtle manner, between two lines of dialogue. At a cafeteria, as Carl-Henning is about to embarrass those present with his child-like behaviour, Paul's girlfriend suddenly reminds him of something he needs to take with him to Aalborg, but she is ignored. Later, in her room, she refuses Paul's sexual invitation by reminding him again. We never hear anyone talking about his departure, and we do not really see any reactions to it that would otherwise have made the importance of it clear to us. As viewers, we have been less than prepared for an event that indirectly causes the death of our protagonist and turns the episodic narrative into a tragedy. Many important events can only be perceived as such after they occured. Thus, our understanding of the narrative happens in a syncopated manner.

This narrative syncopation is combined with a sort of compression of time within each scene. Most films make use of narrative ellipses is but in *Balladen om Carl-Henning* such ellipses can be found several times in each scene, as when someone standing in one shot is suddenly sitting in the next or vice versa. The basic unity of time, place and action in each scene is fragmented. Small slices of time are constantly lost as the camera, the microphone and the spectator unsuccessfully try to get on top of the events.

This syncopated and time-compressed structure becomes evident if compared with those parts of the film that are closer to having some causality to them, as it is the case in the suspense-like night sequence at the dairy farm. Here, the dramatic focus of each scene is in exactly those elements having implications in the next scene.

In opposition to Robert in *Soldaten og Jenny*, Carl-Henning does not show any reflective skills. Whereas *Soldaten og Jenny* is highly informative, *Balladen om Carl-Henning* is less polite about explaining things, making them clear to us as they happen. It is not like there is no connection between events. It is more like the film deliberately downplays those connections that can be established by some afterthought on the part of the spectator. This provides a strong emphasis on each moment in and of itself as the spectator engages in changing situations, only later to get a fuller understanding of their implications.

The documentary style of the film is one form of stylization that allows for an impression of a pro-cinematic world, an experience of perceptual now-ness and some immediate recognition of those situations depicted. But the film involves other kinds of stylization as well, such as achieving contrasts by sudden shifts between a documentary style and beautifully composed pictures. Thus, we see Carl-Henning in the landscape, alone or with Paul, including the windmills, or we hear the quietly sung ballad that frames the film's beginning and ending, and brings the narrative full circle. Or when Carl-Henning wakes up early in the morning and, without a sound, leaves the house. Next he is seen coming out of the dark morning in his white costume, disappearing in the whiteness of the fog at the dairy. The lack of sound adds to this sequence an unreal quality. Or, after his flight from Ballum, the film cuts to a black sky with a small artist seen from a distance, dressed in white and seemingly hanging in the darkness. Or the scenes at the harbor at night in stark contrast. All these moments provide some sort of unreal perceptual experience and supply the baffled spectator with over-condensed but at times under-specified thematic expressions that for this reason tend to stay in mind when leaving the theatre.

Despite its special style and narrative form, the film is classical in other aspects if compared to other Danish films of the sixties. First, its tragic-epic leap at the end is different from the psychological and social dynamics and conflicts among the young couples spending a weekend together in a summer cottage in *Weekend* (1962), or the psychological intimacy surrounding the boy Tim and his sexual attraction to one of his older sister's girlfriends in *Der var engang en krig*. Second, the film's stylization is without the kind of "inner expressionism" typical of many art films. In *Sult* (Hunger, 1966), over-exposed p.o.v. shots signifying perceptual-cognitive dysfunctions resulting from starvation is a recurring stylistic feature. And in *Der var engang en krig* we perceptually witness Tim's recurring dreams, including wish fulfilling daydreams and surrealistic nightmares of sexuality and death.

The central realist, and partly "modernist" films of the sixties exhibit variations in themes and aesthetic sensibilities. *Weekend* develops into an improvised social and ethical experiment that reveals serious misconceptions of self, sexuality and emotional bonding. *Der var engang en krig* is outstanding in its intimacy of tone, its depiction of sexuality and youth, and in its ability to turn narrative into almost nothing but erotic sensibilities. Whereas the postwar films dealt mainly with love or social bonding (be it between a mother and her daughter, a man and a woman, or a group of people), the films of the sixties all contain strong elements of (male) sexuality and eroticism. This is thematisized either through unaccomplished sexuality as in *Weekend*, *Sult* and *Der var engang en krig* or in fleeting and unclear relationships like in *Stine og drengene* (Diary of a Teenager, 1969) or *Dilemma* (1962). Even the "fool," Carl-Henning, tries to flirt but is humiliated. It is not the first time in film history that sexuality has been depicted as impulsive and as a destructive force, very much apart from the more proper prospect of marital life. But this kind of sexuality is no longer connected with passion, action and self-sacrifice. It is rather a more hidden and repressive sexuality always accompanied by the dangers of humiliation as in *Sult*, *Balladen om Carl-Henning* and *Der var engang en krig*.

The episodic narratives, open endings and underspecified characterization of conflicts and characters are common features. But these common features have somehow different effects in each film. In *Weekend*, they create an accumulation of psychological conflicts but without providing conditions for the spectator to engage and sympathize with specific characters, thereby giving the film a disturbing quality. Both in *Sult* and *Der var engang en krig*, the spectator is continuously given access to the thoughts and actions of their main protagonists. What is disturbing about *Sult* is that our attachment to the protagonist does not provide the kind of outcome we might wish for as he knowingly humiliates himself in socially embarrassing scenes. Thus both *Sult* and *Weekend* play on negative social emotions such as shame, humiliation etc.

In postwar realism, the protagonist is often deeply inscribed in a social reality that provides for an ethical orientation from which the spectator judges events. Sometimes a film's protagonist can act as a social agent while at other times, he is driven by social reality. Modernism, on the other hand, often strives to re-invent reality by excessive aesthetic means, and by leaving its anti-heroes in an existential vacuum outside a socially defined space. The films mentioned above seem to fall between realism in its earlier (and more classical) form and modernism (as well as art cinema) as an experimental form beyond given values. We might call these films representatives of a "modern realism." The kind of social intelligence required for the anti-heroes of modern realism has to prove its viability in relations defined by personal intimacy rather than public or family-based social spheres. In short, the films involve a shift from a public and family-based social space to a private and intimacy-based (and thus psychological) social space.

Canonical Realism: Drenge (Boys, 1977)

The film begins in the late 1950s. Ole is a four or five year old boy living in a house on the hospital grounds where his father is a doctor. His world is a small and selfcontained world of children's games late at night. One weekend, Ole's older cousin, Kresten, pays him a visit. On Kresten's initiative they play innocent sex games like "bare" or "shunting engine" (pushing together their naked bottoms) and they peer at a naked female patient. The film moves on to follow Ole and his less than successful relationship with Marianne when he is about 20 years old, and later, we see Ole and his friend flirting with two nurses. Ole seems to have his somehow awkward sexual debut. In its final moments, the film jump backwards in time as Kresten leaves.

The Danish realism of the late 1970s and early 1980s was mostly (but not always) concerned with children and young people, their families and their tentative sexual and emotional relationships. Especially in films by Nils Malmros and Bille August, the intimate world of children and young people is realized in intense psychological portraits, often depicting parents (and schoolteachers) as inadequate or even damaging to the children's self esteem. The social themes of post war realism as well as the intimacy and psychological sensibility of the sixties, so well done in *Der var engang en krig*, find their way into these later films, too. They are part of the formative period of what was later to become a canonical realism in Danish cinema that continues into the mid-1990s. The question is whether or not this realism has any prototypical features apart from often being about children, young people and intimate relationships?

The early films of Nils Malmros include *En mærkelig kærlighed* ("A Strange Love Affair", 1968), *Lars Ole 5c* (1973), *Drenge* and *Kundskabens træ* (1981). *Drenge* might not be Malmros' masterpiece, even though it was received as a masterpiece, described as a breakthrough for a hitherto unseen sensibility. It lacks the perfection of overall form that characterizes *Kundskabens træ*. But at moments, it is the best of its kind and exemplifies the extreme episodic format so typical of Malmros. *Drenge* is minimalistic in terms of narrative structure without ever loosing intensity and nerve.

We are immediately plunged into the unique atmosphere of the film, as the credits on the black screen are supplemented by children's voices in an outdoor environment. It is dusk and we see a birds eyes view of two boys on a lawn, their arms straight out in the air as they spin around themselves and laugh as they pee. The camera moves downward and frames a small boy from behind. In the next shot we see the boy, Ole, as his expression shifts between joy and curious fascination as he watches the other boys. A group of kids climb onto a roof to look through a lighted window, leaving Ole behind.

The setting (the hospital), moods (children playing at dusk), theme (partly sexual curiosity) and the spectator's experience (our attachment to Ole) are immediately established in this first scene. The hospital grounds are established as a selfcontained world rather early, as when Ole's older sister chases some boys away by shouting "only doctors' kids are allowed to be here." The repeated games at dusk, children's voices in open air and the continuing sound of rain in the end of the film create a very nostalgic/distant and at the same time very physical/intimate mood.

Our mode of experience is intimately connected to that of Ole but is never identical to his perspective. After Kresten has arrived, Ole gets his chance to look through those forbidden windows. He and Kresten see a naked woman lying on a couch, the camera slightly shaking as a p.o.v. shot. Then follows a cut to Kresten (glancing with a huge smile) and Ole (with a look of intense but emotionally non-specified attention). An alarm clock rings, and a nurse asks the naked woman to turn around, and the boys go on to the next window. This time it is a man and Ole comments: "Only the men ["mændnerne"] have green light."

This short scene is obviously about sexuality and sexual identity. The boys are knowingly peeping and are obviously fascinated. But there is a difference between Kresten's reaction as he smiles when seeing the lady, whereas Ole is less emotionally specified in his reaction. Clearly, he is fascinated but his fascination seems to be less sexually motivated than Kresten's, as indicated by Ole's attention to the colors of the lights. In this subtle fashion, the dialogue draws the spectator's attention to small differences between how things are perceived by the two boys.

Reviewers tend to draw attention to the authenticity of the children's performances as a major source of the film's realism. Malmros' technique is to make the children repeat his sentences. In this sense, they do not act, but repeat words and a tone of voice.

This makes their dramatic expression less focused than is typical for professional actors. Whereas professional actors usually perform and modulate basic and recognizable emotions, amateurs and children often exhibit a less specified emotional register. Dynamic or kinetic terms like "floating," "explosive," "crescendo" or "decrescendo" are what developmental psychologists Daniel Stern has labeled "vitality emotions" (Stern 1985). This is expressed in our behavior as we move slowly, suddenly, smoothly, in jerks or otherwise. Vitality emotions have no specific emotional value but are more like a qualifier specifying *how* one is happy, angry, sad etc. In a sense, Malmros' children often exhibit emotional qualifiers without qualifieds; the emotional specification has more to do with the context (and editing) than the actors. But it is exactly this emotional under-specification that makes Malmros' films so intense, because every little detail has an openness and a rich potential meaning to it.

All through the film different kinds of dividing lines are revealed: When the boys from outside are not allowed to be on the hospital ground; in an early scene when Ole watches his older sister and her playmates but his sister denies him even that; and in a ritual form, as the children play hide and seek. As the children play hide and seek late at night, Ole leaves for the small lake. When he returns, his father angrily sends him to bed and the following scene takes place: we see Ole, half-lit and in bed, quietly listening to the muffled sounds of his parents downstairs. Steps are heard on the stairs and when his father asks him if he is asleep, Ole pretends that he is and his father leaves the room.

The scene is obviously about Ole succesfully denying his father an opportunity to be reconciled with his son by pretending to be asleep. Technically, this small scene makes use of cuts between semi-close ups of Ole and larger framings of the doorway (his father enters after we have seen the empty doorway three times). Further, we hear low volume sounds from downstairs. The sounds, Ole's face and the repeated framings of the empty doorway create a focal attention *out* of the room at the same time as it gives a strong sense of being *in* the room. This hide and seek is given a sexual dimension after the arrival of the older cousin, Kresten. After playing "shunting engine," they run into their room and lock the door. They throw an eiderdown on the floor and jump on it from a table with their bare bottoms first, each time saying a short sentence that almost sounds like "we are protesting" but with "protesting" slightly changed in its first syllable to sound like "fart." Ole's mother's voice is now heard, and we see the doorknob moving. This is repeated in one of the last scenes of the film when Kresten suggests they play "bare," this time locking themselves in the bathroom. Now it is Ole's father who quite violently bursts through the door and almost shouts at them asking what they are doing? "Nothing," Ole replies.

The strength of the film lies in its sense of details. It contains some short but impressive and significant moments as when Ole is seen watching and listening to the wind in the big and rustling trees beyond the small lake at dusk. Even though it's a situation vague in specified meaning, it has an intense but unspecified perceptual and emotional power to it. At the end of the film, Ole is seen in his father's rubber boots enjoying a walk in the flooded basement. We might (or might not) over-interpret the symbolic nature of this ending but its value seems to be that it succeeds in keeping eyes and ears wide open to those details that are given such importance and are experienced with such open minded intensity in the kind of perceptual world we inhabit as children. Thus, Malmros succeeds in giving an aesthetic form to immediately recognizable experiences that borders on what we can refer to as narrative.

In some sense, *Drenge* is prototypical of the kind of realism that took shape in the late 1970s and early 1980s by having the intimate psychological portrait as its turning point. The central goal of the narrative is for the protagonist to come to terms with something, like in *Johnny Larsen* (1979). After several failures (at work, in the military and in love affairs), Johnny seems to have gained some personal insights thereby indicating that he might be able to create a better life for himself in the future.

The open ending usually forms a new beginning, but it does so in a way that only leaves us guessing as to a more specific outcome, as is the case in the following films: Jens (Claus Strandberg) who is seen in a final shot walking along the quay so as to get hired on a ship in *Honningmåne* (In My Life, 1978) by Bille August; Bjørn

(Adam Tønsberg) after having his final encounter with Sten (Peter Reichardt) in *Zappa*, is seen watching fireworks on new years eve, hand in hand with his little brother in an open doorway; or the once popular schoolgirl Elin (Eva Gram Schjoldager) leaving the end-of-season dance at school with her dress torn in *Kundskabens træ*; or Pelle (Pelle Hvenegaard) running along the ice-filled sea in the last frame of *Pelle Erobreren* (Pelle the Conqueror, 1987). The open ending gives no resolution for its spectator. But quite opposite to what was narrative currency in some modernist films in the sixties, the open ending is more specific in the Danish realism of the late 1970s and onwards. The protagonists are always well defined and so are their problems. So even though the ending is open, we are given the opportunity to make some pretty qualified guesses as to whether he or she will do all right in the future of post plot-time.

Thus, films by Nils Malmros and Bille August often evolve around common themes (sexuality, parents), narrative likeness (open endings, accumulation of psychological elements) and similar style (children playing the major roles, tight economy with details and psychological precision) and thus give access to similar modes of psychological recognition. Nonetheless, many films by August, especially *Zappa* (but also *Tro, håb og Kærlighed*), have a much stronger and classically driven narrative than films by Malmros.

What common features are there to define realism?

One commonality of importance surrounding the three central films examined above is the extent to which they have been recognized as realism by contemporary reviewers and later, by academics. They all enjoy the scholarly status of being considered national masterpieces of film realism.

Nonetheless the films exhibit stylistic variations. *Soldaten og Jenny* and *Drenge* can both be characterized by an "invisible" apparatic style. In the case of *Soldaten og Jenny*, this is combined with an acting style that specifies the emotions involved in a low-key manner, thereby giving it a sense of authenticity and realism.

When the acting style momentarily shows mannerism, this expressive stylistic variation is carefully motivated by specified psychological conditions. The two young boys in *Drenge* exhibit a different and more open acting style. Combined with minimal action and an "invisible" audiovisual style, this open acting style creates an attention to detail, thereby causing an under-specified (in terms of definite meaning) but intense experience. In *Balladen om Carl-Henning* an eye catching and at times disturbing documentary style is used, thereby providing the sense that there is an already present reality to be documented by the camera and microphone. This style is contrasted by abstract and otherwise stylized sequences (although realistically motivated) that can be considered thematic condensations of an otherwise strangely unfocused narrative.

The films can all be characterized as being episodic in narrative form but they also exhibit considerable differences.

Soldaten og Jenny is structured around well defined characters and conflicts but the major dramatic changes come from accidental occurrences and a sudden (and melodramatic) reversal of fortune at the end. Thus the two main characters can only follow this flow of events. Especially Robert is given the role of compensating for their lack of acting possibilities in a prolonged reflection on life and its mysteries.

Balladen om Carl-Henning provides an epic and tragic leap at the end. Overall it is less classical and more modern, as its accidental occurrences are combined with less psychologically defined characters. As their motives appear less clear-cut, their actions become open to interpretation. The ending gives some closure (the end of someone's life) but seems to ask more general social and existential questions, e.g. the pervasive question of the nature of our existential and social capabilities that make us succeed or fail as social beings.

Whereas *Soldaten og Jenny* and *Balladen om Carl-Henning* both have a dramatic structure reaching a peak in the end, *Drenge* has more of an episodic nature based on motives which silently accumulate and group themselves into a strict and impressive pattern. Each scene has its own peak but there seems to be no final peak towards the end of the film. It is more self-contained, accumulating intensifiers that are strongly felt and even more so as they are never released by action.

Another common trend in these three films can be described by what they don't do. Their protagonist is never a man of action following a clear-cut goal. Instead what unites them is the focus on how the main protagonists more or less successfully try to manage certain social and existential situations. Dramatic situations are not defined by specific goals that can be achieved by a simple action. The basic "module" is the situation. Social emotions such as shame, embarrassment, admiration, humiliation, pride and the like are the structuring elements of those situations in which our protagonists have to prove themselves as having the capabilities needed to be a social agent. Socially (and psychologically) defined situations are revealed by the films as a kind of social microcosm, including prototypical scenarios, like the dinner table as a recurring locus of conflict, as seen in: the self-humiliating speech of the father in *Soldaten og Jenny*, the silent and embarrassing lunch in *Weekend* as the young and "liberated" people are visited by an old couple, arguments around the table in *Der var engang en krig*, the angry old father and the servant-like behavior of Carl-Henning's mother in *Balladen om Carl-Henning*, Kresten telling about his humiliation in school at dinner in *Drenge* and loud arguments around the dinner table in *Johnny Larsen*.

The dinner table, school and the workplace constitute central spaces of conflict in Danish realism. The whole point of this realism is not whether to succeed in terms of a limited goal in the outer world but about achieving the general capability to managing social situations and establishing one's place in the social sphere. In a romantic comedy the end is given full closure as the two kiss or get married. And a crime film ends when the crime is resolved or when the protagonist otherwise has decisively failed in doing so. The genre in question defines the kinds of questions raised by the narrative and thereby defines what will count as a true ending. In Danish realism there is no such thing as true closure because there is no clear goal that can be achieved in any decisive way. *Soldaten og Jenny* comes close with its melodramatic ending but *Balladen om Carl-Henning* simply ends when its main character dies. The real goal of realism and its protagonists is, through conflict, to gain that specific kind of social intelligence the film has put forth as needed. The open ending is almost obligatory as there is no final action that can make this social ability salient to the audience. We can only be given the probability of some future turn-around.

Thus, realism is different from the classical narrative as its goal cannot be achieved by simple action. Furthermore, realism is different from art film and modernism as its characters are most often psychologically defined as are the issues addressed, and they all reflect a social space that is most often marginalized in modernist narratives. This is why *Balladen om Carl-Henning* constitutes a modern realism bordering between realism and modernism while *Soldaten og Jenny* is closer to a classical narrative. Modernist films appear more abstract as they deal with existential questions out of social context. Like modernism, realism is more concerned with reaction than with action (Bordwell 1993). However, realism deals with a reaction to more specific and recognizable social conflicts than is the case in art film. It is the lack of ability to manage life that give *Ta' hvad du vil ha'*, *Balladen om Carl-Henning* and *Kundskabens træ* their tragic form, a theme which was later (and again) to be realized in Nils Malmros' *Kærlighedens smerte* (The Pain of Love, 1992).

The analysis above might give some people the impression that there is no such thing as a realism, that realism is always aspectual (Carroll 1993). I believe this is only true if we look at it in terms of international film history. International film history is often about the peaks of certain national film cultures, like Soviet and German films in the twenties, French films in the thirties, Italian films in the forties etc. When realism is mapped in the same way, in terms of outstanding periods of realism, they appear less connected and with good reason. They are different in terms of both nationality and historical time. But looking at realism within a national film culture and across history might reveal some substantial continuities despite their striking differences. Danish film realism is not just "socially extended" but it is socially extended in ways that define its narrative structure and the kind of solutions that will be at the protagonists disposal. It is a kind of film practice between art film (the episodic and open narrative) and classical narratives (well defined characters and conflicts) that can be positively described as dealing with defining oneself as a social agent inside a given social situation. No final action can do it, and no definite narrative closure is possible. Realism is about how personal space is to be defined within a given social space. This can be done in countless ways. Realism is neither a style, nor a narrative form in and of itself. Realism is open to stylistic, narrative and conflictual variations in a continuous revitalization across changing cultural and aesthetic sensibilities of what realism is all about.

Note

1. Three of the films mentioned have no official English title. In these cases, I have made a translation from the original Danish title and identified it as such by quotation marks.

References

Ang, Ien. 1985. *Watching Dallas*. London: Methuen.

Balàzs, Bela. 1970. *Theory of the Film*. New York: Dover Publications.

Bazin, André. 1967. *What is Cinema?* Vol. I. Berkeley: University of California Press.

Bazin, André. 1971. *What is Cinema?* Vol. II. Berkeley: University of California Press.

Bondebjerg, Ib. 1993. "Den danske nybølgefilm". *Sekvens*, Filmvidenskabelig Årbog 93, Københavns Universitet.

Bondebjerg, Ib. 2000. "Film and Modernity. Realism and the Aesthetics of Scandinavian New Wave Cinema". In *Moving Images, Culture and the Mind*, edited by Ib Bondebjerg. University of Luton Press.

Bordwell, David, Staiger, Janet & Thompson, Kristin. 1985. *The Classical Hollywood Cinema: Film Style & Mode of Production to 1960*. London & New York: Routledge.

Bordwell, David. 1993. *Narration in the Fiction Film*. London: Routledge.

Carroll, Noël. 1996: "From Real to Reel: Entangled in Nonfiction Film". In *Theorizing the Moving Image*. Cambridge: Cambridge University Press.

Currie, Gregory. 1995. *Image and mind: Film, philosophy and cognitive science*, Cambridge: Cambridge University Press.

Hallam, Julia & Marshment, Margaret. 2000. *Realism and popular cinema*. Manchester: Manchester University Press.

Jakobson, Roman. 1971. "On Realism in Art". In *Readings in Russian Poetics: Formalist and Structuralist Views*, edited by Ladislav Matejka & Krystyna Pomorska. Cambridge, Massachusetts: The MIT Press.

Jørholt, Eva. 1997. "1940-1949: Voksen, følsom og elegant". *Kosmorama* 220, Winter

Kracauer, Siegfried. 1961. *Nature of Film: The Redemption of Physical Reality*. London: Dennis Dobson.

McCabe, Colin. 1981. "Realism and Cinema: Notes on Brechtian Theses". In *Popular Television and Film*, edited by Colin Mercer & Janet Woollacott. London: British Film Institute.

Nielsen, Hans Jørn. 1984. "Underholdning og beredskab". In *Dansk litteraturhistorie 1901-45*, volume 7. København: Gyldendal.

Shklovsky, Victor. 1965. "Art as Technique". In *Russian Formalist Criticism: Four Essays*, edited by Marion J. Reis. Lincoln: University of Nebraska Press.

Soya. 1940. *Brudstykker af et Mønster*. København.

Stern, Daniel N. 1985. *Barnets interpersonelle univers*. København: Hans Reitzels forlag.

Thompson, Kristin. 1988. *Breaking the Glass Armor: Neoformalist Film Analysis*. Princeton, N.J: Princeton University Press.

Troelsen, Anders. 1980a. "Ungdom, utilpassethed og utopi: Om ungdomsfilm efter anden verdenskrig". In *Levende billeder af Danmark*, edited by Anders Troelsen. København: Medusa.

Troelsen, Anders. 1980b. "Socialdemokratisk Surrealisme: Om *Harry og kammertjeneren* (1961)". In *Levende billeder af Danmark*, edited by Anders Troelsen. København: Medusa.

Williams, Raymond. 1977. "A Lecture on Realism". *Screen*, vol. 18 no. 1.

Reviews

Soldaten og Jenny
Aftenbladet (31-10 1947): "En stor Sejr for Soldaten." [reviewer unknown].

Berlingske Aftenavis (31-10 1947): "En Film med Sammenhæng, med Mennesketale og med glimrende Præstationer", Mogens Lind [M.L].

B.T (31-10 1947): "Fin dansk Film", Kai Berg Madsen [K.B.M].

Børsen (31-10 1947): "Soldaten og Jenny blev en smuk Succes på Saga" [reviewer unknown].

Information (31-10 1947): "Soldaten og Jenny" [K.C.].

Land og Folk (31-10 1947): "Fin, morsom Filmudgave af "Brudstykker af et Mønster"", Werner Thierry.
Politiken (31-10 1947): "Bitter Virkelighed i kunstnerisk Film", Frederik Schyberg.

Balladen om Carl-Henning
Aktuelt (Vestjylland, 29-4 1969): "Miraklerne kan ske i de danske film" [Raun].
Berlingske Aften (8-4-1969): "Helt sig selv", Flemming Behrendt.
Berlingske Tidende (8-4-1969): "En dansk film, der bevæger", Jørgen Stegelmann.
BT (8-4-1969): "Film", Rolf Bagger.
Kristeligt Dagblad (8-4-1969): "Dansk filmtriumf", Irmelin Thulstrup.
Land og Folk (8-4-1969): "Ensomme Carl-Henning", Peer Schaldemose [peer].
Politiken (8-4-1969): "Den hvide klovn – den danske fantast", Henrik Stangerup.

Drenge
Amts Avisen (10-5-1977): "Fremragende film om drenges "alder"", [tt.].
Kristeligt Dagblad (1-3-1977): "Usædvanlig dansk film", Henrik Moe.
Land og Folk: "Følsomt og poetisk dansk filmunder", Mikael Sne.
Politiken (26-2-1977): "Miraklet vi længe har vent på", Herbert Steinthal.

Anne Jerslev

Dogma 95, Lars von Trier's The Idiots and the 'Idiot Project'

> *To me realism is simply the artistic form of truth* (Roberto Rosselini).[1]

> *If I were to describe the real aim of the project it is some kind of search for truth* (Lars von Trier).[2]

The second Dogma film, Lars von Trier's *The Idiots,* was released in Denmark in the middle of July 1998. It had been shot during the months of May and June 1997. Later in 1998 Lars von Trier's film manuscript was published as a book. The book was introduced by the *Dogma 95* Manifesto and after the manuscript followed von Trier's diary recorded on a dictaphone covering the period starting right before shooting and stretching well into the editing of the film. Finally, in 1999, Jesper Jargil's documentary *De ydmygede* [The Humiliated] was released, documenting the shooting of *The Idiots.* Jesper Jargil is credited as assistant director and cinematographer on *The Idiots* in the printed manuscript. But first and foremost he shot director Lars von Trier, his crew and the actors and actresses in the process of making *The Idiots.* Thus, we have five different texts tied to one another, the ten Dogma rules called the "Vow of Chastity," a film manuscript, a diary, a fiction film and a documentary based on the making of *The Idiots.* The texts are all more or less explicitly intertextually intertwined and interrelated, and – at least for the last three mentioned works – are more or less centrally established within the genres to which they each claim to belong.

Jesper Jargil uses selected passages from von Trier's recorded tapes as voice over in *De ydmygede*, and fragments from *The Idiots* seem to be recycled in Jargil's film. Or maybe it is the other way round. The documentary is already folded into the fiction film in the sense that the documentary's cinematographer and one of the

41

cinematographers on *The Idiots* are one and the same person. Evidently from the outset, Lars von Trier's diary is not intended for private use alone. It is in a sense a fake diary, "a kind of diary" as he himself puts it, which is extremely self-conscious and which at times is a denial of the authenticity of the confessions of the most intimate nature which define the personal diary as a literary genre. As von Trier states for example on June 25th, "well, I can barely bring myself to say it, but I guess some sort of honesty is required in a diary" (von Trier 1998: 183).[3] He introduces the diary with a prologue, dated March 1998, half a year after his last recording to the dictaphone, where he states that the diary "true to the Dogma spirit" is "not edited and nothing has been changed by me." Consequently, he continues, "without any dissociation to the text whatsoever" that "no statement is planned beforehand; they occur the very second they are spoken. Since most factual and analytical information contains inaccuracies (not to mention falsities) it is recommended that the text be understood as a kind of author's therapy, provoked by the emotionally tense situation which was also the film's technique (Trier 1998: 159)."

In the sense that von Trier hereby denies that his diary holds any documentary, objective truth, he re-privatizes the text, returning to its original generic form a text that was originally, albeit paradoxically, adressed to the general public. It is a strange document which primarily seems to self-consiously contribute to the general image of Lars von Trier as an excentric artist. He performs himself as neurotically obsessed with his body and with the possibility of bodily illnesses. He is trapped in his body and seems constantly to want to confirm his own mortality. But the body does not quite seem to languish and life goes on. Almost parenthetically he informs the reader at the end of the diary that his wife, whose pregnancy he has recounted earlier, has given birth to twins: "we are editing the splendid scene in the woods which contains the whole philosophy. It is quite a different scene, a bit like Truffaut really, a bit like Fahrenheit, and … What more can I say? Oh yeah, by the way, we had two children the day before yesterday" (Trier 1998: 281).

Besides being a collection of immediate impressions of his daily work experiences, the diary is full of reflections on the relationship between director and actors and on the film itself. The diary is at once a working journal, a written collection of affective moments and a self-portrait, which in reality does not reveal anything more about von Trier than the public already knows. In the same way *The Idiots* is located in a field between performativity and authenticity and it, too, at once confirms and denies its genre. It is a fiction film that acts like a documentary and it extends itself textually into both Jargil's documentary and von Trier's diary in a kind of textual simultaneity or intertextuality. *The Idiots* is thus essentially dialogic and not a demarcated *work* in the usual sense of the word in that it is simultaneously part of a wider body of texts which might be named *The Idiot Project*. Following from this *The Idiots*, with its striking in medias res opening (a close up of Karen in the amusement park "Dyrehavsbakken") and its contrasting classical and sudden ending (Karen leaves her family) might be regarded as a kind of mise en abîme of the *Idiot Project* as a whole. Therefore *The Idiots* adheres to another important statement in Dogma 95's "Vow of Chastity": "I swear as a director to refrain from personal taste. I am no longer an artist. I swear to refrain from creating a "work"." The Dogma Brothers refrain from putting their unique artistic hand on their films. They deny being *auteurs*. Nevertheless, throughout the *Idiot Project*, von Trier is very much constructed as *auteur*.

In his diary, Lars von Trier declares that the many different kinds of material about the film makes it possible to make an "extremely interesting" film about the film: "This is one of the most comprehensive materials ever being made. Also because the film's genesis for the first time … well, maybe not for the first time, but anyway … becomes very conspicuous, not least because genesis and cinematic reproduction takes place simultaneously" (Trier 1998: 237). The paragraph is actually quite strange, as if *The Idiots* was not the finished result of a specific pro-filmic event. As if to begin with pro-filmic reality and the finished work were not separate and different processes of signification. As if becoming, process, was continuous, the end of which only another external camera such as Jesper Jargil's documentary camera could bring to a halt. But the phrase becomes less strange when regarded in the light of one of the important statements that follows the "Vow of

Chastity" in the Dogma 95 Manifesto, signed March 1995. The statement is repeated in different forms throughout the diary: "I regard the instant as more important than the whole." Just as von Trier aesthetically favors the moment instead of the whole, it seems that the creative process in the Dogma 95 tradition is more important than the finished work.

Overall, Dogma 95 may be regarded as a collection of formal and technical strategies implemented in order to accentuate and enhance visual presence and immediacy. The accentuation of the moment at the expense of the whole is one of these strategies of presence. Narrative progression is subordinate to constructions of intense moments. For example, closure is given a low priority compared to moments that exist in and of themselves. *The Idiots* lives up to these strategies beautifully as I shall argue in the following.

In keeping with the Dogma rules von Trier is not credited as director of *The Idiots*, or for that matter, as anything else. Likewise he starts the diary by denying it any value of truth. Nevertheless, von Trier's mark is all over the *Idiot Project* as a whole. Jargil's film opens with a text saying "This documentary follows the making of Lars von Trier's Dogma film *The Idiots*" and the diary tells the story of an honest and hard working director – true or fake. From the director's prologue added ex posteriori, it follows that the diary is completely unreliable. But the prologue simultaneously adds an autenthicating discourse to the diary verifying the text as the true emanation of the inner self. In this way von Trier is doubtlessly inscribed into the *Idiot Project* as *auteur*. Likewise, Jesper Jargil's film is without doubt a film about von Trier's work as a director on a specific film, although the whole project portrays a quite unheroic and ambiguous director.

The only manifest trace of the director in *The Idiots* appears when Lars von Trier lends his voice to an anonymous off screen interviewer, telling the characters what he "has heard" about them. And even though *De ydmygede* initially underlines who directed *The Idiots*, as I mentioned above, the documentary neither documents nor constructs the obvious directorial authority otherwise connected to the famous director of a film. On the contrary. We witness how von Trier's authority is jeopardized time and again in the making of the film; when we see him without pants on or when he acts like a spoiled child in front of his actors and actresses because he feels he is being ignored. Or when he asks his actors and actresses to clean up the house and they immediately start to "spass" and clean as spastic people might clean. But conversely, von Trier's reflective and self-conscious irony in his voice over lends authority to the embodied director Lars von Trier. Thus, in Jesper Jargil's film, the diary extracts are transformed from "a kind of author's therapy" into a more objective and interpretative "voice of God."

In the following discussion of *The Idiots* I am going to draw in more detail upon the aforementioned body of texts consisting of the Dogma 95 Manifesto, the diary, the documentary *De ydmygede* and the fiction film *The Idiots*. I will discuss *The Idiots* as an artistic realization of Dogma 95.[4] Just as Dogma 95 reflects upon film language I shall argue that *The Idiots* might be interpreted as a reflection upon film language and its relation to reality. Clearly, *The Idiots* is about transgression of social and individual boundaries. A small group of young people in a large mansion in a wealthy community north of Copenhagen challenge the Danish bourgeois and their fear of otherness. At the same time, the group seeks an inner freedom by 'spassing'[5] both privately and in public thereby nurturing their "inner idiot" as Stoffer, the group's leader puts it. For Stoffer, the idea is to challenge bourgeois understandings of normality and deviance. Thus, the film resumes the popular debates of 1960s dealing with these matters as well as class differences, suppression and fear of difference. But *The Idiots* is also a melancholy story about a political project that finally comes to nothing. From the interviews in the film given by the group members to an off screen interviewer, it appears that staying in the idiot community was only a parenthetical phase of the characters' lives which they look back upon either with regret or nostalgia. Almost all characters give interviews where Karen is one important exception. By means of the bodily and non-verbal 'spass,' Karen was provided with a means to express a grief much deeper than words and tears could express. When Henrik realizes that he cannot go through with 'spassing' in front of his class, he decides to leave the group. "I'm not going home with you" he says to the others, im-

plicitly expressing that living in the community was only tempo-
rary and that he had to leave in the same manner you leave a home
you are grown up in.

When Karen objects to Stoffer that "some people are really
sick. So how can you defend playing idiot," the film, of course,
comments on society's definition of sickness and normality. Yet
even though the film comforms unequivocally to the Dogma rules
and even though it discusses ideological commitments, it is not
dogmatic in any way. It does not answer unequivocally to the
question about social rules and transgression by turning the relationship between normality and deviance upside down. For example it is never obvious whether Josephine's father is just a powerful patriarch who by bringing his daughter home with him
guides her directly into the sickness that he claims to save her
from or whether the horrible scene points towards the disintegra-
tion of the community from within. At any rate, the eleven young
people cannot prevent one man from dragging his grown child
away. "What the fuck can he do to you," asks Katrine desperately
when Josephine leaves the table on her father's command. But the
scene also raises the question as to what the community is capable
of.

The Idiots is an obvious realization of Dogma rule number two,
which states that genre films are not accepted; it is an art film
claiming a serious theme. But the exciting thing about the film is
not the explicit meaning, the story about social and individual
transgression.

The ten Dogma Commandments and The Idiots.

"It is so wonderful that the Dogma rules have damned aesthetics to
hell," says Trier in his diary (Trier 1998: 236); "This is really what
the Dogma rules are all about – exactly because of the rules you can
get away with a whole lot of stuff" (ibid.: 182). Even though Dogma 95 accuses *nouvelle vague* of cultivating a romantic bourgeois
notion of art, Jean Luc Godard's reflections upon film as a visual
media and questions of visual representation resonates in the quote
as well as elsewhere in the *Idiot Project* and Dogma 95.[6] Like von

Trier, Godard has been occupied with the balance between artistic freedom and aesthetic rules and regulations as a creative force in film making. "I always like to pose restraint upon myself. The freer I am, the more I feel I must force certain basic conditions and rules upon myself" (Collet 1972/1964: 42). Furthermore, Godard was also interested in reintroducing a kind of back to basics cinematic aesthetic norm.[7] Besides *nouvelle vague* there are obvious references to Italian neorealism in Dogma 95 and von Trier mentions neorealism in his diary as well. The Dogma Brothers ten rules are the following:

1. Shooting must be done on location. Props and sets must not be brought in. (If a particular prop is necessary for the story, a location must be chosen where this prop is to be found).
2. The sound must never be produced apart from the images or vice versa. (Music must not be used unless it occurs where the scene is being shot).
3. The camera must be hand-held. Any movement or immobility attainable in the hand is permitted. (The film must not take place where the camera is standing; shooting must take place where the film takes place).
4. The film must be in colour. Special lighting is not acceptable. (If there is too little light for exposure the scene must be cut or a single lamp attached to the camera).
5. Optical work and filters are forbidden.
6. The film must not contain superficial action. (Murders, weapons, etc must not occur.)
7. Temporal and geographical alienation are forbidden. (That is to say that the film takes place here and now).
8. Genre movies are not acceptable.
9. The film format must be Academy 35 mm.
10. The director must not be credited.[8]

Even though Peter Schepelern (2000) in his book about von Trier's film argues that the Dogma rules about aesthetic and technical asceticism may be regarded as a kind of ironic fundamentalistic iconoclasm against Hollywood, they seem to me to be more than just provocations in the usual von Trier manner. They are also more far reaching and complex than merely being an aeschetic countermove against "a technological storm which is the elevation of cosmetics to God" as the Dogma Brothers state themselves in the Manifesto. The interesting thing to me seems to be that Dogma 95 dictates a set of minimalistic technical and narrative rules to which the profilmic has to subjugate itself thereby formulating a broader film aesthetics founded in a notion of realism and the real. This specific Dogma version of realism is directed towards the accentuation of a certain aspect of the ontology of the moving image, namely the photographic presence, the indexical aspect of the image.

Regarded as a coherent cinematic dogmatism, the essence of Dogma 95's realism seems to be the effort to aesthetically accentuate the indexical component of the audio-visual sign – speaking from a semiotic point of view. Or, in a more phenomenological manner, towards aesthetically constructing an impression of an immediate and unmediated almost Bazinian transmission of the represented 'reality' into the cinematic image. This aesthetic aim is accomplished in *The Idiots* more than in any other Dogma film and yet *The Idiots* is neither a barren exemplification of a set of rules, nor is it a naive mimesis. What is interesting about Dogma 95 is that the rules, even though they favor indexicality, also call attention to the fact that indexicality must necessarily be performed. Indexicality is an aesthetic effort. Thus, paradoxically, Dogma 95 may be regarded a set of semiotic procedures aimed at the toning down of visuality as *re-presentation* in favor of a kind of visual *presentation*. Furthermore, what is really interesting about *The Idiots* is that the film's highly reflexive discourse negates the distance usually built into reflexivity. Instead, distance is replaced by immediate transmissions of affect.

Dogma 95 suggests an aesthetics of presence and immediacy in time (now) as well as in space (here). The rules aim at establishing a sense of live-ness,[9] narratively as well as aesthetically, creating a notion of right 'now' by means of the creation of an insecure 'here.' Dogma films must take place in the present. They must come close to the spectator and actions, must take place in a kind of temporal immediacy as if they were transmitted in the very moment they take place. Dogma rule number three demands that actions must not take place where the camera is standing but the camera must seek out actions, and it demands that the camera be hand-held. As such the rules echo a cinema verité "live" documentary aesthetics, where camera movement and (im)balance suggest an immediate attachment to events which unfold truthfully in front of the camera. Correspondingly, it seems that the Dogma rules in a way prescribe the typical contemporary modality of perception that John Ellis (2000) has named witness.

Elsewhere Lars von Trier has elaborated on Dogma rule number three by commenting on the necessity of avoiding conscious framing:

Frame – here you are interested in frames only. Whereas, if you just point with your camera, you are interested in seeking out the content. (…) When you construct an image you are actually going for control. But you might ignore that for a moment and try to put yourself into the frame and find out what's inside, what's in the middle. Then you just point in that direction because then it comes to you … (Schepelern 2000: 233).

Mastery and obsession with control runs as a continuous theme through von Trier's cinematic universe as well as in his work as a director (cf. Grodal 2000). The Dogma rules prescribe another correspondance with the visual material where the director more intimately connects with his scenes without having transformed the profilmic events into visual frames beforehand. The director must first refrain from using his forming and controlling authority and then he can step back in order to adjust the camera to what is really happening on the set. By means of this directorial procedure it should aesthetically be possible to construct the kind of authenticity that von Trier is occupied with in *The Idiots*. The camera must interfere as litle as possible. As such, it seems logical that von Trier himself operated the camera much of the time while shooting. Without being able to survey anything but what he can see through the eye of the camera he has to put his whole presence into the making of the immediate image.

Dogma 95 likewise emphasizes that sound and image must be connected. Music should only be used if the source of the sound has physically been present on the set. It is shown in *De ydmygede* how the beautifully melancholy theme from Camille Saint-Saens' The Swan becomes physically attached to the image because the melodica player is present in the horse cart where Karen sits in one of the very first images in the film. Except, he is, of course, placed off frame. Music is therefore non-diegetic in the sense that Karen cannot hear it. Nevertheless, it also emanates from the image like other kinds of diegetic sound not immediately seen in the image frame. Thus, the actress Bodil Jørgensen who plays Karen is able to hear it.

Von Trier's interpretation of Dogma rule number two thus disrupts classical audio visual perception in the sense that it disrupts the demarcation between filmic and pro-filmic levels. *De ydmygede* defamiliarizes the perception of this scene of *The Idiots* in the sense that after having seen the documentary, there will forever be two persons in the cart that transports Karen into the park. The musical theme from The Swan reappears in *De ydmygede* in an orchestral version and credit information implies that it has been added in post-production. Thus, the documentary uses non-diegetic music in keeping with classical narrative principles, whereas the fiction film inserts the musician as a documentary presence into the pro-filmic event. Dogma rule number two at once expands and narrows cinematic space. It connects organically time with space as well as image and sound. Rule number two thus naturalizes the photographic image or, as cultural researcher Britta Timm Knudsen (2001) has put it, it rejoins what digitalization has separated. Sound is glued to the image which at once emphasizes the film as representation and provides it with a temporal immediacy and a physical presence. Sound points poignantly to the represented objects' having been there just as Roland Barthes would say of the photographic image.

André Bazin, in his famous essay about the ontology of the photographic image, characterizes photography as a "natural image." Likewise, he talks about the "objective nature" of photography, which "confers upon it a quality of credibility": "In spite of any objections our critical spirit may offer, we are forced to accept as real the existence of the object reproduced, actually represented, set before us, that is to say, in time and space" (Bazin 1945/1967: 13-14). According to Bazin, photography has given nature the power to represent itself without the intervention of man. It would be wrong, however, to read Bazin's article as just the naive perception that there is no difference whatsoever between representation and represented, between film and reality. Had this been the case, he wouldn't have ended the article with his tongue in cheek remark that "On the other hand, of course, cinema is also a language" (ibid.: 16). The photographic image is coded; it is also a sign. But the interesting point in Bazin's article is his insistence on understanding that photography is more than a sign system and cinema is more than a language. This *more*, or visual *presence*, is what Bazin is trying to theorize in his discussion of the ontology of the image which he connects to questions of time. This is the really challenging point in Bazin's short article. He tries to conceptualize a 'something' which is unique, a 'something' in addition to the photographic image besides it being coded. Dogma 95 may be interpreted in continuation of Bazin's thoughts but the 1995 Manifesto is not glaringly naive either. Dogma 95 may be understood as an extension into the age of the digital images of Bazin's thoughts of the photographic presence, its temporal actualization of photography's having-once-been-there. On the other hand, visual digitalization must problematize thoughts like Bazin's. Furthermore, Dogma 95 may be regarded as an *audio*-visual transformation of Bazin's thoughts. Sound represents or underlines the enbalming of time, the impression that what once was, is simultaneously here and now; an idea Bazin connected to photography alone.

In the scene where Josephine's father arrives in the community in order to bring his daughter home with him and is offered a cup of tea by the group members gathered in front of the house, the sound of an airplane is heard off screen and Josephine's father turns his head towards the sky. This tiny and quick turning of the body which might be described as either the actor's or the character's response to an aural stimulus is a beautiful example of the realism or, as Barthes would put it, the reality effect, here made possible by the Dogma rules – the presence of mind of actor Anders Hove notwithstanding. We are certain from Dogma rule number one that the airplane is not a prop brought in and we know for sure from Dogma rule number two that the airplane which produced the sound was actually there in profilmic space even though it is never seen within the frame. The sound and the bodily movement is one example of mimetic surplus characterizing realism as a style, according to Torben Grodal (1997) who argues that classical realist writers have tried to simulate "an open and undirected world by increasing the level of description," where objects are "connected to other objects and features by a web of metonymic relations" and "a given element just happened to be there when the camera passed by, metonymically connected to all the other phenomena, and will not appear later" (Grodal 1997: 223). But it is also a very precise expression of Dogma realism's indexically bound *aesthetics of presence*. Because the sound and the source of the sound are physically attached to one another, sound as well as its source were actually there at the very moment the father sits down at the table, and the turning of his head creates an almost documentary authenticity. The movement is not rehearsed; it has not been done again and again before the camera starts running. The scene that we watch in the finished film could never be made in exactly the same manner again.

Dogma rule number two makes it possible for the director to surrender to the small coincidences of reality beyond his control. This would also be in accordance with Dogma commandment number ten that states that the director must not be credited. *The Idiots* is quite close to the original script despite the large number of creative discussions between director, actors and actresses capturered in *De ydmygede*. There is no demand to make improvisations in Dogma 95. But the rules both demand and make it possible to construct a relation of presence and immediacy between image and sound, thus establishing as Bazin puts it, the impression of the "transference of reality from the thing to its reproduction" (Bazin 1945/1967: 14). But whereas Bazin talks about an unmediated transference, Dogma 95 prescribes *an aesthetics*, a *style* of unmediated transformation.

In his discussion of the relationship between photography and the represented object, Bazin claims that "The photograph as such and the object in itself share a common being, after the fashion of the fingerprint" (ibid.: 15). Phenomenology here shares thoughts with semiology in the sense that Bazin's comparison resembles

Charles Sanders Peirce's coining of the indexical aspect of the sign (Peirce 1998). Indexicality points to a physical connectedness between the sign and the represented object. It points out an organic coupling, a natural and inseparable connection, just as the symptom indexically points to the sickness, or the man with the rolling gait points out that he is a sailor or the weathercock points to the direction of the wind; these are all examples in Peirce's elaboration on the indexical sign (Peirce 1998). The weathercock points in the same direction as the wind by means of the wind because it is physically connected to it. The indexical sign, or the indexical aspect of the sign, has a real connection to its object; the weathercock can only do what it does because it is being touched by the wind. But the indexical aspect is simultaneously connected to the two other poles in the Peircian tripolar notion of the sign. Thus, at the same time the sign will always contain the iconic (a relation of likeness) and the symbolic (the arbitrary socially defined relation). The weathercock is thus an index with an icon attached to it. Besides being physically connected to the wind, it resembles the wind by pointing in the same direction as the wind (Peirce 1998: 306). But it would be equally relevant to say that the weathercock is a symbolic sign, at least when you take the cock or the arrowhead into consideration.

Film language is primarily iconic and indexical, contrary to verbal language which is primarily symbolic. As a mimetic system of representation, realism basically stresses the iconic aspect of the visual image. But realism can also be symbolic at least when we keep in mind, as Noël Carroll (1988) so rightly has put it, that cinematic realism is not just one thing but a triangular relationship between reality, one group of films and another, contrasting group of films. In extension, I would argue that Dogma 95's specific aesthetic realization and its claim to realism in *The Idiots* produces an accentuated notion of the indexical aspect of the images, the attachment to the specific visual 'having-been-there.' The inserted interview sequences become very interesting in light of this argument. By means of their ambiguous visual staging of different and interconnected levels of reality within diegetic space, they seem narratively to comment on the idea of indexicality. It seems to me that the interview sequences in particular bring to the foreground the *physical/organic* connection between past and present, between being here and having been there.

In all but one of the nine interviews a disembodied interviewer whose voice belongs to Lars von Trier addresses the characters with questions about what happened in the house while the group was living and "spassing" together. The narrative is interrupted by interview scenes throughout the film, thus dividing the narrative into several separate moments combined into a 'whole' at the very end with the final disclosure of Karen's secret. Characters face the camera. They are not anchored in a recognizable time or space besides the obvious fact that the interviews take place 'later' or 'after.' It is also unclear which function the interviews occupy in the narrative as a whole, because the interviewer never becomes a diegetic character. According to the interviews, none of the characters have any contact with the others anymore, and their memories and reflections have no final truth value. The "spass" period is a thing of the past. Susanne is the last to be interviewed: "I was the one who was with Karen on the last day," she says, "and I was the one who said good-bye to her," she recalls.

Birger Langkjær (1999) has elaborated at length, on how the interviews are a crucial means of establishing the fundamental clashes between fiction and reality, thus creating the ambivalent spectator position and a disturbing experience which according to Langkjær, is the overall point of the film. The question is, must interview persons be understood as fictional characters who reflect upon their fictional character (that is themselves) in another time and place? Do the real actors and actresses talk about the fictional characters that they are impersonating? Or do actors and actresses talk about themselves as private persons? Langkjær concludes that the first mentioned possibility may be the way most spectators understand the interview sequences: fictional characters talk about themselves and the interview sequences are part of *The Idiots'* narrative, even though they are not anchored firmly in narrative time and space. But it is not possible to know for sure. It is not difficult to understand and accept that fictional characters can talk about themselves because we are still situated within the fictional universe. The main problem is that the interviewer's voice undoubtedly belongs to Lars von Trier. The film's director suddenly seems to inscribe himself within the cinematic narrative as a fictional character who remains disembodied and is only heard in these specific sequences. But the voice in the film is definitely not that of the real director. It knows far too little about what has been going on for that to be the case.

The important point to maintain here is that it is most likely characters who are speaking about themselves. By referring to themselves in the first person singular they connect the person speaking 'now' to the person whose past actions they are telling about. In linguistic theory, Roman Jakobson (1957/1990), with reference to Danish linguist Otto Jespersen, has elaborated on the concept of the 'shifter' and, following Peirce expert Arthur. W. Burks, connected it both to Peirce's index and to the symbol.[10] Shifters are for example the personal pronouns, which link the sign physically (indexically) to the person using it. The signified thus shifts constantly, but the sign, the personal pronoun, becomes meaningful only due to the existential connection between the signifying speaker and the signified, the represented 'I', "the word I designating the utterer is existentially related to his utterance and hence functions as an index" (Jakobsen 1957/1990: 388). On the other hand, 'I' is also a symbol "being associated with the latter "by a conventional rule"" (ibid.). The interviews may be regarded as visual dramatizations of the shifter in a symbolic, narrativized form. Therefore, these strange scenes are important contributions to the construction of the impression of indexical presence in *The Idiots*. When we see and hear Susanne say "it was I who was the one who was together with Karen on the last day" the linguistic shifter 'I' is anchored in the physical manifestation which is Susanne. But this visualized 'I' becomes a corporealized shifter in relation to all the earlier pictures of Susanne because Susanne is talking about the 'I' that once was. The fact that Susanne has a different hair colour authenticates the temporal relation even more.

Performing and being

On many different levels, *The Idiots* establishes an indecisive zone between fiction and reality and between performing and being within the fictional universe.[11] *De ydmygede* adds another level of ambiguity since the documentary also oscillates between filmic and pro-filmic. By means of the documentary's editing strategy that several times gives the impression of quoting from the finished film only afterwards to reveal that what we saw was actually the pro-filmic activity, a fluctuation of meaning is established. The interesting and disturbing thing about *The Idiots* is that its authenticity is not derived from the accentuation of 'real' being at the expense of performativity. Nor is it the other way round, where performativity becomes as real as the real. But central moments of seemingly authentic being that affect the spectator profoundly appear, at first, where it is impossible to determine for sure what we see. Are characters performing 'spas' or are characters' innermost feelings being given a means to express themselves through the very activity of being a 'spasser'? Secondly, authenticating moments appear in the parts of the film where character and actor intertwine.

Character and actor intertwine most disturbingly in the nude scenes where the characters' desire is shown most literally. The important scenes are where we see Stoffer in the ladies room in the swimming bath and the group sex, or "gang bang" scene. Being and performing, character and 'spasser' character overlap indeterminately in the scene where Jeppe is left by Stoffer with the bikers, but most of all in the final scenes with Jeppe and Josephine, first during the party sequence where they start caressing in the room upstairs and the morning after when Jeppe tries to prevent Josephine's father from taking her away. This overlapping is also seen most disturbingly in the films' closing scene where Karen goes back to her family with Susanne.

In his critical discussion of Bazin's notion of realism and visual representation, with Beardsley's aesthetics as a point of departure, Noël Carroll (1998) argues that when one talks about visual fiction it is necessary to distinguish between three levels of representation in a film. First, there is what he calls the *physical portrayal* of the model in a live-action film. It is always a concrete person/actor that is being represented, even though this specific person is only there as a fictional character. The actress Anne-Louise Hassing is there whether she is a diegetic character called Susanne or not and whether she is a trained actress or not. This level is what Bazin is interested in in his essay; the physical imprint of an actual thing, or the indexicality of the object.

Secondly, according to Carroll, fiction films also *depict* "a class or collection of objects designated by a general term" (Carroll 1998: 150). Anne Louise Hassing is at the same time as she is a concrete female always there in a more general manner, as 'a woman.' When we look at her on the screen we always see a woman and a specific woman at one and the same time. "What is theoretically important about depiction," claims Carroll, "is that it splits the shot from its source" (Carroll 1988: 151). And continuing from Peirce's tripolar notion of the sign, or of representation, I would suggest that Carroll's term *depiction* which defers focus from *presence* to *resemblance,* can be seen as corresponding to Peirce's iconic aspect of representation. Finally, Carroll discusses a third mode of cinematic representation which he calls *nominal portrayal.* According to Carroll, this third aspect is the most important mode of representation in fiction film, where a person always portrays or represents someone other than the person she or he really is outside the cinematic universe.

Physical portrayal is unavoidable in classical cinematic representation; physical portrayal is thus at the heart of the structure of the star system, primarily in the 1930s spectacular close-ups of stars. Physical portrayal is also commonly subsumed or rather transformed into *nominal portrayal*, though, a fictional character given a particular name by the writer. Susanne (impersonated and played by the actress Anne Louise Hassing) is one such *nominal portrayal.*

It was very important to Lars von Trier that Stoffer "have a real erection," (von Trier 1998: 182) in the scene in the swimming bath where Stoffer insists on following Karen into the ladies dressing room. Von Trier's argument is that a difference in colour grading could easily be recognized when using a stand-in since the Dogma rules make it impossible to colour grade in post-production. Furthermore, von Trier states that it would "simply be the best" (ibid.: 184). The director tells later in the diary about his actors and actresses in the gang bang scene where stand-ins were hired to act in a few "meat shots" (close ups of real penetration, cf. Linda Wil-

liams 1998) that it seemed to be very difficult for them to act together with professional porn actors. He recounts that "it was a big
thing and it was difficult but they went through with it and it was
great, because I can see now that those shots are essential for the
scene. Precisely these shots provide the scene with the danger that
makes it impossible to dissociate oneself from it. That is disturbing
– someone playing idiots and having real sex at the same time. It
adds the tiny transgression to the scene which is needed in this
scene and in the film as a whole. I think this is important at any
time" (ibid.: 250). Put another way; what creates disturbance is
that two different levels of cinematic representation, *physical portrayal* and *nominal portrayal*, are accentuated *at the same time*.
Technically, erection must of course emanate from the actor Jens
Albinus and not from the character Stoffer and this is why *physical portrayal* calls attention to itself much more vehemently than it
usually does in fiction films. The same goes for the gang bang
scene.

The young people have hosted an idiots' birthday party cele-
brating Stoffer and Stoffer suggests a "gang bang" as part of a performance of his inner idiot. Nana, played by porn actress Trine
Michelsen, immediately lies down, legs spread, prepared for a
"spasser fuck," and here, of course, *physical portrayal* is highlighted by means of the extratextual knowledge of the actress' other
profession. But then several of the others follow suit. Susanne,
who throughout the film has been a 'helper' and has therefore not
'spassed' at all, escapes laughing through the door to the garden
but is followed by Stoffer and a couple of the others, who want her
to join the party. In the following scene, most of the community
including Susanne lie naked on the floor on top of each other and
have sex with the exception of three of the central characters, Karen who sits in the background on the windowsill, Josephine who
has fled to an upstairs room and Jeppe who follows her. In this
scene we have young people performaing their 'spasser' character
(and as such are double nominally portrayed – characters playing
characters) and one person who does not play an idiot (Susanne as
nominal portrayal) all on the floor having real sex (physical portrayal). In the scene, complete with "meat-shots," there is an indis-
tinguisable mixture of performance and being. But the very phys-

ical imprint of desire subordinates nominal portrayal to physical portrayal, iconic aspect of the image to indexical aspect. The actors dissociate themselves momentarily from both 'spas' and 'character' and turn into mere physical beings, their own biographical beings. That is what makes the scene so disturbing.

What is interesting about photographic pornography is exactly the ambiguous play with truth and performance, an indexical insisting which at the same time becomes indexical impotence. Rune Gade (1997) talks about the "indexical fetish" in visual pornography, the insatiable insistence upon real physical proofs of desire, erection and ejaculation which relates indexically to the man who was there. Bad acting is of no importance in pornographic narratives. What is important is not nominal portrayal, but rather "representations of authentic desire, situated in a real "having-been-there" body," (Gade 1997: 224) "scattered evidence of a real person's real desire, which *seemingly* breaks through the surface of the "bad" performance" (ibid. – I italicize). This "seemingly" is the fuel of pornography. At least according to Linda Williams who emphasizes the pornographic curse that you never know about the woman, that it is never possible to know for certain whether she is performing, that what you see is actually "the involuntary confession of bodily pleasure" (Williams 1988: 50). Nominal portrayal protrudes in an unpleasant way in relation to the female character in pornography. Therefore pornography has to perform persuasively over and over again the physical being out of control aspect of female sexuality.

Nominal portrayal is doubled in *The Idiots* since the characters play roles, too. They 'spass' together in the house and in front of strangers outside the house. Characters have least at stake when their aim is to place their bourgeois neighbours in embarassing situations, like when they sell Christmas decorations or when visiting the Rockwool factory. There is no doubt here that characters are 'spassing.' The difference between performing and being is less clear in the disturbing scene where Stoffer leaves Jeppe to perform a 'spasser' on his own and places him at a table in the bar with three heavily tattooed, and muscular bikers. When Jeppe suddenly rises from the table in order to leave, the bikers conclude that he needs to pee and they redirect him to the bar's toilet. Here the film crosscuts between close-ups of Jeppe's face turned to the wall and the bikers who wait for him to finish. The question seems to be how to interpret Jeppe's facial expressions. Are they 'spass,' and is Jeppe so much a part of his performance that he acts even though the waiting bikers can only see his back? Does he live up to Stoffer's ideal idiot in the sense that he is performing even when he really does not have to, thus countering Stoffer's accusations after the Rockwool factory incident that Jeppe was not seriously 'spassing'? Or are his facial expressions resulting from fear and exertion that the bikers might realize that he is just acting? The double nominal portrayal raises the possibility that the characters' behaviour is never anchored firmly within the diegesis, thus making several interpretations possible, each of which is not completely satisfactory on their own. An emphatic reading would see the character behind the performer in close-ups in the bar's toilet which are traditionally meant to point to the authentic person behind the mask. Thus the spectator might nervously relate emphatically to Jeppe because he is in a very difficult situation. In this understanding, close-ups reveal the real Jeppe's real tensions – which, on the other hand, do not fit easily into the description of the bikers as nice and helpful persons, whereas seeing only the role within the role focuses on Jeppe's skilled performance and his ability to stand the test that Stoffer has imposed on him. Thus, one is able to laugh at the odd pairing of Jeppe and the bikers. But then again, it would actually be quite difficult to fit the close-ups into this explanation.

Stoffer thinks that 'spassing' touches on an essential suppressed part of the characters' inner life, the subdued 'inner idiot.' But the 'spasser' is simultaneously just a role that members of the group can take on and off at will as part of their transgressive project. Basically the characters are performing when 'spassing.' The important exception are the scenes with Jeppe and Josephine during, and the day after the birthday party, where it seems as if character and idiot character merge imperceptibly. When Jeppe and Josephine start approaching each other they are performing idiots just like they did when they arrived at the birthday party. Their speech is inarticulate and their bodily movements 'spassing' just like we have seen them on earlier occasions when they 'spass.' At the end of the scene, Josephine whispers twice "I love you" and then she starts crying. The verbal expression indicates that Josephine has taken off her idiot performance, her statement a true expression of her inner self. But the point is that *so was the 'spass' caressing* right before. It is not certain when double nominal portrayal has been replaced by a single nominal portrayal. We do not know for sure when performance turns into being in the scene. And it does not matter.

The same goes for the scene that takes place the following day where Jeppe tries to prevent Josephine from leaving and throws himself onto the hood of Josephine's father's car. His movements are firm and goal-oriented when he rises from the table and starts running. But his speech is inarticulate, as if he had put on his 'spass' act. 'Spassing' has in earlier scenes been about challenging society or, more generally, about questioning reality. Just as one of them replies to Stoffer's statement when he realizes that they are preparing a birthday party for him and objects that it is not his real birthday, that "we're fuckin' not idiots either." The division between performance and being has been explicit, acting as an idiot or just being the character, authenticity and inauthenticity has been posed as different levels of nominal portrayal throughout the film. Whereas in this disturbing scene, the doubly constructed nominality is erased. Performance, the diegetic staging of a role, becomes – maybe – sheer authentic emotion. Controlled performance is indistinguishable from pure being or uncontrolled affect. Finally, it does not matter whether the characters projected are Jeppe and Josephine or Jeppe and Josephine acting as idiots. Under any circumstances the awkward, violent and inarticulate bodily movements are carriers of authenticity. Or rather, it feels as if 'spass' is no less than the adequate means of expressing authentic feeling for Josephine, Jeppe, and Karen, too. It seems as if they are conveying their inner feeling with an outward truthfulness and playing the idiot becomes the only possible means of expressing the inner anguish which has no other form of outlet. The point is, that the whole reflexive level in *The Idiots*, the discussion of the relationship between fiction and reality, is not meant to be a distanciating strategy pointing to the constructedness of the visual world. Rather, the function is to break through to reality with the help of emotion. By the end of the film, naughty and ideologically motivated provocation is replaced by existential necessity. Concurrently, with the replacement of a double with a single nominal portrayal, one might say that an indexical relationship between character and idiot replaces an iconic one.

This is made clear in the final scene when Karen's traumatic story discloses that she is the real protagonist in the film. Karen's baby died a little more than a week ago and she disappeared from her family the day before the burial of the little boy was to take place. "Karen's gone into spass," yells Nana to the others who curiously approach the window where Karen is contemplating in order to get confirmation that she has finally joined the group's project. But it turns out that her performance is very different from theirs. And when she returns to her home for the last time, she does not go in order to show that she dares challenge somone who is dear to her, which was Stoffer's notion of the ultimate way of challenging oneself and thus to proof the community's viability. The claustrophobic scene in Karen's home is a profound critique of petit bourgeois fear and pent-up emotions. It is realism's equivalent to the calvinistic family structure in *Breaking the Waves*. But the scene is primarily an emotional *presentation* of Karen's grief. She performs her 'spass' act perfectly because her performance is her being. She is her role. 'Spassing' here transgresses the symbolic order while at the same time, her inarticulate bodily behavior symbolizes this other place. The 'spassing' character is an idiot. Karen's innermost selv resides in a speech-less, non-cultivated emotionality beyond reason – this is the only true place from which her trauma can be articulated.

A true work of art

I have discussed Dogma 95 as an invitation, a serious effort to discuss the necessary renewal of contemporary film language. The imprint of Dogma 95 thus creates the specific reality effect in *The Idiots*. The interview sequences' contribution to a narrative construction reflecting a sense of 'having-been-there' goes hand in hand with a continuous oscillation between different levels of portrayal, thus creating *The Idiots'* realism as an aesthetics of presence.

In an article from 1959, Jean Luc Godard cites Rossellini for saying about film that "One must go to this extreme point where things speak for themselves. Which does not mean that they alone speak, but that they speak of what they really are" (Godard 1959/1972: 141). His formulation is remarkably reminiscent of Viktor Shklovsky's famous notion of *defamiliarization*; that art enables one to "recover the sensation of life, it exists to make one feel things, to make the stone *stony*," (Shklovsky 1917/1988: 20) "art creates a vision of the object instead as serving as a means for knowing it" (ibid.: 20). It seems to me that what Shklovsky touches on here is actually a visual representational strategy of immediate presentation, of speaking directly to the senses. Like Shklovsky, Rossellini speaks about art's ability to affect perception directly and thus, to change our everyday perception in order to make us see and feel in new and different ways. It seems to me that this is what *The Idiots* is really about. The Dogma Brothers signed a Manifesto which prevented them from exposing themselves as artists. Even though *The Idiots* may be a single effort in Lars von Trier's oeuvre, it seems to me to be no more nor less than a true work of art in Shklovsky's notion of the word.

Notes

1 Rossellini interviewed by Mario Verdone in 1952. Reprinted in Forgacs et al (2000).
2 Lars von Trier 1998: 238.
3 All quotes from the diary are translated into English by me. Quotes in English from *The Idiots'* dialogue are taken from the film's English subtitles.
4 Shortly after the film's premiere Lars von Trier accused producers Windeløv and Ålbæk Jensen from Zentropa of having manipulated the film in post-production. It is hard to say whether von Trier was right or wrong and whether he was really angry with his colleagues at Zentropa or not. Or whether the public argument was merely a stunt

that finally established Lars von Trier as the author which the Dogma 95 rules prevented him from being. Surely, the debate is another of the ambiguous texts which constitute the *Idiot Project.*

5 The characters use the verb to spass, the adjective spassing, and the noun spass in order to name their 'idiot'acting or spastic acting. English subtitles use the same expressions.

6 In an interview on the web site www.dogme95.dk titled "The Man Who Would Give Up Control" by Peter Øvig Knudsen, von Trier refers to nouvelle vague himself as a movement which gave "fresh air," "and in the same way Dogma 95 has been designed to give fresh air, to regain lost innocence."

7 Even though Godard may, a couple of decades before cinematic postmodernism, be much more interested in calling attention to the basic *discursive nature* of both film and reality.

8 Dogma 95 is reprinted in Schepelern (2000) in Danish and in Bondebjerg and Hjort (2001) in English. It is also in English on the website www.dogme95.dk.

9 I borrow John Caldwell's (1994) coining of television's different strategies of constructing an impression of live transmission.

10 Rosalind Krauss (1977/1987) also discusses the relationship between the shifter and the index.

11 Britta Timm Knudsen (2000) uses the same difference between 'performance' and 'being.' Cf. also Christensen (2000).

References

Bazin, André. 1945/1967. *What is Cinema? Volume 1*. Berkeley, Los Angeles, London: Univerity of California Press.

Bondebjerg, Ib & Hjort, Mette. 2001. *The Danish Directors. Dialogues on a Contemporary National Cinema.* London: Intellect Press.

Caldwell, John Thornton. 1995. *Televisuality. Style, Crisis, and Authority in American Television*. New Brunswick, New Jersey: Rutgers University Press.

Carroll, Noël. 1988. *Philosophical Problems of Classical Film Theory*. Princeton, New Jersey: Princeton University Press.

Christensen, Ove. 2000. "Spastic Aesthetics". *p.o.v.* no. 10. Århus: Institut for Medievidenskab, Århus Universitet.

Collet, Jean. 1972/1964. "No questions Asked. Conversations with Jean-Luc Godard on *Bande à part*". In *Focus on Godard*, edited by Royal S. Brown. Englewood Cliffs, N.J.: Prentice Hall, Inc.

Forgacs, David, Sarah Lutton & Geoffrey Nowell-Smith. 2000. *Roberto Rossellini. Magician of the Real*. London: British Film Institute.

Gade, Rune. 1997. *Staser*. Århus: Passepartout.

Godard, Jean Luc. 1959/1972. "A Film Maker is also a Missionary: Roberto Rossellini." In *Godard on Godard*, edited by Tom Milne. London: Secker & Warburg.

Grodal, Torben Kragh. 2000. "Die Elemente des Gefühls. Kognitive Filmtheorie und Lars von Trier". *Montage a/v. Zeitschrift für Theorie & Geschichte audiovisueller Kommunikation*, vol. 9, no. 1.

Grodal, Torben Kragh. 1997. *Moving Pictures*. Oxford: Clarendon Press.

Jakobson, Roman. 1957/1990. "Shifters and Verbal Categories". In *On Language. Roman Jakobson*, edited by Linda R. Waugh and Monique Monville-Burston. Cambridge, Massachusets & London, England: Harvard University Press.

Knudsen, Britta Timm. 2000. "Billedernes realisme. Jean-Luc Godards *Vivre sa vie* og Lars von Triers *Idioterne*". *Periskop* 9.

Knudsen, Britta Timm. 2001. "90'ernes visuelle kultur". *Jyllands Posten, Kunst og kultur*, March 6.

Krauss, Rosalind. 1977/1987. "Notes on the Index. Seventies Art in America". In *October. The First Decade, 1976-1986*, edited by Annette Michelson, Rosalind Krauss, Douglas Crimp, Joan Copjec. Cambridge, Massachusets & London, England: The MIT Press.

Langkjær, Birger. 1999. "Fiktioner og virkelighed i Lars von Triers *Idioterne*". *Kosmorama* 224, Winter.

Peirce, C.S. 1998. *The Essential Peirce. Selected Philosophical Writings. Volume 2 (1893-1913)*. Edited by the Peirce Edition Project. Bloomington and Indianapolis: Indiana University Press.

Schepelern, Peter. 2000. *Lars von Triers film. Tvang og befrielse*. København: Rosinante.

Shklovsky, Victor. 1917/1988. "Art as tecnique". In *Modern Criticism and Theory*, edited by David Lodge. London and New York: Longman.

Trier, Lars von. 1998. *Idioterne. Manuskript. Dagbog*. København: Gyldendal.

Torben Grodal

The Experience of Realism in Audiovisual Representation

Prevalent understandings of realism

The aim of this article is to analyze some of the ways in which realism is experienced. Thus, it does not aim to provide a definition of what is real, but to describe and characterize some of the different processes and elements that cause viewers of audiovisual representations to have an experience of 'realism', where 'realism' can be described as an evaluative feeling based on perception, cognition and habituation. The starting point of this discussion deals with how the experience of 'realism' is linked to perceptual specificity, but is also linked to mental schemas that provide typical and familiar 'recognizability.' The article will then discuss how some types of 'realism' are based on the idea of a transparent AV-screen as an 'objective' window, whereas other types of realism emphasise the role of filmmakers, reporters or protagonists, for instance by making subjective deconstructions of transparency in order to indicate the presence of the communicator. The article discusses how some types of realism focus on a specific external reference, whereas other forms, named 'categorical realism' want to portray the general 'essence' of things, yet other forms, described as 'lyrical realism' activate subjective-associative references. Reality can also be constituted by assertions where some human agencies assert that something is real, or constituted by interaction with the represented. Further, the article discusses how and why realism is often connected with seriousness and even with negative and painful experiences. Finally, the article discusses how a postmodern 'reflexive' scepticism towards realism in audiovisual media can be viewed as an emotional stance.

Some of the central terms used to describe media representations are 'reality' and 'realism.' Because they are central, it is no wonder that they are used in many different ways, causing ambiguity or inconsistency in their meaning. Furthermore, the concept of 'reality' (and derivatives like 'real') is not only central for describing media representations but for understanding 'real' life where the concept is also used in many different ways. Our concepts of what is real are based on many different elements and in a given representation, the different elements may each have their own reality status (Grodal 1997). A fiction film shot on location in New York may exhibits a 'realistic' visual picture of New York and realistic acting but have a wildly improbable story. Animators of fantasy films may put a lot of energy into making the movements of fantasy creatures look 'realistic,' that is made in accordance with the viewers' experience-based 'movement schemas.' A non-fiction film may tell a true story but with pictures that only provide a weak experience of reality. That our concepts of 'reality' and 'realism' are based on many different parameters (schemas) in a given audiovisual representation means that the viewer performs a series of different mental operations in order to assess the reality status of each parameter. The viewer may also evaluate the reality status of the film or program as a whole.

Realism is mainly a word used in order to describe the relationship between representations and a physical and social 'reality' exterior to such representations. Realism may be applied to fictitious as well as non-fictitious representations, because realism does not imply that what has been represented is true and 'real' in all aspects. It only implies that the representation is experienced as being a concrete representation that is, or might be true. The evaluation of realism in a given representation is based on three preexisting understandings:

1. A characterization of the representation.
2. Some concept of what the 'real' world looks like.
3. The relationship between representation and concepts of what the 'real' world looks like.

The degree to which there is a positive connection between representation and concepts of 'reality,' determines the degree to which the representation will be evaluated as 'realistic.' Thus, the question of realism does not only imply a characterization of representations, but also a characterization of what different individuals, groups, cultures or epochs understand as 'real,' a rather difficult and complex task. Some parameters, upon which such evaluations of what is 'real' are based, are relatively universal. For instance, our basic perceptions of the physical world are largely based on innate dispositions and on certain anthropocentric presuppositions (like 'earth is down,' 'heaven is up' (cf. Lakoff 1987, Johnson 1997)). Therefore there are universal norms used in evaluating the degree of realism in the perceptual dimensions of representations. However, such an evaluation, does not necessarily express how a given culture experiences a given representation. Even if people in the middle ages perceived the basic features of the world in a way very similar to us, they were not able to represent their perception of exterior reality to the same degree as we can. Therefore they may have perceived their medieval paintings as being more realistic than we do now, because our representational context is different. But other parameters, for instance those norms of human behavior that anchor our evaluations of realism, may vary over time, and from group to group. Even if nonverbal communication is based on innate and universal dispositions, it is well known that different groups enhance or suppress certain features within nonverbal communication (cf. Ekman and Friesen 1975). Moral norms that are 'unrealistic' or deviant in one society may be considered 'normal' in another. Knowledge of what exists in the world differs from person to person and from epoch to epoch. Thus, in evaluating whether a given representation may be labeled realism, we need to perform a historical or cultural analysis that considers the knowledge of modes of representation and knowledge of the world among representation-makers and among intended or actual recipients. The dominant trend within film-and-media studies has been aimed at describing the historical relativism of the experience of reality for several decades, but a description of the pertinent and universal features of reality has often been neglected, thus over-emphasizing the relativism of 'realism.'

A further complication in evaluating 'realism' is derived from the fact that in a central use of the word 'realism,' the representation not only provides a good match for reality, but also for those aspects of reality that are considered to be typical aspects of reality. Thus, many aspects of our concepts of 'realism' and 'reality' are not only descriptive but also imply normative evaluations of what is typical of real life. Representations of the private life of movie stars or millionaires might be just as 'real' as the 'Kitchen Sink' representations of the life of ordinary people, but the latter will often be considered more centrally realistic than the former.

The concept of realism is defined not only with reference to 'reality' but also in contrast to two different terms, the abstract and the fantastic. This complicates things, because the abstract is not necessarily 'unreal,' models within science like abstract models of atoms have very real references to reality. Similarly you might argue that many (although certainly not all) abstract representations within the arts and in media, are representations of general schematic features of objects and thus representations of very real phenomena. Abstractions are not only something that we find in models and exterior representations. Even our basic mental representations use abstractions in the form of simplified schemas. It is therefore evident that realism vs. abstraction provides different meanings than realism vs. fantastic. Thus the contrast between what is 'abstractly' realistic and what is 'concretely' realistic points to an experiential bias in the dominant use of the term realism. What is realistic is not solely nor necessarily real, for many adressees it must also be *experienced* as real. In order to understand the experience of the real in media representation we must look into those basic mechanisms that constitute our *experience* of what is real.

Perceptual specificity

A basic component in our experience of physical and social reality is that what we perceive, what we see and hear, is perceptually determinate, particular and complex. Few objects are exactly identical (except when factory-made), no situations will repeat themselves in exactly the same way in real life. But even if we perceive a given situation or object as being unique, our minds process them as being simpler and more general. We perceive the particular uniqueness of a tree but on the other hand our minds recognizes that it possesses some non-specific features (trunk, branches, leaves). When we store perceptions in our memory we tend to store them as rather compressed, general descriptions, although we may recall specificities when we see the perceived again. Our slotting of what we perceive into schemas provides the superior categorization that provides the background for our comprehension of reality.

In a developmental and historical perspective, representations have their point of departure in abstract, schematic descriptions. Small children and our prehistoric ancestors both draw, or have drawn humans by making circles for head and eyes, lines for limbs etc. Verbal descriptions start on a very general categorical level, man, woman, river, and the ability to provide very specific and detailed 'realistic' verbal descriptions, as shown among others by Erich Auerbach (1974) in his book *Mimesis*, has only been developed through a long historical process. Thus, in a historical perspective, particular and unique objects have been the hallmark of direct perception because only they could provide the necessary complex-specific salience typical of the experience of the 'real,' whereas mental or physical representations might be 'schematic.'

All other things being equal, perceptual uniqueness and complexity enhance the feeling of realism, because the representation is directly simulated in our brains as if we were confronted with reality. Stick figures or textureless computer graphics are less realistic than good photographs. Perceptual realism is often dealt with in relation to 'indexicality': A photograph or film is supposed to be the true imprint of reality via the photographic process. However, seen from an experiential point of view, it is not only our knowledge of the photographic process that provides the feeling of 'realism' but the very salience of the experience where the 'realistic' salience may be created independently of any indexical relation, because it might be 'staged' or computergenerated. Seen in a developmental perspective, knowledge of 'indexicality' is acquired. Small children take film and television for granted and their fascination of audiovisual representations and crude distinctions between more or less 'realist' programs take place even if they do not have the faintest ideas of 'profilmic events' or 'photographic processes.' The impression of reality caused by a complex-particular film sequence is immediate, based on innate dispositions in combination with universal basic experiences of reality.

Some people might find it difficult to understand why 'perceptual existence' experientially precedes a full understanding of reference and its reality status. The simple explanation to this is that except for memories, dreams and thoughts, the innate functioning of our brains presupposes that 'seeing' and 'existence' are the same thing, because our brains were not constructed in a media environment. Thus, for small children, realist films may not be perceived as representations of profilmic events, but as a display of some 'humans' and 'scenes' with a special reality status (they cannot be touched or interacted with). Even for adults it demands a special effort to imagine the 'pro-filmic event' as distinct from the immediate experience. Our increasing knowledge of 'reference' is added to, and enriches the phenomenal experience in the same way as our knowledge of the rotation of the earth etc may be added to and enriching our basic experience of the sun rising each morning, crossing the heavens and setting in the evening, without, replacing the basic phenomenological experience. I know that when watching the evening news a pro-filmic event in some remote TV studio is portrayed, but my immediate experience does not reflect that fact. The news anchor and studio are somehow present in my TV set and in my consciousness, and only a special effort enables me to imagine the profilmic circumstances concretely.

Our knowledge modifies our experience of realism. We know that a science fiction film is staged or animated and we know that even if the famous Rodney King videotape is of a poor quality, it shows something real. Thus there is a potential conflict between 'realism by perception' and 'realism by knowledge.' It has been argued by Wolterstorff (cf. Plantinga 1997) that fiction films do not assert anything about the truth of a given story, but instead invite us to consider that state of affairs, in contrast to nonfiction films which are assertive because they assert that the films' state of affairs have actually occurred in actual worlds as portrayed. However, perceptual salience is an assertion of existence, even when it comes to fantasy creatures. But those assertions may to some degree be contradicted by our cognitive assessment of 'realism,' that is, our evaluation of whether the representation has a possible concrete existence as portrayed. Thus all audiovisual representations are assertions of existence. The specification of which type of existence must be decided by what Branigan (1992) calls "decisions about assigning reference," based on our knowledge about the world, including on our trust in the addressing agencies (filmmakers, TV stations etc) and their assertion of reality status (true, invented etc).

Schematic typicalness and familiarity

The experience of realism by perceptual salience, including uniqueness and complexity (mostly) takes place for the most part based on a basic familiarity and typicality, because our understanding of what reality looks like is based on previous experiences that are stored as 'familiarity' and as 'schematic descriptions' of movements, objects, persons, or situations. We have produced some mental schemas of how people walk or how working class people behave, which we use in order to evaluate whether a given representation is 'realistic' or not. If a representation is very much different from our schemas, we may think that it is not very realistic. But if it looks just like our schemas without any specificity it is not felt as being very realistic either. The purely schematic representation may be felt as being a stereotypical representation that lacks the flavor of the particular or unique time/place/object. As pointed out by the Russian formalists, salience decays over time if we become 'over-familiar' with and habituated to some experiences, and thus the feeling of 'realism' may also decay. Realism could therefore be considered a balancing act between the unique which provides the 'salience of the real,' and the typical which provides the cognitive credibility and familiarity of the real. Since our imagination and our representative capacity often rely on schemas and typicality, the confrontation with non fictional reality is often important for creating specificity.

The bias towards typicality provides a certain normative dimension to the concept of realism, because there are many real phenomena and representations of real phenomena that are not typical or familiar. For instance, as mentioned, realism has, an anthropocentric bias. A high angle shot is experienced as less 'realistic' than a shot from eye level of a standing human being, except when motivated as the vision of a bird or a person flying. But even if a non-typical angle is motivated, the feeling of 'deviation' from the norm persists in the experience. Furthermore, our norms of 'realism' are influenced by considerations of 'canonical view' (cf. Grodal 1997, Humphreys 1989). Recognizing an object is not necessarily easy from all angles. A horse seen from behind is more difficult to recognize than a horse seen from the side. Most people will draw or record objects from a canonical angle in order to allow for easy recognition. Canonical angles may also be considered more 'realistic' or less expressive, even if the object is also familiar from non-canonical angles.

Historically, 'realist representations' have often dealt with the daily routine of uneventful lives, especially that of the middle and the lower classes. Thus, de Sica's *Bicycle Thief* has for many film critics been regarded a prototypical realist film because it deals with the problems of everyday life for ordinary working class people. But such a narrow definition of 'realism' does not seem to correspond to what viewers or even critics perceive as 'realism.' Even representations of intense action, such as emergency rooms or workers strikes as in Biberman's *Salt of the Earth,* may be perceived as 'realistic.' The preference by some critics for notions of 'uneventfulness' and 'daily life' in the concept of realism may be seen as a polemic against those fiction films that stage 'improbable actions' that have a low relevance for ordinary life, and not necessarily a polemic against those representations that portray more extraordinary situations (like sudden illness or social conflict) that may have a high degree of relevance for 'ordinary people.' A common use of the word 'realism' even points to an emotional impact as a valid criterion for 'realism.' Scenes that portray all the gory details of mutilations may be seen as strongly realistic. Kracauer (1960) pointed out that garbage, dirt or sewer grates were important motives for a film's effort to establish 'physical existence' because these things ordinarily went unnoticed. But I might add that the emotional impact of those phenomena that Kracauer called 'the refuse,' is also important in experiencing 'realism.' Thus, our experience of what is real is not only linked to factual existence, but also to the (negative or positive) emotional relevance of what exists. Perceptual realism may not be salient unless it serves to activate emotional concerns.

Transparent access or addresser-and-recording-mediated realism

In several regards typical fiction films are better able to provide a basic 'transparent' perceptual-experiential realism than typical nonfiction films, although their capacity for realism is only one option among several (I shall return to the strengths of nonfiction representations later). The perceptual realism of a 'realist' fiction film provides the experience of a concrete and unique reference, although its realism is general and hypothetical. Ford's *The Grapes of Wrath* or August's *Pelle the Conqueror* portray many scenes that may have been true on a general level, although their specific concrete reference is staged. But while viewing, spectators will often experience the images as if they have concrete references although they know these references are only general and hypothetical. The typical fiction film is based on narrative forms that follow actions and events that develop over time in a way that is similar to that of everyday experience. Fiction films are often focalized by one living being, and the existence of living focalizers provide an experience of online, concrete interaction with what is shown. This is similar to our basic relation to the world by our personal focalization, including our emotions and concerns in relation to that world. Furthermore, the 'classical' 'seamless' presentation especially developed in Hollywood tries to follow the basic perceptual and cognitive rules for experiencing real life events (cf. Bordwell 1986, Bordwell, Staiger, Thompson 1988). But it is just as important to note that fiction films can stage many events that for nonfiction films are inaccessible or only accessible with difficulty. Nonfiction films cannot provide a firsthand view of a murder or the secret negotiations in government or business. Even events that are essentially accessible (a plane crash, street violence etc), very seldom have a camera present at the proper moment. Even if a 'professional' camera is present the circumstances will not allow such optimal conditions that could be made available if a similar scene were shot for a fiction film. The widespread use of privately owned video cameras may provide some footage, but then from a sub-optimal camera position or made with a lower quality than that of a fiction film. The presence of a camera may change the behavior of those filmed, whereas a good actor should be able to perform as if there was no camera present.

Some nonfiction films or programs compensate for the above-mentioned shortcomings in several ways. The simplest way is to emulate the narrative form, although often with some kind of narrating agency in the role as focalizer, whether in the form of voice over or intertitles/subtitles, or by making the reporter or the documentarist into a visually present focalizer. It is also possible to take a more radical step, like the one taken by 'docudramas,' namely to try to restage a real event. Here we get first hand access to information about how a murder happened, to secret negotiations, or to the small everyday dramas linked to accidents and illnesses as seen in docudramas about emergency situations. Thus, the docudrama can provide basic perceptual realism to the events portrayed. The docudrama may even use the real life protagonists as actors in an attempt to capture a basic personal specificity that allows the viewer to have a more accurate real life involvement because the drama and the protagonists are concretely and uniquely real. The possibly unprofessional acting may have a salience and specificity of its own, when compared to professional acting.

However, there are some problems with the docudramas' means of compensating for shortcomings in perceptual realism. The docudrama has to be told after the fact, in contrast to the way in which most fiction films, including realist fiction films, tell the events in a hypothetical presence. Therefore docudramas may provide a similar experience to that of the 'passive melodrama' that is often told from a temporal position later than that of the events. Since viewers are aware of the fact that the story is a 're-enactment,' they may speculate as to its correctness, which is in contrast to the typical realist fiction film in which addressers possess full insight into the hypothetical phenomena. Thus, docudramas may succeed in making some events visually salient, but are in danger of not being able to provide the strong activation that are caused by the feeling that we are witnessing unique and real events.

A more radical or paradoxical 'compensation' for lack of perceptual realism consists of emphasizing its shortcomings by making imperfect perceptual realism into a sign of 'reality'. This implicitly links the perfect perceptual realism of many fiction films with something 'unreal' and 'staged,' thus undermining perceptual realism as an indication of 'realism.' Many documentaries and nonfiction films do not try to achieve perceptual realism. On the contrary. The grainy pictures, the imperfect focus and framing, the erratic camera movements and bad lighting all indicate that this material is shot under un-staged nonfiction conditions, although such images do not emulate the way in which the human eye would perceive such situations. We may follow 'real' policemen or firemen at work, and although we may have difficulties seeing what is happening in the murky alleys of Los Angeles, we are supposed to get a feeling of unstaged 'reality.' Fiction filmmakers, the Dogma film group for instance, have used similar techniques with the intention of making realist fiction films. The method may be exemplified with the fake documentary (the fake home movie), like Myrick's and Sanchez's *The Blair Witch Project.* In this film one of the typical effects of 'imperfect perceptual realism,' namely the subjectivizing effect, is obvious. The erratic, handheld camera and the often poor resolution enhance the feeling of stress, isolation and the strangeness of the experiences in the woods. Furthermore, the amateurish quality of the representation corresponds to the helplessness of its pretended makers, the young persons in the woods.

The production of a subjectivizing effect is an important aspect of 'imperfect perceptual realism' (an 'anti-seamless' presentation). This provides an interesting insight into the relationship between the innate and the acquired aspects of 'realism.' Viewers obviously learn to connect certain features in audiovisual representation to the circumstances of its recording, so that they learn for instance to connect a degraded picture from a satellite transmission to the real difficulties of transmitting over vast distances or they learn to connect imperfect pictures with 'live reporting,' So in the same way that we learn what zebras look like we learn about media recording and media transmission. But on the other hand, the fact that such imperfect transmissions are often experienced as creating subjective experiences points to innate specifications in the way human perception takes place. The 'imperfections' block the easy recognition of objects. Our innate means of categorizing deviating perceptions is to think and feel that subjective factors are blocking the basic 'fusion' of mind and object worlds. Furthermore deviations from perfect vision and hearing destroy our normal lack of awareness of the subjective aspects (the proximal aspects) of our perception. Deviations furthermore create 'stress' and arousal (cf. Grodal 2000a). Given the proper context (such as the horrible experiences in *The Blair Witch Project* or the stressful work of a policeman in the streets of Los Angeles), you might argue that the lack of perceptual realism is transformed into an 'emotional realism' by subjecting the viewer to nervous or stressful experiences and situations. In the more trivial uses of 'imperfect perceptual realism' the aesthetics may either serve as a rhetorical device (the lack of salience in the object is compensated for by camera motion and odd framings and angles that provide a rhetorical salience) or as a 'self-conscious' emphasis on the 'addresser' of the program ('we were here, we did the recording'). Thus the central question is whether the imperfections are motivated by the recording situation or not.

The distinction between 'perceptual realism' and 'emotional realism' is linked to the problematic of the 'aspectualization' of the word 'realism.' The producers of many different modes of representation claim they are 'realists,' but only portray certain aspects of reality. Terms like 'magic realism,' 'extreme realism,' 'poetic realism,' 'psychological realism,' or 'social realism' show how different modes of representation may claim that they are portraying chosen aspects of reality. (Later in this paper I will argue for the relevance of the term 'categorical realism'). Even standard films may use elements derived from e.g. expressionism in order to provide 'realist' descriptions of divergent mental states. These different 'aspectualizations' of the word 'realism' are a logical consequence of the fact that reality is a multi-faceted and open-ended concept because new knowledge adds new elements to what is understood to be real. We can only deal with this problem of 'aspectualization' pragmatically: Some aspects of reality are typically evaluated as being more 'normal' and 'intersubjective' than others. There are some representations that can be called 'realism' without any specifications, like *Bicycle Thief* or *High School,* whereas other representations need specifications that mark them as belonging to special types of realism, like the 'psychological realism' of Polanski's *Repulsion.* There are not only different types of realism corresponding to representations of different aspects of reality, but some types are evaluated as more prototypical or central than others.

The aesthetics of imperfect perceptual realism is the very opposite of a Bazinian aesthetics of realism. According to Bazin (1967) the essence of film art is its ability to perform an objective 'mechanical' recording of the world that leaves no trace of an intervening human subject. Films and photographs should represent a perfect replica of the world. We thus have two different ideas of realism: one centered in the subjective vision of the experiencer, the addresser, the other centered in the object world, based on the presupposition that such a neutral representation is possible. Some scholars and filmmakers have disputed that a neutral representation is possible. For instance, Bill Nichols' book about documentaries, *Representing Reality* (Nichols 1991)*,* is based on the presupposition that neutral representations are ways in which ideological representations pose as neutral and natural, and that nonfiction programs therefore must be self-reflexive and admit that they are specific in their representations. Imperfect perceptual realism is one possible way of marking the presence of an addresser or experiencer. But it might also be argued, following Bazin's ideas, that we are sometimes able to minimize our awareness of our subjective situation of observation and therefore sense this type of 'disinterested' objective observation of the world. That the experience of being disinterested may be characterized as feeling does not necessarily make it subjective, because (as argued in Grodal 1997) certain feelings and emotions are central tools for marking the reality status of given experiences. Thus, addresser-based and object-based realism are different and equally valuable ways of representation.

Nevertheless, perceptual realism is not the only way in which we experience reality, just as the narrative form is not the only form that we use in order to assemble data (cf. Branigan 1992). Many audiovisual representations use a categorical form (cf. Bordwell and Thompson 2001), the aim of which is not to provide a vivid portrayal of concrete situations and experiences, but on the contrary, to extract a more abstract understanding out of concrete examples. Even if the famous documentary *Night Mail* makes use of narrative elements (a train ride from London to Glasgow) and illustrative visual examples of some of the activities, the purpose is not only to provide a concrete experience of a night on the night mail train. The purpose is also to provide a more general knowledge and abstract impression of some aspects of the British mail system. Even if an important segment of nonfiction programs try to portray some very specific concrete and unique situations, another important segment try to portray general, and thus 'non-perceptible,' non-concrete and non-unique situations. Thus, categorizations and mental models serve a quite different function than being a 'silent background' or than organizing tacit knowledge for our understanding of concrete situations. In the categorical film the abstract schematic level is the focus of the representation. For example, photographs of a tiger in a dictionary do not denote the concrete and specific tiger, but tigers at a schematic level (cf. Branigan 1992). Monty Python derives much humor out of conflating the concrete and the schematic use of images of trees and larks. The experience of reality that might be provided by such abstract portrayals of phenomena, I will refer to as 'cognitive realism' or 'categorical realism' as opposed to 'perceptual realism.'

The difference between 'perceptual-narrative' representations and categorical representations may be illustrated using the nonfiction montage sequence at the beginning of *Beverly Hill Cops.* We are presented with different shots that obviously have no narrative connection to each other. But they seem to have a common 'theme': all the shots show some aspects of the poor life in a black ghetto in Detroit. The different persons and locations have a very concrete and unique 'realistic' specificity. Had the scenes been linked by narrative elements they might just have been perceived as concrete perceptual realism. But as the viewer cannot find a narrative link, by default they search for a 'thematic,' or categorical connection, and may find 'poverty' and 'black ghetto life.' This process does not fully deprive the individual images of their concrete reference, but nevertheless it gives them a double status as concrete reference as well as concrete illustration of a more abstract theme, poverty. The narrative part of the film mostly takes place in the rich Beverly Hills, and although it is very possible to see the scenes and events as focally describing the opposite theme 'richness' and 'white upper-class life,' the categorical understanding is now only felt as a background for the concrete events, because the narrative form evokes a concrete focus.

What is the source of that feeling of 'realism' that is connected to categorical presentations? Plato and other thinkers within the 'idealist' tradition thought that 'ideas' were more real than appearances (or 'perceptual realism' in the language of this paper), they were the essence of reality. But this of course does not provide a psychologically satisfying explanation, especially because perceptual realism is such an important elicitor of 'feelings of reality.' However, as mentioned, when small children draw, they often draw the 'formal essence,' legs as lines, stomach and head as circles. The schemas are the mentally pertinent features in the experience of the ever-changing phenomenal world. Therefore I propose that there is a kind of 'schematic salience' that provides a feeling of reality that is abstract and atemporal and the power of which comes from being the mental essence of many different experiences, in contrast to the feeling of perceptual salience that is connected to the temporal, specific and unique. In fiction films they are often dealt with as redundant themes in the concrete narrative progression. To activate this 'schematic salience' the presentation needs to make concrete illustrations and exemplifications so that the schematic salience is supported by perceptual salience. But schematic realism presupposes that the final reference is not only to the concrete and unique but also to the general and pertinent. *Night Mail* is not a documentary about a specific night and a concrete train, the concrete illustrations refer to the general and a-temporal-repetitive.

The illustrated and focused categorical presentations provide a feeling of both realism and reality. Its exemplifications provide the unique perceptual salience, and its categorical presentation provides the categorical essentialist salience. The reason I emphasize that the presentation must be 'focused' is that if not, the presentation will lead into yet another type of experience, the lyrical mental-associative experience that to a much lesser degree points to an exterior, inter-subjective reality. It is often pointed out that many documentaries provides a lyrical experience, and Plantinga has described three typical 'voices' in nonfiction films, the formal, the open, and the poetic voice. However, no explanations have been provided for the seemingly paradoxical phenomenon that a type of presentation that should be 'facts-oriented' often intentionally or unintentionally provides a lyrical experience. Let us take a look on one of the famous lyrical documentaries, Ruttmann's *Berlin, Symphony of a Great City.* The film provides a long series of shots from life in Berlin supposedly taken on one specific day, because it starts early in the morning and ends late in the evening. Sometimes the film shows several shots of similar events sometimes it contrasts different events. But except for the fact that all shots are taken in Berlin and exhibits a diurnal cycle, there is no clear focus, no arguments are put forward, and no clear categorical analysis is provided. Therefore, viewers 'by default' build up a web of associations between the different objects and events that only have a diffuse center in the idea that this shows 'life' in a modern city, Berlin.

In 'real life,' everything is concrete and is fixed in a continuous forward-directional time and a contiguous space. Associations between widely different time periods, spaces and objects, as well as associations based on similarity and other formal features, typically only exist in our minds (we may associate New York and Tokyo as important capitals, link different historical periods, find a similarity between eyes and sun), or as representations. An experience based on associations is typical of a lyrical experience, which contrary to most narrative fictions and contrary to the concrete documentary, does not primarily refer outwards to a concrete reality, but refers 'inward' to the existence of the experiences in the mind. In the focused categorical audiovisual representation, categorical 'assertion' provides the link between the exterior world and mental representations, but in the unfocused presentation this assertion of an external existence is lacking. This provides some curious effects. Many lyrical films are in essence straightforward or even extreme 'documentaries,' such as some films by Marguerite Duras (cf. Grodal 2000a), but are nevertheless experienced as strongly lyrical. The reason for this is that the viewer cannot find the focused categorical assertions and therefore 'by default' searches the mind for possible associations, thus establishing a subjective associative web, cued by the film. Even a typical documentary like *Night Mail* lingers between a concrete, focused reference and a lyrical 'mental' reference, helped by the lyrics of Auden on the sound track. The film's apotheosis of 'speed' and 'efficency' sometimes evokes a purely 'idealistic-internal' reference.

Assertions of existence and realism

Many scholars have been interested in assertions from an epistemological point of view. Thus Wolterstorff and Plantinga (1997) point to the fact that non-fiction films perform pragmatic acts asserting that what is shown and told is true in the world. Some theoreticians like Nichols (1991), are very sceptical in relation to the overt assertiveness of non fiction films as is found in what Nichols calls the expository mode, for instance in the form of the 'voice of God,' an all-knowing voice over. However, the problem of assertion in establishing reality and fiction could, however, also be approached from a psychological point of view. As discussed earlier, our basic experience of reality is not only linked to the perceptual processes but is also linked to the enactive processes (our motor-based relations to the world, cf. Grodal 1997). Those things, those perceptions are real that can guide our (re)actions. Thus, the question of 'reality' and 'realism' poses the problem of 'agency.' In the typical narrative fiction film, the question of 'agency' is solved through the existence of a protagonist for whom the perceived serves to orient actions. In some types of 'observational films' the non-fictitious protagonists have a salience that provides the viewer with some kind of agency that allows for the necessary 'enactive relevance.' However, many types of film, for instance the categorical documentary, do not have any 'onscreen' agency that can provide relevance. But the explicit or implicit addresser of such films may for the viewer serve as an agency that performs non-concrete actions by asserting that a given thing is true. To utter the specific kind of performative or symbolic actions which claim something exists, is (as shown by Austin and Searle) a central feature of human communication. Assertive-performative activity is a central means of transmitting a feeling of reality and factuality. Assertions need not be verbal. Any framing or presentation is in principle an assertion, although it may not be felt if the viewer cannot reconstruct the principles on which the assertions are made.

As discussed in relation to *Night Mail*, the assertions made during the film are central to providing a concrete focus, the concrete reference of the representation that might otherwise be perceived in a subjective-lyrical mode. Nichols' distrust of overt assertions as an ideological mode is a rather severe exclusion of a central way of communicating about reality. Abuse of addresser-agency is of course possible, but we cannot abolish addresser-agency in general just because it might be abused. It might also be argued that there is a certain 'honesty' surrounding overt assertions that makes it possible to have a clear impression of the asserting agency. This may become clear when we compare an 'expository' film and its overt assertion with a so-called 'observational' film that pretends to be recorded by 'a fly on the wall,' as an objective recording without any asserting agency. However, most viewers watching Wiseman's brilliant 'observational' documentary *High School* will expect the film to provide some general assertions about the American High School system, albeit on the basis of concrete observation. But because Wiseman hides his asserting agency responsible for the concrete shooting and editing the film is seemingly asserted 'by reality.' This 'problem' with the 'observational' mode has been noted (cf. for an overview Carroll 1996: 224-52), and scholars like Nichols are therefore fond of the 'reflexive' film that overtly thematicizes itself as a specific representation. However, it might be argued that an average informed viewer of an overtly 'assertive' expository film is very well aware of the fact that it is a film made by a human agency and that a reflexive representation is not the only option for representing the asserting agency.

Realism and virtual or actual interactivity

Assertions are a unique example of the way in which reality is experienced based on actions and interactions. The addresser 'interacts' with the represented by making assertions. The simplest form of interactivity is based on immediate proximity that allows a person to react on what she hears and sees, either verbally or physically. Media representations are in principle non-interactive (except for the telephone and some computer applications). Films and programs may use different procedures in order to veil or overcome this problem. The simplest form of interactivity is 'passive' interactivity or interactivity by proxy. Passive interactivity consists of speaking to or looking 'towards' the viewer-listener. In this way the viewer may have a feeling of being a passive participant, a concrete listener-viewer and may have a very concrete feeling of sharing a real experiential space with the persons that are present in the media and have a feeling of situational uniqueness. Interactivity by proxy means having an audience that serves as a mediated proxy for the viewer-listener or an asserting addresser. The viewer-proxy may even use an interactive media, like the telephone or the net. However, a strong feeling of reality by interactivity is however produced by certain computer applications, and most prominently in some computer games. Despite an often rather poor perceptual definition, such games can produce a strong feeling of reality because players can physically interact with the represented world. This provides us with an insight into those powerful elements in the experience of reality that are linked to our (inter)actions, our output (cf. Grodal 2000b).

Reality and realism as genuineness, seriousness, and as pain

Our experience of reality is often linked to evaluations of the seriousness of intentions and consequences, and to evaluations of 'genuineness.' Even the most realistic fiction film is not fully real, because the actors do not intend to kill each other, they only pretend to have that intention. This is a specific consequence of a more general principle in our experience of reality and 'realism' demanding that vital human (or animal) concerns be at stake. When playing or pretending, we are supposed to be free to discontinue that behavior, as opposed to those acts that are the consequences of our 'genuine' self and its vital concerns. A transmission of a football game might rarely be described as 'realistic' whereas a transmission of a fight between police and demonstrators might be seen as a piece of 'realism' because vital concerns are supposed to be at stake in the latter case. But if a documentary peeps into the locker room and shows how real concerns are at stake for the players, showing their 'true backstage' identity, it might easily be termed 'realism.' In the television genre often called 'reality TV' (*Survivors, Big Brother* etc) based on staged performances by ordinary people (a kind of 'amateur actor'), it is often emphasized by programmers that the participants act in accordance with 'serious' and therefore 'real' motives.

It is difficult to draw a clear line between what is just pretension, a 'role,' and what is 'genuine.' Motives that make people act and pretend in real life (their 'front stage' appearance as it is called by Goffman, cf. also Meyrowitz 1985), may be controlled by stronger motives than their 'relaxed' private and intimate (back stage) behavior, although probably a 'behind the scene' documentary about actors, politicians or football players would be evaluated as a more 'realist' representation than a presentation of 'front stage' performance. To sing a song, play an act or perform a sketch might be seen as being just as 'real' as working on an assembly line.

However, it seems that the concept of 'seriousness' and genuineness serves a vital function in the evaluation of what is real or realistic. It might be an implicit reflection on the problem that 'realist' representations often prefer situations in which the agents are supposed to have a limited capacity to 'act.' Even if the life of the hero of *Bicycle Thief* from one perspective is trivial and uneventful, the loss of his bicycle and therefore possibly his job is an 'existential crisis' that guarantees that his behavior is serious and genuine. The reality TV concept *Big Brother* emphasizes its ability to evoke genuine behavior by pointing to possible deprivation. Confined for a long period of time in limited space that is under surveillance, nine out of ten participants have to be excluded by painful processes, the participants should be reduced to a basic or even deprived situation compared to present day life standards etc.

A consequence of the principle that a strong feeling of reality demanding that vital human or animal concerns be at stake is that 'realism' is more often attributed to representations that portray negative emotions than those that portray positive emotions. This is perhaps based on the assumption that 'pain' is more real than 'pleasure,' thus evoking more genuine behavior. A documentary about deprived and suffering people would probably be labeled 'strongly realistic' more readily than a documentary about happy jetsetters, even if it is not clear whether the first group is more typical than the other. Some of the classic realist films, like Ford's *The Grapes of Wrath,* or Biberman's *Salt of the Earth,* focus on deprivation and pain. Some philosophers and artists think that 'death' is the ultimate reality. Freud even called those mechanisms that were linked to pain the 'reality principle' as opposed to the 'pleasure principle.' Although Freud's terminology does not make sense from an evolutionary perspective, it might represent a fundamental feature reflecting the way in which humans experience reality. The psychologist Nico Frijda has claimed the existence of a 'hedonic asymmetry.' Frijda states that, "Pleasure is always contingent upon change and disappears with continuous satisfaction. Pain may persist under persisting adverse conditions" (1988: 353). Thus, the bias in realist representations for describing suffering or deprived people may not only reflect a political wish for advocating empathy, but also a feeling that pain and deprivation are more real than pleasure.

Realism in an age of pervasive representations

A series of scholars, for example Jean Baudrillard (cf. Grodal 1992), have argued that the fact that people in the age in which 'online' experiences play a decreasing role in comparison to experiences linked to audiovisual representations, leads to a dissolution with our experience of what is real, which entails that the concept of realism becomes increasingly problematic. The salience of images does not warrant any real concrete and unique reference, and as even the perceptual world becomes increasingly man-made, there are no absolute and natural norms to anchor an authentic experience of reality.

The present pervasiveness of representations even in every day life certainly questions what is true or probable (realist), and what is only invented and improbable (fantastic or just lies and misrepresentations). However the question about the reality of representations is at the heart of even the most rudimentary pre modern verbal or iconic representations. From the invention of language, sculpture and painting, strange tales have been told about gods, magic causations or Cyclops, or visual representations of gods and other fantastic beings have been shown, asserted and believed to be true representations of the real. Even if premodern humans typically only had visual and acoustic access to a relatively small concrete environment, many of their beliefs about the world were molded by what they were told existed elsewhere. Modern viewers of fantasy and science fiction films do not trust the realism of such representations more than premodern humans had in fairies and gods, quite the contrary. Even if 'perceptual realism' activates innate dispositions, the massive exposure to audiovisual representations probably does not create more credulous viewers than verbal communication created credulous listeners. Some questionable representations are even more easily performed verbally than in an audiovisual media. Thus generalizations like 'New Yorkers are happy and active' are easy to make verbally, but if they are illustrated visually, even naïve viewers might have some doubts about the validity of the generalizations.

Therefore, it is not obvious that the world is moving in the direction of a crisis of representations of reality (except in the sense that the increase in knowledge increases the awareness of possible problematic relations between the concrete world and representations). Even heavy media users have an extensive experience of the non-media world, including the experience of media-platforms as physical objects, and their first-hand experience of other cultures will typically be greater than ever before. There is no reason to believe that the basic 'perceptual' realist experience of the everyday intersubjective world has changed radically. It still provides the norm in relation to which special represented phenomena are evaluated and characterized. Furthermore, there are more complex public discussions about the validity of representations than ever before, so the proliferation of (audiovisual) representations is matched by an expansion of critical discourse. This does not mean that people cannot be seduced into believing that biased and stereotypical representations are real or realistic. All types of human communication are possible learning processes, but the physical co-existence of slaves and masters, or Nazi-officers and victims did not prevent strange concepts.

Those high modernist and postmodernist discourses that have centered on a crisis of representation and 'reality' may therefore be explained better from the point of view of the emotional dimensions of the cognitive appraisal of what is real and realistic. As briefly mentioned earlier, a vital component of our experience of reality is emotional, the feeling that something exists and thus can serve as a possible object of, or scene for, action. A central aspect of this feeling of reality is the feeling of a certain basic familiarity. Periods of rapid change, including expansions of representations may cause alienation, an emotional dissociation that makes feelings of familiarity, and thus the feeling of 'reality,' more difficult for many people. Therefore, to some extent, some aspects of high modernism and post-modernism do not reflect 'the essence' of the present period seen from within, but are on the contrary emotionally and experientially rooted in the conflict between past and present. Thus, those modern and 'postmodern' critics and artists that express their scepticism of 'realism' and their interest in 'metafiction,' 'reflexivity' and 'intertextuality' may be seen as symptoms of a cognitive and emotional period of transition that for emotional reasons need to bring to the foreground the representedness of representations. Even if postmodernism in principle should be against grand narratives and grand generalizations, their negative epistemological claim of 'uncertainty' and scepticism is a grand historical narrative, that implicitly expresses a longing back to a Cartesian world in which a divine principle guaranteed the link between world and mind.

However, the feeling of reality and realism is based on, and serve, our pragmatic interaction with the world. Whether we communicate with grunts, with words, or by means of audiovisual media, we make and use concepts of what is actually and uniquely real or what is 'typical,' and we trust some communicators or representations as being better guides for our actions and concerns than others. I therefore think that concepts like 'real,' 'realism' and 'truth' are pertinent even for a postindustrial society with pervasive audiovisual representations.

References

Auerbach, Erich. 1974. *Mimesis. The Representation of Reality in Western Literature.* Princeton N.J: Princeton University Press.

Bazin, André. 1967. *What is Cinema?* Berkeley: University of California Press.

Bordwell, David. 1986. *Narration in the Fiction Film.* London: Methuen.

Bordwell, David, Staiger, Janet and Thompson, Kristin. 1988. *The Classical Hollywood Cinema. Film Style & Mode of Production to 1960.* London: Routledge.

Bordwell, David & Thompson, Kristin. 2001. *Film Art. An Introduction.* 6th edition. New York: McGraw Hill.

Branigan, Edward. 1992. *Narrative Comprehension and Film.* London: Routledge.

Carroll, Noël. 1996. *Theorizing the Moving Image.* Cambridge: Cambridge University Press.

Ekman, Paul and Friesen, Wallace V. 1975. *Unmasking the Face: A guide to Recognizing Emotions from Facial Clues.* Englewood Cliffs, NJ: Prentice Hall.

Frijda, Nico. 1988. "The Laws of Emotion". *American Psychologist* vol. 43, no. 5

Grodal, Torben. 1992. "Romanticism, Postmodernism and Irrationalism". *Sekvens 92. Filmvidenskabelig årbog.* København: Københavns Universitet.

Grodal, Torben. 1997. *Moving Pictures. A New Theory of Film Genres, Feelings, and Cognition.* Oxford: Oxford University Press/Clarendon.

Grodal, Torben. 2000a. "Subjectivity, Objectivity, and Aesthetic Feelings in Film". In *Moving Images, Culture and the Mind*, edited by Ib Bondebjerg. Luton: University of Luton Press.

Grodal, Torben. 2000b. "Video Games and Pleasures of Control". In *Media Entertainment,* edited by Dolf Zillmann and Peter Vorderer. Mahwah, N.J.: Lawrence Erlbaum Associates.

Humphreys, Patrick R. and Bruce, Vicki. 1989. *Visual Cognition: Computational, Experimental and Neuropsychological Perspectives.* Hove: Lawrence Erlbaum Associates.

Johnson, Mark. 1997. *The Body in the Mind: The Bodily Basis of Meaning, Imagination and Reason.* Chicago: University of Chicago Press.

Kracauer, Sigfried. 1960. *The Nature of Film: The Redemption of Physical Reality.* London: Oxford University Press.

Lakoff, George. 1987. *Women, Fire and Dangerous Things: What Categories Reveal about the Mind.* Chicago: University of Chicago Press.

Meyrowitz, Joshua. 1985. *No Sense of Place. The Impact of Electronic Media on Social Behavior.* Oxford: Oxford University Press.

Nichols, Bill. 1991. *Representing Reality.* Bloomington: Indiana University Press.

Plantinga, Carl. 1997. *Rhetoric and Representation in Nonfiction Film.* Cambridge: Cambridge University Press.

Johannes Riis

Is a Realist Film Style
Aimed at Providing an Illusion?

The experience of realism in cinema is intricately tied to the impression that the events and persons depicted are somehow real. We know the film to be screened, yet we experience the depicted events to be occurring. This 'experiential realism' is not identical to the application of the term often used by critics, that is, to designate films that portray the real world, especially its social aspects, in a recognizable way, in contrast to other films of the same or a previous period. However, I shall be concerned here with the theoretical problems of our *experience* of the story world as being realistic, independently of our recognition of events, persons, and places. There are emotions involved in this kind of film realism and even though we do not recognize reality, I believe that we feel the object depicted to be real.

The appropriate term for an experience of realism in which reality need not be imitated, might be *illusion*. Although I am not entirely confident with the term's connotations of deceit and wishful thinking, I believe that 'illusion' may very well provide the most coherent explanation of what a realist film experience means. In order for illusion to accomplish this, it is necessary that we remove the term from the realm of epistemic concerns and situate it within aesthetics and the analysis of style, without carrying with us the burden of epistemically wronged spectators, duped into having false beliefs as to what is real. This is the task that I set forth in this article, arguing that the term illusion may be slightly better at getting to the heart of the matter than terms like 'imagination' and 'simulation,' at least with respect to style analysis.

The paradox of fiction and Dial M for Murder

The major problem can be stated like this: How can we experience the depicted events as realistic while also being aware that this is a screened, recorded, and enacted reality? For example, we may feel that the concerns at stake are so important that they require immediate response by the protagonist and, consequently, feel inclined to warn him or her, while at the same time we may self-consciously look for our companion's response to see if our distress is shared. We may attend to the techniques that the film deploys in order to heighten our sense of realism, while at the same time responding to the action as it unfolds.

It is crucial that we do not experience a scene as realistic *only* when dealing with the scene's content, independently of techniques and our self-awareness as spectators. When watching the attempted murder on Margot Wendice, played by Grace Kelly in Hitchcock's *Dial M for Murder* (1953), we do not necessarily experience the event as less realistic relative to our awareness of the music score and the camera's movement in a half-circle around her, both initiated at the moment she picks up the phone from the desk where the murder is about to take place. As long as there is no exclusive focus on music or camera work, these prominent elements do not destroy the illusion of the event taking place. In *Dial M for Murder*, we are still full of suspense when the hands of the assassin, Lesgate/Swann, played by Anthony Dawson, enter the picture with a pair of stockings as he reaches for her neck. When we cut back to a two-shot allowing us to see him standing right behind her having stepped out from behind the curtains, the suspense is almost unbearable. She keeps repeating "Hello!" and taps the phone to get a clear line, while he holds back because she keeps putting the phone to her ear, making her neck inaccessible. We might say that the artificial nature of the music and the camera movement allows for a suspension of the scene. The scene goes on for 30 seconds from the moment she picks up the phone until he throws the stocking around her neck, allowing her to say "Hello!" no less than seven times. Moreover, I take this as an example of the fact that as long as there is no exclusive focus on aesthetic means, we may be aware of them with no serious consequence for our experience of realism with respect to the scene.

Noël Carroll (1990) has suggested that the kind of situation described here may be stated in terms of a general problem, the paradox of fiction. The paradox of fiction involves three propositions that appear true in isolation, but reveal a contradiction when combined (Carroll 1990: 87).

The propositions are as follows.
1. We are genuinely moved by fiction.
2. We know that that which is portrayed in fictions is not actual.
3. We are genuinely moved only by what we believe is actual.

Carroll notes that viewers may then resolve the contradiction by denying that they are genuinely moved, implying instead that our emotions are qualitatively different from the ones we have in real life. Others may deny that they know that they are only watching fiction, forgetting this fact momentarily, and yet others may deny that genuine emotion only follows from what we consider to be actual.

I shall try to demonstrate that a theory based on our experience of the depicted events as realistic may be able to capture all three propositions with no contradictions, if formulated in terms of an illusion. The kind of illusion in question is best understood to be of an emotional as well as cognitive and perceptual nature. When talking of cognitive illusion, I should hasten to add that 'cognition' in this sense merely designates that memory and inferences are involved. Thus we are drawing on the information we have received in earlier scenes of *Dial M for Murder* concerning the murder plan so that we are not surprised when he enters the frame from behind the curtains, even though we did not see him hiding there. I do not mean to say that we are suffering from what might be termed an 'epistemic' illusion, which is akin to an hallucination in which we are convinced that what we are watching is actually occurring before us, and not just represented.

The reality of illusion and its cognitive components

Understanding our experience of realism as a kind of illusion seems at odds with modern conceptions of the spectator. Since Noël Carroll in *Mystifying Movies* (1988) rejected analogies linking film viewing and dreaming, or analogies between film viewing and being locked into certain viewing positions where the viewer only sees shadows on a wall, there have been few attempts at developing an illusion based account of our film experience. An illusion based account seems to underestimate the intelligence of spectators, characterizing them as unable to think for themselves. Incidentally, this may also serve as a critic's first move against realist styles, calling instead for reflexivity (see Plantinga 1997: 214-18).

However, an illusion based account of our experience of realism does not have to be tied to particular aesthetic values, nor does it have to misrepresent the spectators as mere dupes, falling victims to techniques that the critic alone is able to see. An illusion based account of our experience of realism may explain the apparent paradox by recourse to the way perception, cognition, and emotion are embodied. This is the path taken by ecological-cognitive film theorists. Thus Joseph Anderson has explained our perception of movement in film as the result of the way our ancestors interacted with the environment in our past (Anderson 1996: 90-110). Due to contingencies at the point where human vision evolved, perhaps before, we are only aware of changes, called *invariances* that occur at a certain speed within our perceptual field. Similarly, Torben Grodal has discussed the spectator's perception as centered on the representation of character goals, termed *cognitive identification with subject actants* (Grodal 1997b: 88-93). If we see Harrison Ford running for his life with a huge stone on his trail in *Indiana Jones*, or if we see Jerry the Mouse being pursued by Tom the Cat, we respond to the concern in question, survival, by experiencing the importance of escape ourselves. Thus we have an experience that seems realistic due to the forming of action goals relative to the story world.

The implications of the cognitive-ecological perspective are first, that the functions performed by human perception, cognition and emotion are materially and physically grounded. Secondly, that they have evolved in order to facilitate interaction with the environment at a certain point in time. The precise environment in which these capacities originate is unknown. Uncertainty as to the processes by which these capacities are carried out is considerable. Yet we have to recognize that capacities and purposes are embodied, for if we do not, we risk a mere rationalization. We end up describing the way the system *ought* to perform in order to be purposeful and rational. From the point of view of epistemology, our system ought to adhere to what we know to be true and actual. To the extent that we react otherwise, we may attribute this to the flights of fancy, the imagination. However, the 'embodied' view acknowledges that even though a conscious 'I' knows that the representation of the film is not actual, another part of the subject reacts as if it were indeed actual. The distinction 'actual' and 'non-actual' cannot and does not penetrate all cognitive, perceptual and emotional processes. In these embodied processes lies the "reality of illusion," as Anderson puts it in the title of his book. This is also where we find what Grodal in this volume has called a perceptual input's "claim of existence."

An illusion based account of the experience of realism puts emphasis on the spectator's response as essentially involuntary. If we speak of an illusion, we speak of the impression and feeling that the scene in the film is really there, and depending on how the style is carried out, it demands considerable concentration and willpower to be detached in our viewing of a scene such as the one in *Dial M for Murder*. The fact that we know that Grace Kelly is only acting, is not necessarily of great consequence for our embodied processes of perception and cognition. Even when we watch a film repeatedly and know what the outcome of a suspenseful situation will be, we may still react as if what we see is a unique situation (Gerrig 1996). Nevertheless, we may still acknowledge that the boundaries are fuzzy between an involuntary and automatic response on the one hand and a response on the basis of voluntary and deliberate thought on the other (see Frijda 1988: 357).

How might we conceptualize the experiences of the film as a work, as a screened event or as a story world unfolding freely in front of us as being non-paradoxical. A strong possibility is the concept of *situational meaning structure* introduced by the Dutch psychologist, Nico Frijda, in his elaborate theory of emotions (Frijda 1988, Frijda 1986). Briefly, his idea is that the emotions we experience are the result of the way in which we cognize an event or object. 'Apathy' is an appraisal that one cannot act in any way to alter a given situation. 'Hope' may be characterized by believing that a situation may be altered by chance or by the intervention of others. Similarly all the emotions we have names for may be described in terms of their situational meaning. The difference between 'anger' and 'hate' is the difference between focusing on an event and its agent and focusing on a person independently of any present and actual actions. Generally, emotions are the result of monitoring concerns, defined as "a more or less enduring disposition to prefering particular states of the world" (Frijda 1988: 351). Frijda points out that once an emotion is elicited, it tends to persist and be closed to judgments that relate for instance to probability assessment or other concerns (Frijda 1988: 354). The latter point relates to the way we may glance at our companion or be momentarily disturbed, only to feel that we *have* to look back and attend to the concern depicted in the film. Equally important and relative to the point made above regarding the embodied nature of cognition is that we often react to what *appears* to be real, trusting our senses rather than what we know – a loss may not be felt to be real until the moment we want the desired object to be present (Frijda 1988: 352).

Using the concept of situational meaning to understand the cognitive components of emotion, we are now in a better position to see why the three propositions which Carroll described as contradictory need not be viewed as a paradox. (1) "We are genuinely moved by fiction." Yes, but our experiences, including the intensity of our emotions and our subsequent actions regarding the scene in *Dial M for Murder*, are strongly influenced by our knowledge, confirmed by the presence of screen, camera, and by other spectators. The fact that we know the film is intended to be fiction rather than documentary also matters, but it is less clear whether this distinction needs to affect the intensity of our feelings, at least in the case of graphically depicted violence (Meade 2001). (2) "We know that that which is portrayed in fictions is not actual." Yes, but due to the fact that we respond emotionally to concerns that appear to be at stake, our reactions is then made ambiguous for a few seconds when we detect Dawson's confusion or even desperation in that he cannot attack. We are much less responsive to the fact that Anthony Dawson and Grace Kelly are actually presented in an acting situation since no concerns appears to be at stake here (for instance that they are overreacting or in other ways exposing themselves). (3) "We are genuinely moved only by what we believe is actual." Yes, but due to the way in which cognition and emotion are embodied, we partly believe that the situation is real. Nonetheless, due to a realist style the situation appears to be real.

Narrow formulations of illusory properties

Exactly why are we not allowed to say that our experience of life really at stake is based on mistaking appearance for reality? Two conceptual obstacles seem to be at work. First, the fact that even when illusions are discussed in the context of aesthetics, they are traditionally formulated in terms of material properties, and secondly the fact that other terms such as imagination or simulation seem better suited for describing our experience.

Traditionally, illusions have been considered in terms of two-dimensional drawings and pictures that seem less relevant to the kind of object that we are concerned with here. However, an attempt has been made by Richard Allen to defend the thesis of illusionism by forming a theory of 'projective illusion' in which the illusion depends on contextual factors (1995). In trying to respond to Carroll's critique of psychoanalytic illusion theories for portraying spectators as dupes, Allen accepts the idea that we exercise some measure of voluntary control over what we see. Later, however, he withdraws this claim of voluntary control:

[In projective illusion], I can bring to bear my knowledge of the fact that the representation is a depiction to prevent projective illusion taking hold, or to break the hold of the illusion entirely. This idea of projective illusion is both empirically false and conceptually confused. What is distinctive about an illusion is that it is a special form of representation that is configured in such a way as to confound our senses: our senses become unreliable guides to what lies before us (Allen 1997: 79).

This characterization of illusion is simple and adequate: if we become aware that our senses deliver unreliable information about what lies before us, we may speak of an illusion. However, the reason why Allen considers his own account of illusion incoherent, is that one cannot choose freely what one sees. The theory of projective illusion, as he points out elsewhere, lacks *objectivity* (Allen 1998: 62): an illusion involves the impression that something actually lies before one, independently of one's own mental acts.

Traditional theories on illusions have focused on two-dimensional pictures, such as Müller-Lyer illusion of lines with arrowheads and the duck-rabbit figure. These are not necessarily of any relevance to theoretical considerations in film studies. In the duck-rabbit drawing, we are free to choose what object we want to look for and we are sure to see it. In *Dial M for Murder*, we may look for Grace Kelly's intentions and beliefs as an actor or we may look for Margot Wendice as a woman of little knowledge of the crime she is to fall victim to – the latter of which has strong control precedence. Due to realism in acting and the film as a whole, we can only know the existence of the actor's intentions and beliefs by inferring from knowledge of context. Here, our illusion is more like the Müller-Lyer illusion. We cannot choose to see the lines to be of equal length. They appear to be of different lengths and the fact that they are identical in lengths can only be known by context or from one's own measurement. Our experience of the film differs from traditional illusions in that in the latter we do not feel that an event is unfolding freely in front of our eyes.

We may try to grasp the difference by distinguishing between properties provided to us unreliably. Properties given to us unreliably in the illusions traditionally discussed concern the material and categorical nature of the objects (for example, *either* rabbit *or* duck). However, why should these basic properties be more central to what an illusion is, at least in the context of film studies, than those previously discussed in relation to *Dial M for Murder*? In the latter case, we see a man's *intention* to kill a woman and we see her *belief* that she is alone, also due to our knowledge from previous scenes. Surely this intention and this belief qualifies as an illusion by the definition given so far. They are unreliable guides to what lies in front of us. It may very well be that there is a hierarchy among these various properties. That is, appearance of intentions and beliefs that put important concerns in jeopardy are likely to create a sense of realism. One of the implications of Grodal's comparison of the lack of realism in the drawing style of various cartoons outweighed by the perception of action-centered goals and extreme violence, to the realism of a photographic medium where action-centered goals are absent, is that the animation is more likely to be felt as realistic whereas with photography one gets the feeling that someone is pointing the spectator's attention toward certain objects (Grodal 1999).

The illusion of intentions and beliefs being in front of us does not necessarily go away, at least not entirely, when we glance at another spectator. It persists because cognitive processes concerning emotions have been initiated, and it is of no great consequence that I direct my view and even my attention to other matters for a brief moment. If other matters are not assessed as requiring my attention, chances are that I will feel that I must look back at the screen. The world of Margot Wendice and Lesgate/Swann appears to exist, to some extent, independently of what I look at and what I attend to.

Is the spectator imagining things?

The point is that objects and events do not enter our conscious mind with only material and physical properties assigned to them. When we experience a depiction as realistic, certain properties, such as intentions and beliefs, seem to lie in front of us independently of what we choose to do. This is at the heart of an illusion based account of our experience of realism, and it is, in my view, inconsistent with describing the spectator to be 'imagining' the objects as fictional.

At first glance, the proposition that we merely imagine something to be the case and therefore become engaged in this 'inner image' of imagination, seems to solve the paradox of fiction. Our emotions are disconnected from an exterior reality as a result of what we *imagine* to be the case and not what *is* the case. We know that Dawson does not actually intend to kill anyone and that he is only acting, but we play along and imagine that he is about to kill her. There are many versions of imagination-based theories, but what they have in common is the way they disconnect our response from the exterior world, focusing instead on the way in which the representation is transformed by means of an imaginative act.

One imagination-based theory stresses the continuity with language in watching fiction as a question of unasserted thoughts. Thus Noël Carroll, drawing on Roger Scruton, points out that we are able to entertain a thought *unasserted* (without supposing that it refers to any exterior reality) (Carroll 1990, Scruton 1982). Similar to how we might be moved by the prospect of an event if we imagine it in detail, we may also be moved by a thought or proposition unasserted, that is, without assuming that it refers to the real world. In another version of this theory, Kendall Walton (1993) stresses the continuity between being moved by fictional representations and being moved by playing make-believe. This is a theory that relies less on language as a model, and more on psychology. Make-believe, whether a social or individual act, whether conscious or unconscious, is believed to be essential to the institution of fiction. "Imagining aims at the fictional as beliefs aims at the true. What is true is to be believed; what is fictional is to be imagined" (Walton 1993: 41). In yet a third version of the imagination based theory using computers as a model for the mind, Gregory Currie suggests that we run our belief system in a kind of *off-line* mode. "When I engage with fiction I simulate the process of acquiring beliefs – the beliefs I would acquire if I took the work I am engaged with for fact rather than fiction" (Currie 1995: 148). The point is, that the representational content may be identical in simulations of fiction and beliefs acquired from fact, but the simulations "lack the connections of belief to the exterior world via perception and behavior" (Currie 1995: 150). Nevertheless, they also "function as internal surrogates of beliefs because they retain belief-like connections to other mental states and to the body" (ibid.). Currie also speaks of secondary imagining, stating that we simulate character beliefs and desires within what is already an imaginary construct, namely the fictional story. I shall discuss only the first kind, primary imagining here.

'Imagination' is a term with nominal value. As Walton suggests, the term can serve similar functions as 'film viewing' or 'film watching,' and in order not to confuse an epistemic illusion with an aesthetic one (since they are both cognitive), it may define our experience with respect to what is fictional. Nevertheless, I believe that the term's connotations that a spectator constructs what is there as a result of a voluntary act, are too strong to serve us well at least in style analysis where the term illusion is to be preferred (although illusion is probably not preferred in relation to more permanent media effects). Historically, imagination has at least two distinct meanings. The empiricists of the 17th century saw imagination as the bridge between what is there at all times and what we contribute, whereas the romanticist Coleridge stressed the importance of imagination as a creative act or as a way of seeing something in a new perspective, which has the quality of a synthetic view (Beardsley 1975). However, the way imagination is used to explain emotions in relation to fiction is closer to the 17th century definition of the term, in which something other than what is there is supplied. It is by supposing that we relate emotionally to an inner image rather than to what is represented in a film that an explanation is gained.

Notwithstanding their individual differences, we ought to be cautious of imagination-based theories on two accounts. First, they put too much emphasis on the importance of voluntary decision making relative to fiction. It is true that I can decide at will whether to see a duck or a rabbit in a certain drawing (Scruton 1995: 216) but many cases, as Richard Allen has pointed out, can be seen as a matter of *aspect seeing* where both images make perfect sense. Drawing on Wittgenstein, he points out that this is a general feature of perceptual reports. We may see a face in the clouds, or a physical resemblance to a family member in someone else etc (Allen 1997: 77). That is, the fact that we are 'free' or 'able' to see whatever aspect of a person, thing, etc that we want to is true also of real phenomena (that is, non-fictional, non-representational phenomena). This is the very reason why we say that people who for example fail to realize what is at stake in a given situation have willfully misinterpreted what we say.

Filmmakers may have gone through considerable pains to make sure that the scene possesses sufficiently realism to convince the spectator. This constrains freedom in regards to what we can see. Nevertheless, it is a fact that *a specific kind* of film or film sequence may require that I imagine what the representation is supposed to mean. At the end of Emir Kustorica's *Underground* we see an abstract representation of the way in which Yugoslavia has broken up. In this case, imagination is necessary in order to transform what is there, not by responding merely to what is represented in terms of properties such as objects, character beliefs and intentions, but seeing instead the small islands as representative of states. In order to appreciate this kind of film sequence, I need to see the represented not in the illusionary manner which is difficult to sustain anyway, but seeing instead what is represented *as a sign.* This means that I try to imagine what the intention is, thus in a sense supplying what is not there and bridging a gap. It is part of my experience that I contribute to what is there, deliberately and willfully. In this type of case, the concept of imagination is an adequate term.

My second reservation concerning the concept of imagination is that it is assumed that objects and events enter the mind or are initially processed according to the distinction between 'fiction' and 'reality.' Thus using the asserted/unasserted theory it is presupposed that we can somehow bracket what we experience and put it into a distinct category before processing it with the mind's eye. Here, the idea is that "real" and "fictional" become labels, which can then be removed when they have dissociated themselves from the exterior world. As for the analogy to playing make-believe, it may very well be that a kind of make-believe is involved, which is likely to be the case in for instance non-realist styles of comic acting. Here it seems to me that actors often highlight for example that they are not really hurt. However, even if make-believe could be done unconsciously, we still loose sense of what is foregrounded by the term 'illusion.' That what seems to be in front of you is there independently of any agency other than the one present. We also loose sight of the way the world is presented because filmmakers and actors have succeeded in making convincing representations. A convincing appearance is not required in games of make-believe where a new framework lends meaning to the represented through context.

A similar objection can be raised against the notion of an off-line simulation. It seems to me that this particular theory puts too much confidence in either the power of consciousness or the intelligence of the 'system' in detecting the mode in which input should be processed. We must assume that some of the perceptual and cognitive processes are identical regardless of what we know their status to be in terms of being true and false. From the fact that we are generally able to distinguish between the categories of fiction and fact it does not follow that they each need their own mode of reception. One of the implications of an off-line simulation in which all fiction is processed is that it is difficult to see how recognition of real events, persons or periods may contribute to our experience of realism. That is, it is difficult to see how a film might play upon various beliefs regardless of their source, in achieving a sense of realism by imitating reality.

Imaginings and the historical realism of Burnt by the Sun

I take it that the overarching categories of 'fiction' and 'fact' function as important guides which ask the extent to which we *ought* to let ourselves be influenced by our beliefs about the world. Generally we are good at this but we may occasionally be wrong, especially when the beliefs acquired from viewing feature films are not supplemented by beliefs acquired from personal experience or factually based representations, such as documentaries and news reports. In many cases, the nature of a belief may render the question of the sources of its acquisition relatively insignificant, and in those cases where a truthful account is important, we may inquire into the matter by supplementing with factually based representations.

What I believe to be true about the US judicial system is learned mainly from feature films, and in the absence of factually based representations or personal experience, the films constitute my knowledge of the judicial system. Whether I am right or wrong, can only be ascertained afterwards, and it is only relevant if I get in trouble with the law in the US or if I am somehow able to affect the beliefs of persons with direct or indirect legislative or administrative power. If I were to make a film that questioned the US judicial system such as *Hurricane* (2000) with Denzel Washington, I would try very hard to represent the events with direct bearing upon the crime as truthfully and accurately as possible. It is worth noting that we are often informed as to what portions or aspects of a story a filmmaker intends to be true and which are merely a free adaptation or interpretation of events. We can be informed for instance by extra-cinematic discourse such as interviews but we may also assume that a film's representations correspond to actual historical events and that they are so significant that the filmmakers aim is a relatively truthful depiction of for instance, what it was like to live in a certain historical setting. Because we are not fully aware of the information sources on which our beliefs are based, we may incidentally learn something about the world, but we may also acquire false beliefs. To what extent one or the other is true in regards to my beliefs about the US judicial system requires an inquiry of its own.

It is perhaps more interesting to look at which ways the blending of beliefs acquired from the film itself or other films and beliefs acquired from factual sources may enrich our viewing of a film. In watching Nikita Mikhalkov's *Burnt by the Sun* (1994), the story is given additional weight if one knows that random prosecution and a widespread use of informers were the order of the day under Stalin in the 1930s. Although I may have acquired false beliefs from the film, I may also have acquired an understanding of the experience of victims under this regime, similar to the understanding which a documentary may provide but achieved by different means. Either way, I have certainly had an experience that causes me to reflect on the nature of the Stalinist regime, and I have a difficult time letting go of the film and it stays with me perhaps because of the blending of history and an imaginative story.

I suspect that inconsistencies will abound if my experience of historical realism in *Burnt by the Sun* is to be explained under the assumption that we view this film through a special kind of mode such as imagination. The theory of off-line simulation makes particularly strong demands of our perception and cognition if we are to separate the 'pretend-beliefs,' for instance acquired in the film's first scenes or from other films, from the beliefs acquired by reading or watching non-fiction. While watching historical films we have to separate our factual knowledge from "knowledge" acquired during the film's exposition. Indeed, the reason why a historical film such as *Burnt by the Sun* may leave one feeling the affects of the horror of Stalin's regime is exactly because the emotional experience hinges on the inability to distinguish between beliefs and 'pretend-beliefs.' Moreover, even if we ought to, and generally succeed in, distinguishing between beliefs acquired from factual sources and from fiction, we achieve this not necessarily because the two have entered our mind in two fundamentally different modes (on-line or off-line; asserted or unasserted; trusting or make-believe), but because we are able to reason and make sound judgments. Watching a film like *Burnt by the Sun* may prompt one to study the period, but even here I doubt that we will be inclined to discover precisely what aspects of the film were truthful and which were invented.

Is recognition engaging?

I noted earlier that there were cognitive components to emotion and that this could be described in terms of the relationship between an emotional experience and situational meaning. I want to discuss now the ease with which we seem to recognize that certain concerns are at stake in a film. This requires a broader discussion of recognition.

When we recognize that life is at stake in *Dial M for Murder* this is done on the basis of recognitional capacities that we naturally possess and it is hardly any extra effort to exercise them in response to a film. We may thus speak of perceptual realism (see Riis, in print). Perception does not only serve to inform us about the size and relative position of objects in our close environment, but it serves to inform us as to what can be expected from other beings on the basis of their behavior. In written or verbal narrative fiction, we must have the intentions and beliefs communicated by way of a narrator, but in film we seem able to pick up intentions and beliefs through a perceptual process, in continuity with cognition, from the actor's actions.

We may distinguish between various levels of recognition. To recognize an object by seeing how it belongs to a group of tomatoes is one thing, but to recognize the tomato as belonging to Italy or even to a specific sort of regional tomato is recognition on a more refined level. Similarly we may recognize intentions and be-liefs in the story world to different degrees. We may recognize the intention to kill in *Dial M for Murder* even if we saw the scene in isolation, but the hesitation or confusion that arises when she does not hang up the phone faster, is recognized at a more refined level if we have seen the previous scenes in which the murder was planned and in which Lesgate/Swann shows doubt and only yields to blackmailing. That is, the cognitive processes, especially involv-ing memory, may work with intentions and beliefs analogous to objects such as tomatoes.

I believe that when we speak of a realist style or experiencing of realism, we do not simply mean that the film has given us a chance to exercise recognitional capacities that we naturally have come to possess. An additional requirement would seem to be that we find what we recognize with ease to be emotionally engaging. That we have come to possess these recognitional capacities naturally means that we have come to possess them with little or no effort. In relation to the perceptual and cognitive capacities discussed above, it means that we will have to have lived in an environment in which there are human beings who interact in correspondence to a number of concerns. If we have come by these capacities with ease, chances are that we will find the opportunity to exercise them less than exhilarating when watching a film. It is not even taken for granted that the opportunity to exercise recognitional capacities that require particular or formally acquired skills is engaging, even though the case can be made that avant-garde films test our recog-nitional capacities (see Peterson 1994).

If the events conveyed to us in a film are to appear to exist in-dependently of the agencies of filmmakers and ourselves as specta-tors, emotional activity of some sort seems to be required. Grodal highlights the need for a motivational theory in cognitive film the-ory in his discussion (Grodal 1997b: 1-4). Drawing on Gibson's concept of affordance, he points out that for something to be ex-perienced as being realistic, it is required that an object or event not only 'be there' but 'affords' something (Grodal 1997a: 39). However, in his writings, Grodal prefers the term *simulation*, meaning that we are immersed in the story world by means of identification with subject actants (making plans for the characters, etc). This usage is not that dissimilar from what Currie termed 'secondary imagining,' only in Grodal's case, simulation seems to be supplementary to a perceptual process rather than to imagination and pretend-beliefs.

However, in my view, there are problems in choosing the term 'simulation.' Apart from the fact that it carries the connotations of either being off-line or disconnected, or alternatively, even of 'faking' one's emotional response, it suggests in Grodal's usage that we have somehow lost ourselves in a realistic experience of the story world. This is often the case, but only relative to the way a concern is depicted. In experiencing the scene from *Dial M for Murder*, I am well aware that as a spectator I cannot interact with the participants in the scene, which is part of the emotional effect suspense films aim for. I am frustrated and aware of my own position as a spectator, a world apart from that depicted. In spite of this, the experience of film realism is not reduced.

Realism as a means of establishing an illusion (rather than fiction)

Having dealt with imagination in various forms, I will now compare the concept of illusion to that of 'fiction.' Fiction seems to be a relatively neutral term in regards to descriptive value, but it does not necessarily describe the kind of relationship we have to films with actors in them. In fact the term may be slightly misleading in that it may function as a corollary to imagination, designating the film as somehow 'untrue.'

In short, I believe that fiction is the best term to describe and categorize a film, made for the purpose of providing an experience without necessarily making any claims about the real world. The extent to which factual claims are made, for instance in a historical film, is an additional feature or value to the primary purpose of the film, to facilitate an experience. This is a definition of fiction and non-fiction that accords with central work on the nature of non-fiction (Plantinga 1997, 2000) as well as a naturalist conception of art. The latter stresses the continuity between the experiences we may have in real life and those we have in response to art (Dewey 1995, Livingston 2001).

My reason for bringing up both fiction and art is that even if we define the intention of non-fiction as seeking truth, it is misleading to say that the opposite is the case with fiction. Fiction films do not necessarily intend to be untruthful. As we saw with *Burnt by the Sun*, we may value fiction films because they intend and succeed in giving an accurate representation of a historical period and milieu. As film critics remind us when they characterize something as a 'realist representation,' the borders between what we categorize as fiction and non-fiction are not necessarily characterized by the intention to be untrue and true. On similar grounds, it is also misleading to speak of a 'simulated reality.' Imitating an actual situation as truthfully as possible is required if we are to design a flight simulator, but if we are to 'design' an experience for a film spectator, realism is yet another means of enhancing the illusion. In this sense realism is not an end in itself, but a means.

The reason that the term 'fiction' does not serve us well in understanding our experience of what is represented in a film is perhaps best illustrated by bringing into focus the performance of Klaus Kinski in the credit sequence of Werner Herzog's *Woyzeck* (1978). Here we see Kinski in a soldier's uniform running into a close-up, apparently being exercised by his superior officer, and throughout the scene we see him in fast-motion with only a musical score on the sound track. When we see him in close-up, in a frontal as well as two profile shots, the credits start appearing across the screen: first "Klaus Kinski in," then "Woyzeck." Next we see him run up to the camera again, only to be commanded to do push-ups, after which he is kicked by by his commanding officer when he finally surrenders, evidently exhausted. What gives this sequence its impressive force is not our imagining the pain and suffering his character goes through, it is the thought that the actor Kinski actually goes through this masochistic exercise in order to achieve a characteristic sense of realism in the acting. The sequence is in no way experienced as realistic in a stylistic sense, as we are constantly reminded of cinematic form through fast-motion, music, and credits.

Here we are reminded how the actor can be acting in a realistic style, evidenced in the photographical reproduction, without the film necessarily as a whole intending to provide an illusion. The reason we are moved here is *not* because of an illusion. What we are experiencing is a photographic sequence organized in such a way as to make us aware of the realism of the acting. We could speak of illusion or false beliefs if we are later informed that Kinski actually faked his expressions, that he neither experienced his situation as painful in the slightest way, nor did he imagine in any way that he was being humiliated. However, according to two reliable documentary films, Kinski's means of achieving the results he aimed for was in part through psychological realism, that is, trying to experience the emotions himself. The way in which we experience a film is not determined by the way it is categorized, and in this case, Herzog has highlighted the documentational aspect of photographical films by drawing attention to the actor's work.

I also fail to see how we can talk of 'fiction' in trying to explain our viewing experience. It is true that Kinski no doubt intended his acting to be used in the kind of film that we categorize as fiction or feature film (in German a 'Spielfilm' which translates to 'photoplay'), and it is true that the purpose of his realist method is to make it convincing that he be a soldier in a historical setting. Even if we acknowledge that he merely pretends to be a soldier in a historical setting, and that this may be termed fictional or make-believe, this does nothing to explain the striking experience the viewer has here.

Woyzeck's credit sequence is impressive because the acting strikes us realistic in the sense that it appears to represent, and for all we know actually does represent, the experience of an actor. As was the case with historical realism, we can only judge a posteriori whether our impression corresponds to a historical reality or whether we will end up with false beliefs. Whether the film turns out to be 'ficticious' or 'illusory,' meaning here that Kinski only pretended to be feeling humiliated or suffer, or whether the 'acting' was entirely constructed in a computer, can only be decided afterwards. Our decision is in this case likely to require considerable corroboration to convince us.

Theoretical claims that stress imagination, a term closely associated with fiction, tells us that our knowledge of the objects, we are experiencing makes a difference as to the way the object is experienced. However, in this case, it is the other way around. Due to our knowledge of the film as a photographic reproduction, we are impressed by what it documents in terms of acting. Despite it being a fiction film, *Woyzeck* believably documents and represents Kinski's realistic acting style. From Kinski's own words in which he characterizes the experience of playing Woyzeck in terms of suffering, suicide and self-laceration (Kinski 1996: 280), and from Herzog's documentary *Mein Liebster Feind – Klaus Kinski* (1999) and Les Blank's *Burden of Dreams* (1982) we also become aware of the pains actually involved.

In conclusion

Currie has objected to using the term illusion since it requires the possibility for error, and this condition is generally not met when we look at moving images. Therefore illusion ought to be replaced with 'appearance' (Currie 1995: 42-47). However, 'illusion' is adequate on the grounds that our response to the film, that is, the perception, cognition, and emotion carried out and leading to an experience of realism when viewing the film, has as its function to respond to a situation that *is* real.

Two kinds of realism are at issue in my discussion above, and only the first can be seen as being of an illusory nature. There is no recognition of actually existing intentions and beliefs in experiencing that important concerns are at stake among characters in an event that appears to unfold freely and independently of what one as a spectator does. Intentions and beliefs were merely performed by the actors and in this sense our impression of realism is unreliable. Likewise, we may say that Kinski was only pretending, but since the context is such that we are strongly focused on the profilmic event, the impression we get is framed in terms of Kinski's acting methods (rather than in a freely unfolding event). As it turns out, this impression is reliable.

One way to understand this distinction, as I noted earlier, is to view emotions in terms of cognitive components of situational meaning. The situational meaning of *Woyzeck*'s opening scene is in large part comprised of the actual events during the film's recording, whereas in *Dial M for Murder*, this is not the case. One may object that we are free to see whatever aspects we decide to focus on, but as I argued, drawing on Frijda's notion of control precedence and the way emotions tend to close off other aspects than their own, it is difficult to focus on Anthony Dawson's intentions as an actor instead of his character's intention to kill Grace Kelly's character. For the same reason, we continue searching for the situation's emotional concerns even though music sets in and the camera circles, both in an abrupt manner.

My suggestion is that we should not care too much whether our impression of realism turns out to be truthful or illusory (or, fictional, imagined, or simulated). However, the point is that we need to acknowledge that a feature film can actually make true claims and accurate representations of the world, and that this may be an important component of our film experience. We saw this in relation to historical realism. I have pointed out that our experience of realism in cases such as *Dial M for Murder* is not the same since it is *not* characterized by a relationship between represented events and really existing conditions. What are we to call these films if not illusion?

The illusion proffered by a thoroughly realist style is at best a weak one, since emotion is always comprised, in part, of awareness that the actors are only acting. Yet this knowledge tends not to affect our film experience, unless cued by the film as in *Burnt by the Sun* and *Woyzeck*. Emotional responses tend to favor appearances, and the emotional and involuntary nature of what we as spectators experience as being before us is what is stressed by the term 'illusion,' in contrast to the competing term 'imagination.' If this turns out to be a lost battle of words, leaving illusion as unattractive as ever, I would like to think that I have highlighted some relevant properties of realism in film, regardless of what we call them.

References

Allen, Richard. 1995. *Projecting Illusion: Film Spectatorship and the Impression of Reality*. New York: Cambridge University Press.

Allen, Richard. 1997. "Looking at Motion Pictures". In *Film Theory and Philosophy*, edited by Richard Allen and Murray Smith. Oxford: Clarendon Press.

Allen, Richard. 1998. "Film Spectatorship: A Reply to Murray Smith". *Journal of Aesthetics and Art Criticism*, vol. 56, no. 1: 61-62.

Anderson, Joseph. 1996. *The Reality of Illusion: An Ecological Approach to Cognitive Film Theory*. Carbondale: Southern Illinois University Press.

Beardsley, Monroe C. 1975. *Aesthetics from Classical Greece to the Present: A Short History*. Tuscaloosa: University of Alabama Press. Orig. 1966.

Bordwell, David. 1985. *Narration in the Fiction Film*. London: Methuen & Co.

Carroll, Noël. 1988. *Mystifying Movies: Fads and Fallacies in Contemporary Film Theory*. New York: Columbia University Press.

Carroll, Noël. 1990. *The Philosophy of Horror*. New York & London: Routledge.

Currie, Gregory. 1995. *Image and Mind: Film, Philosophy, and Cognitive Science*. Cambridge: Cambridge University Press.

Dewey, John. 1995. "Having an Experience". In *The Philosophy of Art: Readings Ancient and Modern*, edited by Alex Neill and Aaron Ridley. McGraw-Hill: New York. Orig. 1934.

Frijda, Nico H. 1986. *The Emotions*. Cambridge & New York: Cambridge University Press.

Frijda, Nico. 1988. "The Laws of Emotion". *American Psychologist*, vol. 43, no. 5: 349-58.

Gerrig, Richard. 1996. "The Resiliency of Suspense". In *Suspense: Conceptualizations, Theoretical Analyses, and Empirical Explorations*, edited by Peter Vorderer, Hans J. Wulff and Mike Friederichsen. Mahwah, NJ: Lawrence Erlbaum Ass.

Gibson, James J. 1979. *The Ecological Approach to Perception*. Boston: Houghton Mifflin Co.

Grodal, Torben 1997a. "Audiovisuel virkelighedsfremstilling". *Sekvens. Filmvidenskabelig Årbog*. Københavns Universitet.

Grodal, Torben 1997b. *Moving Pictures: A New Theory of Film Genres, Feelings, and Cognition*. Oxford: Clarendon Press.

Grodal, Torben 1999. "Film, Character Simulation, and Emotion". Paper presented at the *Film, Mind, Viewer* symposium in Copenhagen.

Kinski, Klaus. 1996. *Kinski Uncut: The Autobiography of Klaus Kinski*. London: Bloomsbury. Orig. 1991.

Livingston, Paisley. 2001. "Aesthetic Value". Paper presented at *Filosofisk æstetik, ph.d. seminar*. Copenhagen.

Meade, Ben. 2001. "Emotional Response to Graphic Violence in Film: Realism Revisited". Paper presented at *Problems of Representation in a Cognitive Theory of Film*. Pecs.

Peterson, James. 1994. *Dreams of Chaos, Visions of Order: Understanding the American Avant-garde Cinema*. Detroit: Wayne State University Press.

Plantinga, Carl. 1997. *Rhetoric and Representation in Nonfiction Film*. Cambridge, U.K. & New York: Cambridge University Press.

Plantinga, Carl. 2000. "The Limits of Appropriation: Subjectivist Accounts of the Fiction/Non-Fiction Film Distinction". In *Moving Images, Culture and the Mind*, edited by Ib Bondebjerg. Luton: Luton University Press.

Riis, Johannes. In press. *Spillets kunst – følelser i film*. København: Museum Tusculanums Forlag.

Scruton, Roger. 1982. *Art and Imagination: A Study in the Philosophy of Mind*. London: Routledge & Kegan Paul.

Scruton, Roger. 1995. "Imagination". In *A Companion to Aesthetics*, edited by David Cooper. Oxford, UK & Cambridge, Mass., USA: D.A. Blackwell.

Walton, Kendall L. 1993. *Mimesis as Make-Believe: On the Foundations of the Representational Arts*. Cambridge, Ma: Harvard University Press. Orig. 1990.

Mikkel Eskjær

Observing Movement and Time – Film Art and Observation

As soon as we start considering the reality status of cinema we are confronted with different, and often contradictory, positions. Traditionally, cinema has been defined as the registration of reality; the divergence of reality and cinematic representation; linguistic or semiotic structures; or the perceptual and cognitive processes of the spectator (whether pre-conscious, conscious or sub-consciuos). Thus, questions about the reality of cinema and the nature of cinematic representation have led to endless discussions and a variety of answers, ranging from the idea of pure reality, to a culturally, ideologically or mentally dependant reality.

In order to avoid the diverging positions in film aesthetics, this article argues for an approach put forward by system theory and second order cybernetic. In a discussion of the reality of cinema, Dirk Baecker suggests using an ontogenetic approach that retreats from asking about the ontological status of a given phenomenon, focusing instead on how this phenomenon is produced. Applied to cinema, this approach does not focus on the reality of cinema, but rather on how this reality is produced and communicated (Baecker 1996). Bracketing ontological categories all together (realism, formalism, structuralism etc) it looks upon the reality of cinema as constituted by processes of observation. Cinema offers a way of looking at the world. This way of looking is an observation of reality, being itself a part of the social world it observes. The processes generating this observation based reality is the subject of this article and will be described in relation to both cinema and the social system of art.

This article will be addressed from two perspectives:

- First, following a formal definition of observation, I will turn to a description of cinema as being reflecting the reality of communication (Baecker 1996). Cinema is an observation of communication, produced by psychology and the audio-visual registration of human behavior, thereby capturing the reality of communication.

- Second, the notion of observation will be expanded to include Niklas Luhmann's definition of art as a social system and a medium for communication (Luhmann 1995). I intend to show that cinema has turned its own form (movement and time) into a medium for communication. This thesis will be discussed and illustrated by referring to Deleuze's theory of the movement-image and the time-image.

The second perspective illustrates my approach to system theory. Whereas most system theories start by explaining the general architecture of differentiated social systems, I intend to exploit the possibilities offered by system theory by starting from below, through a process of re-specification offered by Deleuze's theory of cinema. Focusing exclusively on cinema, I follow Luhmann's theory of art, limiting my investigation to that part of the art system identified as film art.

Above all, within the framework of an existing film aesthetic, the aim of this essay is to give an account of the reality of cinema based on the concept of observation. Such an approach can be seen as the initial step toward understanding the social role and function of cinema as a communicative medium. It also helps to explain how the reality of cinema cannot be separated from the social reality.

Cinema is "a human fact" as Morin stated, thereby becoming a part of social reality (Casetti 1999: 108). Whether the project outlined here falls under the traditional categories of film sociology is hard to say.[1] Nevertheless, it points to a relevant dialogue between aesthetic theory and sociology, which, compared to the vast area of film studies in general, has been somewhat neglected in recent years.

The observation of communication

In describing cinema as an instance of observation, we need a formal definition of observation. Defined by Niklas Luhmann, observation is the capability of psychological systems (e.g. a spectator) as well as social systems (e.g. the legal system or the art system) to handle a difference that defines only one side of the difference, and not the other (Luhmann 1994: 15). This is indeed an extremely formal definition, dealing only with the formal operation within an observation, and without referring to the content of the operation. Making observations always implies a distinction (e.g. new/old) to mark what is at the center of the observation (e.g. new) and what is external to the observation (old), even though the external is still an essential part of the observation. The external is just momentarily neutralized, thus constituting the virtual side of the distinction. For instance, talking about what is right implies a notion of what is wrong. In the same way, observing something as new depends on the difference between old and new, though the unmarked part of the distinction (old) never actually becomes part of the given observation.

In watching a film, we distinguish between what happens on screen and the screen itself. We do not see the screen, though it is a precondition for watching the film. If we do focus on the screen, we do not see the film, but a flat surface upon which there are flickering lights. The distinction here is that the observations' blind spot remains invisible, unless we create a new distinction between observer and observed, observing the distinction used by the observer (the difference between the screen and what is on the screen), for instance as a process of self-observation. This new distinction also creates a blind spot, that is, the point from which we distinguish between observer and the observed. Evidently, the process is continuous. Each observation creates a new blind spot, which is only observable from a new observation point building on a new distinction, which also remains invisible, and so on.

According to Baecker, cinema represents a particular form of observation. The reality of cinema is produced by the audiovisual registration of the world of communication. Baecker claims that cinema has developed its own way of investigating the nature and reality of human communication, which separates it from, for instance, the novel:

The movie revels in trying to find out how human emotion, which the novel and its corresponding psychologies had related back to conscious and unconscious thought, translates into, and is evoked by, mere behavior, thus triggering a different, behavioral and cognitive, psychology. The movie rarely, if ever, distinguishes between behavior, communication, consciousness, and situation. Yet one can observe how movies employ these distinctions in order to create the puzzles which motivate the story. Their blurring of the distinctions in one sequence of pictures leads them to make a distinction that solves the puzzle in the next sequence, which, however, blurs some other distinction (Baecker 1996: 561-562).

To a certain degree, cinema can be described as a communicative mise-en-scène. However, this mise-en-scène leads to a blurring of behavior, actions, and consciousness, thus creating puzzles, motivations, narrative gaps, cause-and-effect relationships, indecisive moments, connections and irritations, which all take part in securing the narrative drive and visual dynamics of cinema. The blurring of different forms of communication and communicative action is an essential part of the reality of cinema.

Describing cinema as an observation of communication through behavior, actions and situations, does not necessarily imply a human agent, as long as the film revolves around an anthropomorphic project, a fact emphasized since Béla Balázs (Balázs 1970). Thus, we have no problem following the communication between two desk lamps (mother and baby) playing ball with each other in the animation film *Lux Jr.*

The idea of cinema as an observation of antropomorfic communication is not particularly new or original (let alone exhaustive), but it does allow Baecker to investigate an important distinction within cinematic observation. According to Baecker, cinema's observation of communication establishes a distinction between "staging communication and communicating" that is, the difference between aesthetic communication (cinema, a novel, a painting) and an "ordinary" act of communicating (asking what time it is, asking for a cup of tea, or ordering somebody to close the window). This distinction indicates the difference between reality and the reality of cinema. During the ordinary act of communicating reality is not the product of communication, but rather a part of it. Aesthetic or staged communication on the contrary, is communication made symbolic or fictional, where reality is produced through communication, and external to communication. Reality becomes fictionalized, or as Luhmann puts it; art is a fiction with *"eine befreiende Distanz zur Realität"* (Luhmann 1997a: 353).

However, the problem is that we tend to forget this distinction when watching films. The produced reality of communication is taken for granted because cinema's audiovisual universe so readily reminds us of reality, that is, the reality of an unstaged communication. As a result, cinema is perceived as communication without communication, as unstaged communication and not as the reality of aesthetic observation.

According to Baecker, we need to install the distinction of communication within cinema in order to realize cinema as observation of communication. Only then will we grasp the nature of cinematic observation. From Baecker's perspective, such an approach becomes a sociological concern, since it maintains the difference between reality on the one hand, and the (communicated) reality of cinema on the other. He thus emphasizes the reality of cinema as a communicated reality, thereby inscribing cinema in the social circuit of communication.

The two-sided objects of fiction

Cinema and entertainment can be described as playing with the distinction between reality and the reality of fiction in a very subtle way. In his book on mass media, Luhmann defines entertainment as a special optical and acoustic game which creates its own fictional reality. However, although this reality is fictional, it is not unreal. The fictional world of entertainment makes use of real objects, but these are two-sided objects whose structure allows us to cross the boundary between fictional and real objects. When seeing a bicycle in a movie, it is a real bicycle that turns into a bicycle in the fiction because our knowledge of the real object enables it to become a fictive object in the world of imagination (Luhmann 1996: 98-99, Eskjær and Helles 2000: 54).

Baecker illustrates the idea with the human face as an example. According to Baecker the face can be described as a two-sided object. In a movie we watch the expression of a face change, e.g. from concentrated and happy to concerned and scared. However, changes in the facial expression occur within the fiction, thereby taking us from reality to fiction. In this way, changes in an object in reality become attributed to the world of fiction.

Attributing an object to the realm of art allows for different reactions and possibilities. (1) The two-sided object allows for a crossing between fiction and reality. (2) The status of the object allows for an oscillation between fiction and reality knowing that the attribution of the object belongs to the realm of fiction. (3) The possibility of focusing on the technical creation of the object (what Metz called the fetishism of technology, the function of which is to defend one self against the seducing power of fiction (Metz 1977: 74-77)).

Cinema's communication of observation is thereby made up of two-sided objects, permitting the passage from reality to fiction. This passage is never absolute (resulting in psychotic viewers not knowing the difference between fiction and reality, that is, observers who are unable to handle the difference between communication and staged communication), but rather represents a delicate balance between the two. Baecker observes that "Stories, pictures, sounds, and casts all have to tread the narrow line between a fiction that tells something about reality, and a reality that opens a space for fiction" (Baecker 1996: 574). This narrow line is the balance upon which cinema builds its powerful expressions creating a reality pregnant with meaning.

Film, art & communication

In order to expand the notion of film art as observation we will turn to Niklas Luhmann's notion of art, and the reading of Luhmann by Ole Thyssen (Thyssen 1998). The role of art in Luhmann's theory needs to be understood as being a functional system. It is well known that Luhmann was not interested in art for art's sake, but rather the functional differentiation of art as a sub-system of society (Luhmann 1995: 10, Reese-Schäfer 1999: 111). As a sociologist, Luhmann seeks to understand the emergence and development of structural complexity in the region of society called art.

As with any functional system, art is neither based on persons, actions, genres nor schools, but rather on communication. According to Luhmann, communication is the smallest unit of a social system (Luhmann 2000: 217). The art system is itself especially apt to demonstrate his idea, since it is neither possible to point to something in the artwork (a technique, an action, the artist, an intention) nor to construct an analytical unit (a genre, the viewer) that defines art. Everything seems to have the ability to be called art, from cave paintings to ready-mades, from the unique to consumer products in the age of mechanical reproduction. Only through communication may something be established as art, either when a work of art communicates itself as art, an artist declares his work as art, or an observer (a viewer, an institution, a system) observes something as art. Thus, the art system is based on communication and the unity of differences between artwork, producer and observer. Art is a product of this triangulation, where no one part determines whether a given work should be considered art. Thus, art is a genuine social relation neither dependant exclusively on objective criteria (mode of perception) nor subjective criteria (judgment) (Thyssen 1996).

From a systemic perspective, communication is the unity of the differences between three selections: information, message and understanding, where understanding depends upon the distinction between information and message (Luhmann 2000: 181). In order for an action to be called communication, all three selections are required. The phrase "nice weather" contains information about the weather. But it also contains a message, whether it is an objective phrase or an ironic statement. The distinction between information and message, in this case the decision whether the information is objective or ironic, depends on the understanding. Only then does communication take place.

Art is communication based on perception. Indeed, every communication builds on some kind of perception whether visual, aural, tactile or otherwise. But art is unique in that it focuses on the perceptual part of the communicative act. When we see the handlebars and the seat of a bicycle turned into the head of a goat, we are not so much interested in *what* it is (the information), as we are in *how* it came to be (the message). In this way, aesthetic communication is about making the difference between information and message explicitly clear within every communicative act.

Art does not so much offer information as it offers an almost infinite number of different ways of presenting information. The fact that *Berlin, Symphony of a Great City* still fascinates has less to do with the information about Berlin during a day in 1927, than it has to do with the particular perceptual way in which the film observes the changes during that day.

Art's perceptual observation differs in two important ways from other types of observation. It contains a perceptual surplus compared to (a) The everyday observation of individuals (b) The observation belonging to other social systems. Looking at the former, everyday observation tends not to see the dynamics of for instance urbane space; the movements, the rhythms, the patterns and the sudden disappearing of shadows etc, all of which are brought to life in films like *Berlin*, or *Man With a Moving Camera*. Art deals with a radically different and complex observation of the world, which would be dysfunctional outside the system of art. Thus, art may force us to observe differently and communicate differently about things and relationships that remain hidden in ordinary observation and communication. It is evident that such a functional understanding of art has many similarities with formalistic positions within art theory (Lemon 1965).

Furthermore, looking at the latter of the two differences, the observation of art represents an alternative world to perspectives offered by other sub-systems. For instance, the cinematic observation of the dynamics of urbane space contains a sensuous precision, surpassing any theoretical description within the system of science. Perhaps that is why we find a number of modern architects referring to the cinema rather than theory of architecture, when describing their work.

Art may be described as an "invitation" to observe the world in a different way (Thyssen 1998) by playing with the difference between reality and the reality of fiction. This new observation might even change one's observation of the world outside the art system. For instance, visiting an apparently idyllic American small town will perhaps never be the same after David Lynch's deconstruction of the American middle-class.

124

The instability of observation

The invitation to observe, leads to a general definition of the role and function of art as a differentiated social system. Art illustrates the implicit foundation of a differentiated society build upon functional systems, namely the plural and partly contingent nature of observation (every system observes reality, and thereby each other, in accordance with its own order and code, the economical system through +/- payment, the political system through +/- majority, etc). Art accepts that it is built on the loose ground of observation, that it is a construction of a world independent of physical reality, and that it only becomes art if somebody observe it *as* art. A set of handlebar and a bicycle seat may become a goat, if observed as such. Each work of art confirms that it could have observed otherwise. And art simply lives by always presenting new observations. An observation can never be repeated. In this case it will be regarded as a copy and fall out of the art system (unless, of course, it is the act of copying which is declared a work of art).

The system of art is thus stabilized by always being unstable, a paradoxical situation that Thyssen defines as a meta-stabile system (Thyssen 1998: 349, 1994: 123). Art is able to challenge existing orders by presenting alternative observations of the world, and by not obeying rules or orders other than those of art. For instance, an artist may declare a tiny island an independent state, or establish an alternative government consisting of artists (who allegedly should be more human than politicians). Such actions are allowed within the art system because art is an autonomous system detached from the rest of society, and because such happenings will most likely be followed by new events. This degree of innovation and instability is unique to the art system. Unlike all other systems (especially the economical system), art permits a very high degree of variation and much less redundancy. Within the political system, the same actions would either be regarded as nonsense (and thereby be invisible to the system) or as a very serious threat to the system (and it would be treated as such).[2]

Thus, the art system confirms that the world is built on observations by conflicting observers, and that the observer is always contingent, though possible to identify and realize. Art also states that a monolithic view of society is impossible since world and society is the product of competing observations. A first order observation of the world such as unity is impossible in a differentiated society. The function of art as autonomous is to refer to the inaccessibility of world unity, and to make an invisible condition visible.

The communicative contribution of the art system is to represent the universal nature of observation by confronting reality with the many possible fictive realities of art.

Art thus directs attention to the processes involved in every observation and social communication. Art manages to show, that another world exist behind the world of art, although this ability is realized within art itself, that is, through art's own operations. Thus, the relationship between art and reality is to be understood as the unity of art and reality within art. In that sense, one can speak of art as symbolizing the world (Luhmann 1990: 16, Roberts 1999), or rather, as Luhmann puts it, "um die Unbeobachtbarkeit der Welt zu symbolisieren" (Luhmann 1995: 192).

This is achieved not by showing what can't be shown, but by indirectly referring to everything that is not observed or by referring to that which remains unmarked by stressing the artwork's own observation. A paradigmatic example is seen in the use of irony, which pays attention to what is external to itself, by directing attention to the limitation of its own form (Roberts 1999). Also described by Luhmann as: "was im Kunstwerk selbst nicht gesagt, sondern nur als nicht-gesagt markiert ist" (Luhmann 1995: 192). This is the reason why Luhmann claims that modern art deals with the observation of the un-observational sides of the world (Luhmann 1990, 1994).

Form & medium

So far, we have been looking at the communicative contribution of the art system as a functional social system. A further description must focus on the operations behind the aesthetic observations of art and cinema. This step requires an introduction to another important concept in Luhmann's discussion of art.

When presenting Luhmann, his authorship is often divided in

two: an early period influenced by the American sociologist Talcott Parsons and a later period influenced by the concept of autopoeisis. The transition between the two periods is marked by his major theoretical work *Soziale Systeme, Grundriss einer allgemeinen Theorie* (Luhmann 2000). However, even in Luhmann's later period we see a theoretical shift away from the system theoretical concept of system/surrounding, in favor of a more distinction theoretical approach (Borch 2000, Baecker 2000). Such a shift can be seen in Luhmann's use of the concept of form/medium, originating from the Austrian-American psychologist Fritz Heider (Heider 1959).[3]

The concept becomes prominent in Luhmann's late works (Luhmann 1997a: 190 ff.), and is particular important in his theory of art (Luhmann 1995: chapter 3). It allows him to grasp art differently from traditional aesthetic theory. Art is normally defined through ontological differences, for instance between the ontological status of material and form as in the classic example of the difference between marble and a statue. The problem with such a distinction is that the statue is still marble, not just form, and marble is never just material but always has a form. Such problems disappear the moment we use the distinction between form and medium since it belongs to an observer, and not to a world of objects. Form/medium is a "beobachterabhängige Unterscheidung" as Luhmann says (Luhmann 1997a: 195). It is an internal distinction made within an observing system, thus "Es gibt keine entsprechende Differenz in der Umwelt" (Luhmann, 1995: 166). The air wherein words, lyrics, music takes form, is to be true of something on a molecular, atomic or sub-atomic level. But not to the observer. To the observer, it is only a medium where forms are formed. The same goes for the screen, which physically is a flat surface, but to the spectator it is only a medium transmitting the visual universe of moving pictures.

Art communicates meaning. This requires a medium through which the communication takes place. The problem is, that a medium can never be experienced by itself. We only have access to a medium through its form. A form is a strong coupling of elements, which permits us to experience the medium. It is therefore important to stress that form and medium presuppose each other: "Das medium wird gebunden – und wieder freigegeben. Ohne medium kcinc Form und ohne Form kein Medium, und in der Zeit ist es möglich, diese Differenz ständig zu reproduzieren" (Luhmann 1997a: 199). Formally, Luhmann defines form as exhibiting a strong coupling and medium as exhibiting a loose coupling of elements occurring in time. A form is thus an aggregate of elements which either exists momentarily before perishing and dissolving into its medium like an utterance, or lasting for a long time like a marble statue. Nevertheless, forms are subject to change and/or disappearance, whereas the medium remains stable. Luhmann therefore concludes that "Medien sind invariant, Formen variabel" (Luhmann 1997a: 209).

At first sight, this definition may seem weak, as Luhmann himself notes. However, it contains a number of useful points. A medium may for instance be light or acoustics. Such media are preconditions for the subsequent emergence of forms, for instance a sequence of tones, colors in a painting etc. Through the condensation of elements, forms let us experience the medium. The ticking of a watch indicates the medium of air, although we normally do not notice the medium. The alphabet is the medium for words, though we do not read the letters but the words, at the same time as we do not see light, but the objects that light is thrown upon (Luhmann 1997b, Heider 1959).

The important thing in this particular context is that art constitutes a special relationship between form and medium. On the one hand, art has been defined as a medium for communication. On the other hand, artistic expression requires a medium such as light or acoustics to be realized. Therefore Luhmann (1997b) put forward the hypothesis that art creates the medium in which it expresses itself through its own form. This is a reversal of the established relationship between form and medium, where the form chooses a medium. In art however, the medium is a product of the form.

It sounds more cryptic than it actually is. Music requires a medium (acoustics) that renders different forms possible. However, these forms become media themselves, as seen in e.g. a certain pitch or tonality, meaning a particular constellation of sounds, wherein a variation of forms takes shape. In the same way one can speak of the difference between language and poetry or between language and prose: both of which have stabilized as media for other forms.

In systemic terms, this means that art becomes a medium of second order, where the difference between form and medium is used as a medium for communication (Luhmann 1997b: 105). When John Cage performed his piece *4.33* (1952) (4 minutes and 33 seconds with no added sound to the environment of the performance) he was already presupposing the distinction between music and silence as a medium for his particular work of art.

Since our aim is to understand the reality of cinematic observation, we will not be satisfied with a general definition of art as observation, here as being a particular relationship between medium and form. However, Luhmann's theory only offers a general theoretical framework and no extensive specifications; it is an isomorphic theory describing common features of all parts of the same system. This is both the strength and the weakness of Luhmann's theoretical work. In order to more fully understand the nature of film art in contrast to other aesthetic disciplines, we have to enter a process of re-specification. The concept of medium and form offers a basis for such a re-specification.

Cinematic re-specification: the medium of movement and time

Cinema differs from its predecessor, photography, by capturing motion and by being time based. Following Luhmann, I will claim that cinema has turned its own forms of movement and time into different media in which cinema expresses itself. Through movement and time, film art has created a particular reality of observation.

It seems obvious that one should combine such an interpretation with theories dealing with cinematic movement and time. The most elaborated work in this field is Gilles Deleuze's two books on the movement-image and the time-image (Deleuze 1986, 1989). Although this work is encumbered with certain problems, such as its rather elitist view of cinema, an anachronistic emphasis on the author (ideas that have both been challenged by contemporary film theory), and an uneven explication of the many images of cinema (Rodowick 1997, Casetti 1999) Deleuze's theory still represents one of the richest, most thorough discussions of the reality of movement and time in cinema.

This it is not the place for an extensive presentation of Deleuze's complex theory and its philosophical references to Bergson and Peirce. Rather the presentation can be limited to a few general points, outlining Deleuze's theory, read through the lens of a theory of observation. However, any account of Deleuze's film theory, even a short one, will have to include the following topics:

- The nature and possibilities of film theory, i.e. cinema as an instance of thought.
- A new conception of the image, i.e. cinema as an instant of movement, or rather a modulation of reality caught in movement.
- A classification of the movement-image and time-image.

Regarding the first topic, Deleuze defines his theory as a theory about the concepts that rise out of cinema: "A theory of cinema is not 'about' cinema, but about the concepts that cinema gives rise to and which are themselves related to other concepts corresponding to other practices" (Deleuze 1989: 280). Cinema itself does not produce concepts, but signs and images, which theory and philosophy may capture as a "conceptual practice." Cinema is an observation of the world built on particular sign- and image practices, thereby offering a special kind of observation.

The second topic represents Deleuze's alternative to previous film theory, presenting a different conception of the image. This alternative unfolds through a critique of the semiotic understanding of the cinematic image. Linking the image to an utterance, semiotics makes a double reduction of the picture: "on the one hand the reduction of the image to an analogical sign belonging to an utterance; on the other hand, the codification of these signs in order to discover the (non-analogical) linguistic structure underlying these utterances" (Deleuze 1989: 27).

This transformation violates the moving image and deprives it of its most authentic feature, namely its visible movement. As a consequence, Deleuze operates with a totally different conception of the image where "the movement-image is the object, the thing itself caught in movement as continuous function. The movement-image is the modulation of the object itself" (ibid.). Thus the image does not resemble the object, but a modulation of the object through movement.

This definition places us at the heart of Deleuze's idea of the relationship between image and reality. The movement-image is an image between other images (drawing on Bergson's definition of matter as image). It originates from what Deleuze calls the plane of immanence (Deleuze 1986: 58-59), described elsewhere as "plane of consistency" or "planomenon," (Deleuze & Guattari 1988: 69), where from paintings, words, books etc originate. Thus, the image is neither an analogical nor a coded sign, but something from the plane of immanence, which takes the form of a picture, e.g. a bicycle becoming the cinematographic picture of a bicycle. Thus cinema represents one among many kinds of observation where an observation turns its own form of movement and time into the medium of a movement-image and a time-image, both of which lead to a variation of different images.

The third topic concerns the taxonomy of images. It is impossible to give an account of them all in this essay, but I may point to their main characteristics and differences. The revolving point in Deleuze's theoretical construction is the emergence of the movement-image, which constitutes cinema as a new independent form of observation. However, it is also the historical break with the movement-image that turns cinema in a new direction with the appearance of the time-image.

A rather crude distinction between the two images defines the movement-image as an observation built on movement and space, plugging different parts into a new whole. Contrary to the movement-image, the time-image observes qualitative change and becoming in the whole (or Duration), meaning the world according to time and memory: how it could have been, or how it is remembered and understood. As Casetti writes:

Reality as perceived from a precise perspective, caught in one of its aspects (the movement-image), and reality that condenses a whole series of possibilities, open to totality (the time-image) [...] the world as it is and as it develops, as it appears and as it can be conceived (Casetti 1999: 41).

The movement-image organizes the relationships between objects and actions in different areas such as shots, sequences, connections of sequences etc. In this way the movement-image observes how behavior and consciousness emerge when persons, situations, and actions are confronted and related to each other in a sequence of time. We thus observe communication in its many sensory-motor forms, including the observation of observation (the perception-image), expressions of the human face (the affection-image), the behavior of human actions (the action-image), and the psychological relations involved in human actions (the mental-image).

In the movement-image time is only indirectly portrayed and always subsumed to (the sensory-motor link of) movement and the structuring of time according to the montage. Thus, time emerges in the form of "empirical progression" derived from motor-sensory logic, although we naturally encounter regressions such as flashbacks and the like (Deleuze 1989: 273).

The time-image is the only image where time appears in its pure form, without being subordinated to movement or to sensory-motor schemes. Therefore, the time-image is organized around the appearance of pure time, and is an observation of the duration of time. The distinction between a movement-image and a time-image matches Bergson's distinction between matter and memory, the two forms (or tendencies) that constitute the precondition for any experience (Bergson 1991). Therefore, Deleuze's 'Bergsonism' operates with two different categories: on the one hand pure perception of matter and movement; while dealing with pure memory, on the other hand. However, the two categories are mixed in normal experience, combining both perception and memory ("This mixture is our experience" (Deleuze 1988: 26)).

Only by separating the function of the two categories into their pure tendencies, do we understand the nature of experience as constituted by both perception and memory. Therefore, the separation is only a "moment, which must lead to the re-formation of a monism" (Deleuze 1988: 29). Furthermore, the distinction between a movement-image and a time-image should not be conceived as absolute. The two types of images are related and work simultaneously, illustrated by the emergence of the time-image as a result of the crisis of the movement-image, and by the movement-image's status as an indirect time-image. But each of them represents two different forms of observation.

Communicating perception

Despite the very different aim and nature of aesthetic theory and sociology, we can still use the theory of the movement-image and the time-image to enrich the discussion of the social function of film art. According to Luhmann, art installs itself in the insurmountable gap between mind and communication, perception and communication, psychological and social systems. The theory of autopoietic systems presents us to social systems that communicate but can't perceive, and psychological systems that perceive but can't communicate. Or as Luhmann puts it, "Das Bewusstsein kann nicht kommunizieren, die Kommunikation kann nicht wahrnehmen" (Luhmann 1995: 82). The reason is, that mind as a psychological system is operationally closed. The mind can never convey its own operations to another mind (resulting in an immediate breakdown of any form of communication). Only through the operations of communication is it possible for ego to inform alter about perceptual and/or psychological experiences. Only through stable forms like words or moving images (perceptible to an audience), may the artist express otherwise inaccessible feelings or experiences. In other words, art turns perceptual and intra-personal experiences inter-subjective accessible as well as subject to social communication. Therefore, Luhmann claims that:

Kunst macht Wahrnehmung für Kommunikation verfügbar (…) Sie kann die Trennung von psychischen und sozialen Systemen nicht aufheben. Beide Systemarten bleiben füreinander operativ unzugänglich. Und gerade das gibt der Kunst ihre Bedeutung. Sie kann Wahrnehmung und Kommunikation integrieren, ohne zu einer Verschmelzung oder Konfusion der Operationen zu führen (Luhmann 1995: 82-83).

Thus, art integrates communication and perception through a perceptual arrangement of elements and forms, making perception and cognition accessible to communication. This idea is not for-

133

eign to film theory. Indeed, one of the earliest theories of cinema proposed by Hugo Münsterberg in 1916, described cinema as equivalent to the mind, that is, an objectification of "our world of perception, our mental act of attention" as exemplified by the close-up imitating the processes of focused attention (Münsterberg 1970: 38). Following Deleuze's definition of movement and time, we will argue that film art is the communication of perceptual experience related to movement and time.

Limitations and further investigations

In conclusion, the ideas presented here can be recapitulated by mentioning some reservations towards the chosen approach, thereby suggesting further investigation. The general idea of this article has been to problematize the question of the reality of cinema, focusing instead on how the reality of cinema is produced through the operations of observation. This was achieved by giving a general account of cinema as observation of communication involving two-sided objects that play with the difference between reality and the reality of communication.

In accordance with the isomorphic nature of Luhmann's theory, we also looked at a few general features involved in aesthetic communication and observation. In cinema, these observations take form within the medium of movement and time, forming the basis of our re-specification of cinematic observation. The movement-image and the time-image each offer observations of different forms of motor-sensory and temporal reality, such as the perception of the urban space, or the significance of the past and present in our experience of duration.

So far, the description of cinema as observation has mostly been conducted in relation to the art system. Focus has been on the immanent observing processes of the work of art. However, observation as a fundamental operation not only belongs to the artworks, but also to the observers of artworks (Luhmann 1994: 15). Are we to fully understand cinema in terms of observation we will need to include how observers (spectators, organizations, social systems) observe cinema as art and how they contribute to communication about cinema as part of the social system of art. As pointed out earlier, Luhmann only offers a general framework, passing the process of re-specification over to his readers.

Another question concerns cinema as a product of popular culture. In this case, cinema is not only observed as part of the social system of art. From a quantitative perspective, the majority of films are perhaps observed as entertainment rather than art. Therefore we have to investigate operations of cinema when observed as part of the social system such as the mass media. In this case, cinema contributes less in order to make observation and perception the subject of social communication, than conforming to a social picture of reality upheld by the mass media (Luhmann 1996). Apparently cinema has a special ability to circulate within two social systems, that of art and that of mass media. How can this be? Does it point to theoretical incoherences or shortcomings in system theory, or can it be explained by the characteristic features of moving images that permit an oscillation between the two systems?

These questions require further investigation of the social reality of cinema as observation. However, on a more general level, they also point to the importance of bridging the gap between aesthetic theory and sociology in order to investigate the communicative complexity of cinema.

Notes

1   Francesco Casetti distinguished between four main traditions within sociology of film; Cinema as industry, Cinema as Institution; Cinema and the Culture Industry; Cinema and the Representation of the Social (Casetti 1999).

2   Other systems may also be described as meta-stabile, or as creating their own *Eigenvalues*, as when the political system maintains its stability despite, at times, great fluctuations in the opinions of voters (Thyssen 1994: 122). Nevertheless, the art system displays an extreme degree of flexibility, even permitting it to challenge the notion of art within the institution of art, as when a urinal or Drillo box is declared a work of art.

3   Originally published in 1926, Heider's text "Thing and Medium" has a purpose other than that in Luhmann's theory of distinction. Heider (1896-1988) wants to investigate how the processes of perception and cognition are determined by the structures of the physical world (Heider 1959: 2). However, the description of how distal stimulus affects the sense organs (proximal stimulus) through a medium, shares many similarities with Luhmann's use of the concept in relation to observation.

References

Baecker, Dirk. 1996. "The reality of Moving Pictures". *MLN* no. 111, 560-577.

Baecker, Dirk. (ed.) 1999. *Problems of form*. Stanford: Stanford University Press.

Baecker, Dirk. 2000. "Interview med Dirk Baecker". *Distinktion* no.1, 123-131.

Balázs, Béla. 1970. *Theory of the film*. Dower Publications.

Bergson, Henry. 1991. *Stof & Hukommelse*. København: Munksgaard.

Borch, Christian. 2000. "Former, der kommer i form – om Luhmann og Spencer-Brown". *Distinktion* no. 1, 105-122.

Casetti, Francesco. 1999. *Theories of Cinema, 1945-1995*. Austin: University of Texas Press.

Deleuze, Gilles. 1986. *Cinema 1. The Movement-image*. London: The Athlone Press.

Deleuze, Gilles. 1988. *Bergsonism*. New York: Zone Books.

Deleuze, Gilles. 1989. *Cinema 2. The Time-image*. London: The Athlone Press.

Deleuze, Gilles and Guattari, Felix. 1988. *A Thousand Plateaus. Capitalism and Schizophrenia*. London: The Athlone Press.

Eskjær, Mikkel and Helles, Rasmus. 2000. "Mediernes Realitet – en introduktion til Luhmanns teori om massemedierne". In *Sekvens, Årbog for Film- & Medievidenskab*, edited by Frank Henriksen. København: Københavns Universitet.

Heider, Fritz. 1959. "Thing and Medium". *Psychological Issues* no. 1, 1-35.

Lemon, Lee. T. (Ed.) 1965. *Russian Formalist Criticism, Four Essays*. Lincoln: University of Nebraska Press.

Luhmann, Niklas. 1990. "Weltkunst". In *Unbeobachtbare Welt. Über Kunst und Architektur,* edited by Niklas Luhmann et al. Bielefeld: Verlag Cordula Haux.

Luhmann, Niklas. 1994. *Kunstsystemets evolution*. København: Det Kgl. Danske Kunstakademi.

Luhmann, Niklas. 1995. *Die Kunst der Gesellschaft*. Frankfurt am Main: Suhrkamp.

Luhmann, Niklas. 1996. *Die Realität der Massenmedien*. 2. erweiterte Auflage. Opladen: Westdeutscher Verlag.

Luhmann, Niklas. 1997a. *Die Gesellschaft der Gesellschaft*. Frankfurt am Main: Suhrkamp.

Luhmann, Niklas. 1997b. "Kunstens Medium". In *Iagttagelse og Paradox*, edited by Ole Thyssen. København: Gyldendal.

Luhmann, Niklas. 2000. *Sociale Systemer. Grundrids til en almen teori*. København: Hans Reitzels Forlag.

Metz, Christian. 1977. *The Imaginary Signifier*. Bloomington: Indiana University Press.

Münsterberg, Hugo. 1970. *The Film, a Psychological Study. The Silent Photoplay in 1916*. New York: Dover Publications.

Reese-Schäfer, Walter. 1999. *Niklas Luhmann, zur Einführung*. Hamburg: Junius.

Roberts, David. 1999. "Self-Reference in Literature". In *Problems of form*, edited by Dieter Baecker. Stanford: Stanford University Press.

Rodowick, David. N. 1997. *Gilles Deleuze's Time Machine*. Durham: Duke UP.

Steiner, Dietmar. 1988. "Billedernes og følelsernes by. *B*, no. 1, 28-31.

Thyssen, Ole. 1996. "Æstetik som systemtvang. Om Niklas Luhmanns Samfundets Kunst". *Kritik* no. 120, 52-59.

Thyssen, Ole. 1994. *Kommunikation, kultur og etik*. København: Handelshøjskolens Forlag.

Thyssen, Ole. 1998. *En mærkelig lyst. Om iagttagelse af kunst*. København: Gyldendal.

Tornabene, Francesco. 1990. *Federico Fellini, the Fantastics Visions of a Realist*. Berlin: Benedikt Taschen.

John Corner

Documentary Values

A new interest in documentary

Documentary film and television have achieved a much stronger visibility within international media studies over the last few years. The 'Documentary' category has moved out from its rather marginal position as a topic for study (crudely put – too aesthetically fancy for media sociology, too messily referential for mainstream film studies) to a more acknowledged space. A number of books, articles, journal special editions and conferences have helped this shift along. They have significantly boosted the take-up of documentary as a topic on courses and attracted the attention of young scholars to a research area growing in liveliness and opportunities. There is an ironic dimension to this, given some of the factors affecting the health of documentary practice itself. These factors are brought out more clearly in what I have to say below.

One cause for the new interest may well be belated recognition of the real fascination of the documentary mode of working, placed as it uncertainly is between the realms of reference and imagination and between the imperatives of information and entertainment, of knowledge and spectacle. Here is a form that has been blurring boundaries and mixing categories long before the ideas of transgression and hybridity became exciting for critics in the Humanities. Analytic enthusiasm for discursive complexity, contradiction and self-subversion is well satisfied by the traditional as well as the more innovative forms of portrayal. Together with this, there has undoubtedly been more recognition of the sheer *achievement* of documentary, aesthetic and social, within the academy. This has modified, if it has not entirely replaced, a dominant idea of documentary as essentially a suspect practice, one in which quite often dubious political ideas are combined with naïve representational tactics to manipulative ends.

The very way in which documentary practice interconnects the various elements of its depictive endeavour, often in relations of tension as well as of fusion, tends, I think, to encourage in documentary scholarship a productive combination of sociological and aesthetic lines of appreciation and analysis. This links film studies' core concerns with questions of scopic allure, mise-en-scène and narrative system to an agenda about the social protocols of knowledge, institutionalized practice and the relationship between what is on the screen and those specific events and circumstances that are the grounding, often tantalizing, referent of all documentary projects. One might judge that the artistic and the referential are so intimately compounded here that commentary finds less room to reproduce the kinds of reductive one-dimensionality that can so easily be applied to other areas of media output. The student of documentary is simply too challenged by the audacity and complexity of the documentary work to be lazy or to impose an entirely 'external' reading. This is to over-state the case, of course, but the real benefits of introducing considerations of documentary within the frame both of research and of teaching are now widely recognised. That double cut – into the density of 'text' on one side and the density of 'world' on the other – is invigorating.

However, allowing for this heightened awareness of documentary achievement and its interest, there is little doubt that the primary cause of a renewed enthusiasm for examining the genre has been the growth of the different varieties of 'reality television' throughout the 1990s and the debates that they have generated. For journalists writing about broadcasting, for academics and certainly for students, the dominance of new and often surprising kinds of audio-visual documentation in the schedules has highlighted the established lines of documentary practice as a key point of reference for explanation and, often, for contrast. At its crudest, documentary and its study have become attractive by association. They are now part of 'required background' (it helps to know a bit about the vérité tradition when trying to assess how the appeal of *Big Brother* works!). More positively, though, the new forms of popular factual output have provoked a very useful and widespread reconsideration of just what is involved in following the imperative 'to document' using a camera and a microphone. They have generated a debate about 'documentary values' which has been pursued intensively within the television industry itself. This industry has not been much given to openly reflecting on the fundamental problems of the form and, until quite recently, it has been largely insulated from academic contexts of debate. The newer internal disputes have then been mediated, with different levels of seriousness and rigour, to the public at large, where they have joined a wider, more diffuse set of arguments coming from the audience experience in the form of letters to newspapers and the writings of television reviewers. It is awareness of the new output and the consequent debate (amounting almost to a 'running story' in British newspapers during the late 1990s) that has helped, alongside the other factors noted above, to give the whole issue of documentary its sharper profile in the academy. For those of us working in the area for many years, the transition to the fashionable, to the cutting edge, has seemed to happen fast. The growth in the literature and in student interest have presented an unexpected challenge.

In this chapter, I want to pursue some questions about 'documentary values', framing much of what I say in terms of the last few years of debate and dispute. By 'documentary values' I mean to refer to a number of different dimensions of the documentary project but in particular to two broad realms. First of all, to questions concerning the *technico-aesthetic production* of documentary. By this, I mean the practices and the forms through which documentaries variously achieve what Brian Winston has called their 'claim on the real' through their claim first of all on our perceptions and imagination and on our trust. I want to emphasise techniques as well as technology here, in their development, imitative but also transformative, alongside established codes of depiction at work elsewhere in the culture. Dispute about these questions has, of course, followed documentary work since its beginnings. As I noted above, it has quite often been taken up from a position that judges the entire documentary project to be an exercise in depictive fraud. Documentary has been seen to be an 'impossible' venture, even by those who have goodwill towards it (in his recent, perceptive review of the genre, John Ellis sees it as 'based on a fallacy' (Ellis 2000: 115).

Secondly, there is the question of the *social function* of docu-

mentary. This has always been an important, if often only assumed, property of the documentary project in its various strands
(John Grierson was notably keen to stress the 'sociological' prov-
enance of documentary when it suited him to play down artistic
aspiration). Indeed, assumptions about seriousness of content and
approach in relation to social purposes are a stronger factor in discussion of the new 'reality television' than assumptions about
technico-aesthetic propriety, though quite frequently the two are
implicitly linked and read into each other.

I want to start with some observations about the recent debate
on the state of documentary in Britain, particularly as this debate
has been pursued by those working within television.

Crisis? What crisis?

By the mid 1990s, there was a growing recognition in the television
industry that new forms of factual output, initially those following
the format of reconstructed or observed 'emergencies', like the
BBC's highly successful *999*, were achieving unexpected levels of
success with the popular audience. These new 'reality programmes' were quite quickly changing not only the character of
the schedules but also the pattern of commissioning. Documentary
in British television had for some time seemed to many commentators to be an 'endangered species' as a result of radical changes in
the television economy and the emergence of much more intensive
terms of competition for the popular audience. An emphasis on
popular fiction had seemed to put a question mark against documentary output of all kinds (as well as against serious drama) and
academics had joined broadcasters in voicing concern at what appeared to be a shrinking area of programming. However, the threat
now was not that of generic displacement by completely other
types of output but of an unexpected displacement 'from within',
by new forms of the factual, often drawing on documentary exper-
tise. Not surprisingly, given the internal nature of developments,
there was some disagreement within the industry as to whether
these circumstances constituted a threat at all. Speaking at the 1997
Sheffield International Documentary Festival, John Willis (then a

Commissioning Editor for Channel 4) noted that documentary was 'surfing on a new wave of success' (reported in Fry 1997: 20). Others were quick to disagree with this triumphant claim. A 'Genre Audit' for the trade magazine *Broadcast* noted the way in which the investigative documentary in particular was being neglected as a result of the shift towards 'reality show' productions with stronger human interest. It reported a strong bias towards documentaries that had an observational narrative against those grounded in inquiry or exposition (Fry 1997).

In the following year, anxieties about the consequence of the new formats grew as the 'docusoap' model, more closely emulating the methods of observational documentary, proliferated across the channels. Writing in the *Daily Mail* early in the year, the acclaimed observational film-maker Paul Watson noted:

I despair of what's happening, for this rash of docu-soaps sums up the very worst of programme-making. This is television at its cheapest and laziest, fobbing off the viewers with something not much better than moving wallpaper (Watson 1998: 9).

He went on to comment:

What saddens me about such stuff is that it's pushing better programmes to the margins. Why pay a fortune to put on original drama, or invest in a serious, investigative documentary, when you can get away with a cheap series simply by pointing a camera at someone wanting self-promotion? (Watson 1998: 9).

A number of points are worth noting here. The claim that viewers were being 'fobbed off' fitted uneasily with the indications that large numbers of viewers were enjoying the new programmes and making them weekly favourites. This tension between critical judgement and audience response (amounting here to a kind of 'false consciousness' diagnosis of audience choice) was to continue as a problem in mounting a popular attack on the new formats. It is also interesting how Watson raises questions both about technical accomplishment ('lazy') and about the integrity of the documentary subject (people who are 'self-promoting'). These judgements were variously taken up or contested by other commentators. However, the point about the implications for the television economy (and, within this, the economy of documentary production) continued to provide the core issue – the bad was driving out the good[1].

The 1998 'Genre Audit' for *Broadcast* showed an internal debate much sharpened from the previous year and once more focussed around contributions to the Sheffield Festival. Peter Dale, A Commissioning Editor for Channel 4, lamented the fact that 'today, documentaries are cherished because they entertain' and urged the need to 'demand from our documentaries the rigour, passion and insatiable curiosity we expect from the highbrow award-winners' (Dale 1998: 17). Yet in the same edition, Tim Dams reported how many directors felt that docu-soaps had been unfairly targeted for criticism in a way that neglected their reviving influence on the genre as a whole. He quoted BBC director Chris Terrill's robust views on the new developments:

Terrill admits factual programmes have been taught a lot by the docu-soap. 'If you look at some of the classic documentaries, they are bloody boring', he says. 'We commanded post-watershed graveyard slots. We weren't challenged enough to reach a bigger audience' (Dams 1998: 17).

Dams noted that a 'Trojan horse' view was held by many docu-soap directors, one in which the new work was seen as helping documentary as a whole 'burst into the meanstream' rather than putting it at risk. Docusoap, here, was a benign not threatening newcomer.

This tension between a sense of serious documentary being in peril from new developments and a sense of it being subject to an exciting extension of range is reflected in much other commentary. Sometimes, rather than a dispute, it produces a genuine ambivalence of judgement, both positives and negatives being perceived in a play-off whose final outcome it is still too early to assess. John Willis, writing more recently about the general situation (in a collection subtitled 'breaking the boundaries', well indicating the predominant academic tone of excitement as well as of concern) reflects this more cautious approach:

Our own schedules are full of documentary soaps about airlines or hotels, doctors or vets. As one BBC producer inelegantly told me, 'We're drowning in a tidal wave of vets with arms up cow's bums'. Now to some commentators, this renaissance is a disaster. Documentary soaps are more akin to entertainment and can be intrusive, sometimes dishonest. They're the Big Macs of documentary, bland and rather tasteless, a symbol of the terrible commodification of factual television. And I think that's partly true. But for those of us who've seen years of documentary budgets being cut and documentaries pushed to the edges of the television schedule, it's a pleasure to see so much factual programming, at peak time (Willis 2000: 100).

The new developments are seen here as a 'renaissance' for documentary as a whole, the new factual programming has reversed the budget cuts rather than caused them. In a sense, Willis' comment above commits itself to a notion of the genre shorn of social function in order to be so inclusively positive about recent shifts. Documentary variety becomes, in this view, a matter of *taste*, with a concession to the negative, 'Big Mac' view of docusoap that does not compromise the upbeat conclusions about the general state of things. The 'part truth' of 'commodification' is not allowed to undercut the overall assessment. Not surprisingly, academic commentary, though it has reflected these tensions, has tended to place them within a far more critical sense of the industry and its current orientation than those who work within it would normally find acceptable.

'To document': Vectors of value.

In the light of these recent shifts, I have started to think that 'documentary' may now be a rather unhelpful category with which to pursue assessment. It is particularly unhelpful in thinking about the new links between popular knowledge and audio-visual experience. The problem is that it carries too many assumptions and, I think, too many idealisations. The notions of the 'social' and the 'public' which the term mobilises (albeit differently in its different European language variants) have value, certainly – as a teacher of work on documentary for 25 years or so I still cannot hear the word without responding positively. But there is a danger of nostalgia blocking a clear response to current developments. This is so even if the final aim is to critique, rather than to welcome, the new. The term needs pressing back towards the broader category of 'documentation' from which it initially sprang (most explicitly, for Britain, in John Grierson's written advocacy of a documentary cinema during the early 1930s – see Hardy, 1979). In doing this, we are not only going from narrowness to breadth, we are being descriptive rather than evaluative. We are trying to re-locate the rich, generically ambitious idea of 'documentary' within the bewildering range of practices now available for depicting the real on screen, including the screen of the computer.

I have noted in recent writing (Corner 2000) that the term 'documentary' is always much safer when used as an adjective rather than a noun, although its noun usage is, of course, a form of abbreviation, championed by the cinema pioneers and established through sheer familiarity. To ask 'is this a documentary project?' is more useful than to ask 'is this film a documentary?', with its inflection towards firm definitional criteria and the sense of something being more object than practice. This is particularly true of documentary work within television. Documentary within cinema (in most countries a marginal form) still has the strong contrast with its dominant Other – feature film – against which it can be simply defined as 'non-fiction'. Television non-fiction describes half the schedule, a very lively, rapidly changing half at that, and so the question of generic identifiers becomes immediately more troublesome.

Documentary functions: Value and form

It seems to me that there are three classic functions to which documentary exposition, testimony and observation have variously been harnessed and around which questions, and assertions, of documentary value have gathered.

1. The publicity project of modern civics. Documentary is regarded here as providing a new and exciting mode of promotion

for citizenship within the context of liberal democratic government and changing modes of social and industrial organisation. This is documentary cinema in its classic, modernist-realist phase, funded (directly or indirectly) by official bodies. In Britain, it is certainly this function that Grierson saw the documentary as primarily fulfilling in the 1920s and 1930s. Not surprisingly, extensive and 'heavy' use of commentary is a defining feature. It should also be noted that a directly affective, as well as cognitive, impact is often sought, an intention for which the use of music and a range of rhetorical tropes, visual and verbal, give support. This fits in with the idea of documentary film as a work of cinematic creativity not just of social information. The protocols of informational rationalism that are a regulating factor in much news production have not held such general sway across documentary discourse, given these origins both in a form of promotionalism and a form of artwork.

2. Documentary as journalistic inquiry and exposition. This is essentially the documentary as *reporting*, possibly the most extensive use of documentary methods on television (at least, until very recently). Through in-camera presentation, or commentary voiceover, and perhaps with interviews interspersing either or both, the documentary work grounds itself not in an idea of 'art' or 'publicity' (see above) but an idea of 'reportage', one which importantly includes an experience of kinds of *secondary witness* (see Ellis 1999 on the importance of this notion).

3. Documentary as radical interrogation and alternative perspective. This is documentary as developed within the independent cinema movements which have maintained a presence in the audiovisual culture of some countries (the critical commentaries of Bill Nichols – see Nichols 1991 – provide the major body of work on U.S. developments and an essential reference for all writing on this topic). The authorial position is not 'official' nor does it claim journalistic warrant. Implicitly, sometimes explicitly, the documentary discourse attempts a criticism and a correction of other accounts in circulation. There is often a level of formal experimentation here not usually found in broadcast forms, although some public broadcast systems have tried to develop work of a parallel kind. A wide range of styles has been deployed, including tech-

niques of disruption and distancing taking their cue from non-realist cinema but also including direct-cinema styles of observationalism and kinds of personal testimony extending well beyond both
the duration and format of the conventional 'interview'.

This typology leaves out many important variants that have
flourished within different national television systems, but I believe it has a certain rough adequacy (in Corner 1996, I explore examples across the three categories over a 60 year period). It is
worth noting that all of the above functions tend to produce, by
design, work quite low in commodity character. Intended use-
value is stronger than exchange value (leaving aside for the moment
the question of how the audience realises this use-value).

To these three functions, there has been added, by a process
of steady development (involving one or two periods of faster
change) a fourth function, the debate about which I outlined at the
start of this chapter.

4. Documentary as diversion. This is documentary as 'popular
factual entertainment' to use the recent British coinage. As I suggested in my opening section, it is in many countries a quite new
form of documentation, albeit with partial precedents. Performing
this function, documentary is a vehicle variously for the high-
intensity incident (the reconstructed accident, the police raid), for
anecdotal knowledge (gossipy first-person accounts) and snoopy
sociability (as an amused bystander to the mixture of mess and
routine in other people's working lives). Propagandist, expositional or analytic goals are exchanged for modes of intensive or relaxed
diversion – the primary viewing activity is onlooking and over-
hearing, perhaps aligned to events by intermittent commentary. In
seeking its new pact with the popular, documentary work in this
vein has tended to 'shadow' previously established fictional formats[2]. So the early Reality TV shows, focussing on the activities of
police and emergency services, learnt a lot from the style of dramatic action narratives (Bondebjerg 1996 and Kilborn 1994 are
suggestive accounts). 'Docusoaps' have clearly learnt a lot from the
more relaxed rhythms of the Soap Opera and a good bit, too, from
the newer styles of talkshow (Dovey 2000 offers a critical review
in the context of broader inter-generic shifts). We are presently
seeing a range of documentary-style projects emerge that have

made strong and successful connections with the format of the traditional gameshow. As I write, the second series format of Channel 4's *Big Brother* – pre-planned group surveillance within a 'game frame' that has an element of viewer voting – has reworked key aspects of the television/real life interplay to huge success, following that of the previous year. The show marks, I think, another decisive stage in actuality-based entertainment.

I would not want to underestimate the real degree of innovative adaptation and creativity that has gone into these developments. Questions of scopic appeal, forms of talk and narrative system have been vigorously re-addressed in all but the most dull and imitative of formats. In documentary as diversion, by contrast with the previous three functions, we have forms that are very high in exchange value, strategically designed for their competitive strength in the television marketplace. They are far less clear in their use-value, which necessarily centres on their status as objects of pleasure rather than as resources. Television documentary producers have often produced work which entertains, sometimes in surprising and subversive ways, sometimes with populist calculation, but when a project of documentation is entirely designed in relation to its capacity to deliver entertainment, quite significant changes occur both to the forms of representation and to viewing relations.

Documentary values in a 'post-documentary' culture

There has, then, been a decisive shift towards diversion. This has not had the effect of completely displacing 'serious' output but it has certainly had the effect of reworking the identity of this output both within television's generic system and within the pattern of viewing habits and expectations. In what ways might this constitute a 'post-documentary' setting, one in which the older set of identifiers, practices, functions and expectations will simply not carry across? One in which the matrix for valuation has been transformed?

First of all, and most obviously, it might do this because audio-visual documentation, under the drive of diversion, has become too extensive and varied to allow 'documentary' what one might see as its minimum sufficient level of generic identity. There has been a quite radical dispersal of documentary energies across the schedules. As a category of work, 'documentary' has required certain things to be assumed, taken as given (it is, indeed, a question-begging category and always has been). Looking and sounding very different from other kinds of programmes helped this process along, supporting what we might call 'documentary authority'. Extensive borrowing of the 'documentary look' by other kinds of programme, and extensive borrowing of non-documentary kinds of look (the dramatic look, the look of advertising, the look of the pop video) by documentary, have complicated the rules for recognising a documentary and for attributing documentary status.

Secondly, a performative, playful element has developed strongly within factual production. This is evident not only in relation to depictive styling (including the much wider scope given to musical accompaniment) but also in such features as the degree of self-consciousness now often displayed by the participants in observational sequences. This self-display is no longer viewable as an attempt to feign natural behaviour but is taken as a performative opportunity in its own right (*Big Brother* displays this in its own, calculatedly non-natural, setting). As such, it constitutes a staple element of docusoap in contrast to the self-restrained ('consciously unselfconscious') naturalism of demeanour, speech and behaviour sought in classic observationalism.

The new levels of representational play and reflexivity will undoubtedly impact upon the conventional rhetorics of documentary seriousness, requiring in some cases quite radical adjustments and accommodations to be made. Here, I am very much in agreement with the director Chris Terrill's point cited above about the need to respond to the challenge of repositioning with the new landscape of popular television. Documentary is no longer classifiable as a 'discourse of sobriety' to use Bill Nichols much-cited phrase (see Nichols 1991) with the implications of the dutiful, both in address and in viewing relations, that this carries. Terrill's comment above about the 'graveyard slots' of old also warns against too sentimental a view of past achievement, as does Winston's more recent remark about 'the traditional, small-audience, elite-demographic ghetto' from which the new material, whatever its unevenness of quality, has escaped (Winston 2000: 55)[3].

As yet, it is hard to gauge the implications of the new playfulness for documentary credibility. Newspaper stories about representational fraud in the newer formats have combined with the brazenly performative nature of much on-screen action in a way that must have raised popular audience awareness of just how '-constructed' audio-visual documentation can be. But this also appears to have gone along with, if anything, an increased viewing enthusiasm. In the 'diverting' mode, it is clear, belief in the veracity of what you are watching is not a prerequisite to engagement and pleasure. Indeed, quite the reverse rule would seem to apply. What also seems clear is that the generous license accorded to the more diverting modes cannot, as yet, be simply transferred across to more serious kinds of documentary claims-making. In the notable British case of Carlton Television's *The Connection* (1996), a documentary purporting to show the activities of a Colombian drugs cartel, there was widespread and deep public disquiet when revelations of 'staging' and falsification appeared in newspapers (see Winston 2000 for details of this instance). Only research on viewing groups will enable us to understand what new blurrings, and perhaps what new differentiations, now inform the interpretative frameworks and criteria of credibility used by different segments of the audience[4].

Thirdly, and related to these questions about style and performance, the broader range of cognitive and affective investments which people make in audio-visual documentation is likely to have undergone a shift. However, once again, only audience research (now very much required in this area, see the suggestive work of Hill 2000) can begin to establish its scale. The very terms of the value placed on documentary programming by viewers, the way it works for them as a viewing experience and as a resource of social knowledge, have changed. The 'back story' to this shift involves transformations in the nature of public and private life over the last two decades and the complex ways in which both the contours of social knowledge and emotional experience have been reconfigured. Such processes have strongly national dimensions, of course, but at their broadest, they involve the way in which selfhood is set within culture and culture set within a particular political and economic order. The terms of 'seeing others' and 'seeing things' on the screen today are very different from those of the defining moments of documentary history, those moments when an expository realism seemed to resonate at least partially with a public, democratic rhetoric of reform and progress. These stealthier and more long-term changes are ones to which the newer forms of factual programming seem to have brought an accelerated momentum.

'Documentary' is a category that has very largely been defined and applied in relation to a sense of the 'Public'. Of course, there has been considerable variety in just how the 'Public' has been thought about, institutionalised and positioned in national life. Ideas have been framed by a range of authoritarian, liberal and radical perspectives. In many countries, however, there is a quiet but deepening crisis developing around 'publicness'. This is something to do with changing terms of citizenship and a move away from the once established (whether coercive or voluntary) forms of solidarity. It is very much to do with the changing character of the national and international economy and the increasing emphasis on market systems, market values and the volatile dynamics of production and consumption. These have generated a version of the 'popular' which is often in direct tension with notions of 'the public' (throughout the 20th Century, these two terms display a developing history of tension, often overlaid by an assumed synonymity). All media researchers know the extent to which 'public service' broadcasting has been redefined and, in some countries, displaced both as a practice and as an aspiration, by these changes.

The varieties of conventional broadcast documentary are, in fact, more vulnerable here than news since they are premised upon both a deeper and a broader engagement with perceptions of social community – its varieties, rhythms, problems and tensions, the interplay of the specific with the general. They have assumed and fostered rhetorics of belonging and involvement, albeit with elements of the manipulative or the sentimental, that are now increasingly difficult to sustain, even in revised form.

The survival of documentary

I have described a situation in which subjective factors to do with audience expectations, social affiliation and modes of cognition and affect combine with the objective factors of a multi-channel and more intensively commercialised television industry. The pattern varies across Europe but its main features are now widely recognisable. Only a more systematic attempt to measure what is going on in the schedules under different programme categories, as well as sustained inquiry into viewer choice, expectation and judgement, can allow us to be confident about the scale and direction of change. However, the aesthetic, political and cultural co-ordinates which helped hold together 'documentary' as an unstable but viable generic enterprise have both reduced in strength and shifted apart.

I would not expect the production of serious documentary simply to disappear in these circumstances. My use of the idea of 'post-documentary' is not meant to signal that 'documentary' is now finished but to signal the scale of its relocation as a set of practices, forms and functions. Some established strands of practice will undoubtedly continue in recognisable form across the kinds of disjunction I have discussed (although serious observational studies will find it hard to regain their impact and hold after the reworkings of docusoap). They will win viewers and deserve critical support. But they will do this in what, for many national television systems, will be a radically changed setting for audio-visual production and consumption. To the extent it wishes to enjoy a popular reach, documentary will need strategically to redevelop itself within the new economic and cultural contexts for engaging the popular audience, with an acknowledgement of the pattern of tastes that are newly established. The diverse commercial and socio-cultural conditions of the contemporary popular resist a neat separation, which makes any strategies for successful programme innovation within popular space hard to formulate. Getting a chance of being *seen* by a general audience, never mind about being liked by it, increasingly involves a stronger element of risk in calculation, given the present grid of channels and scheduling. Much of the uncertainty of the present debate in Britain reflects these new difficulties not only of production (including those of programme design) but of distribution, together with a genuine wish to avoid both too alarmist a response to popular factual entertainment and too easy an accommodation to its stylings. The exchange of views between Brants (1998) and Blumler (1999) provides a very useful framing for the issues involved in evaluating the shift to 'infotainment' more generally, against a background of established knowledge values.

As use of the internet becomes a more routine part of popular knowledge and entertainment, the possibilities of multimedia supplementation and of different 'platform' strategies are opened up. The first series of *Big Brother* in Britain showed how a reality show could use a website to extend its values of co-presence and duration. It remains to be seen what other kinds of combined documentation can work in different settings to enhance the terms of audience experience and use.

'Documentary' is an evocative but complex category, hiding many variants. It points essentially to a range of projects located within the terms of political modernism, predicated on quite specific contexts of mediation, of public and private experience, and informed by a factual aesthetics contained by given, limited, technological possibilities. Its characteristic modes have shown expositional and analytic energy together with a real ethnographic zeal in the portrayal of forms of living. It has a mixed representational legacy in many countries – of investigative, exploratory energy and yet also of epistemic and aesthetic containment. It has served to open up but also to close down ways of looking at the world. With some confidence we can note how, across its varieties, it has most frequently worked within a strong dynamics of social change, using its revelatory and expository energies to help initiate or to shape this change to different radical or socially ameliorative ends. It has been a tradition of documentation with a strong teleological emphasis, often a discourse of disquiet and discontent but also one of aspiration and hope. Among the new formats, a tone of relaxed acceptance (perhaps ironic more often than celebratory) reduces a sense of political horizons beyond the programme, even as it may open out the space available for observation and testimony and regenerate our enthusiasm for the delights of engaging the real through style.

'Endangered species' status has long been conferred on documentary by some commentators. But few of them could have foreseen the impact that a new range of popular images of the real are bringing to the traditions of its practice, the discussion of its future and the whole broader, and ramifying, question of 'documentary values'. It is highly probable that these values will increasingly be perceived and debated under other kinds of heading – as for instance 'journalistic values' where these criteria are appropriate, or as part of a broader ethics of actuality portrayal (Winston, 2000 outlines what the scope of this might be). Once again, however unwelcome many of the pressures that have caused it may be, a move towards thinking outside and beyond the documentary category, rather than working exclusively within its parameters of assumptions, will aid clarity of argument about the quality and purpose of those 'realities' we find on our screens.

Notes

1   John Ellis (2000) makes some illuminating points about the way in which 'docusoap' emerged in British television at least partly as a tactical solution to a problem of competitive scheduling. The BBC found that the relaxed narratives, 'soft' content and sociable terms of address of docusoaps were very succesful when run up against popular series drama on the ITV network. This, more so than reality shows in the harder, more urgent 'emergency services' mode. See Ellis 2000: 138-142.

2   It is clear that by following observational models of documentary, the new 'reality' formats have not only been able to offer audiences the pleasures of a social voyeurism, aligned to the various rhythms – urgent or expansive – of observed events and settings. They have also found it possible to generate something akin to the pleasures of following a fictional diegesis, with its continuities of space and time and the opportunities these provide for engaging with characters in action and interaction. Expositional documentary formats, including journalistic accounts, make their claim on the real extensively through the explicit verbal proposition of commentary, on-camera address and

interview. Observational models, however, rely more on an implicit truth guaranteed by the authenticity and depth of the primary depiction and its flow of observed and overheard behaviour. Their 'realism' is therefore much closer to that of dramatic narrative. This proximity of observational values to dramatic values, achieved according to different directorial recipes in different series, is of course a key element of docusoap's success and also of the success of *Big Brother*. Too strong a resemblance to dramatic fiction risks undercutting credibility, too weak a resemblance risks a reduced audience engagement. Such a 'border-crossing', from observational spontaneity towards dramatic crafting, also creates the cultural conditions for a kind of comedy drama that gains its impact precisely from reversing this process. In look and dialogue, such drama replicates through careful scripting and acting some of the uncertainty, hesitation and looseness, the infiltration of self-consciousness and display into an apparent 'normality', of observed behaviour in the new formats. (In Britain, the series *The Office* (BBC2) is a recent and deserved success in this vein). All of which relates to the more general point, significant for documentary studies, that 'realism' may best be used as a term of analysis for documentary output when that output trades on the codes of visual fiction.

3 Interestingly, in the light of my earlier comments on the debate about how to relate the success of reality shows to documentary's future, Winston also entertains the view that docusoap might have been 'the price of survival' of television documentary (Winston 2000: 55). This is to put the matter much more cautiously than celebration of some 'renaissance' in the genre as a whole, of course. But it reverses the verdict of those who see documentary as being squeezed out by the budgets and ratings regime encouraged by new formats.

4 As I finish this article, a survey for the *Radio Times* by the polling agency, MORI, offers some interesting data (Pile 2001). Whatever the scale of audience it attracts, the category of 'documentary' certainly seems to have kept its status in public esteem. In a listing of 'best programmes' on television, documentary came top with a 42% vote. Soaps managed 27% while 'Reality TV' was tenth (and bottom) with just 8%. When it came to the 'like to watch' category, documentaries came top with the over 35's and second (behind comedy) with the under 35's. Once again, 'Reality TV' came bottom, scoring only 2% with the under 35's. Whilst these figures certainly cannot be seen as a reliable guide to viewing behaviour, they still indicate a significant durability in the public presence of the category. More finely-tuned inquiries into essential and desirable generic features and into the perception of variety would be very useful.

References

Blumler, Jay. 1999. "Political Communication Systems All Change: A Response to Kees Brants". *European Journal of Communication* vol. 14, no.2: 241-249.

Bondebjerg, I. 1996. "Public Discourse/Private Fascination: hybridization in "true life story" genres". *Media, Culture and Society* vol. 18, no. 1: 27-45.

Brants, Kees 1998. "Whose Afraid of Infotainment?". *European Journal of Communication* vol. 13, no. 3: 315-335.

Corner, John. 1996. *The Art of Record*. Manchester; Manchester University Press.

Corner, John. 2000. "What Can We Say About Documentary?". *Media, Culture and Society* vol. 22, no. 5: 681-88.

Dovey, Jon. 2000. *Freakshow: First Person Media and Factual Television*. London: Pluto.

Dale, Peter. 1998. "Docs in Danger". *Broadcast*, 23 October: 17.

Dams, Tim. 1998. "Time To Move On". *Broadcast*, 23 October: 16-17.

Ellis, John. 1999. *Seeing Things: Television in the Age of Uncertainty*. London: I.B. Tauris.

Fry, Andy. 1997. "Factual's New Soft Sell". *Broadcast*, 17th October: 20-21.

Hardy, Forsyth. (ed.) 1979. *Grierson on Documentary*. London: Faber.

Hill, Annette. 2000. "Fearful and Safe: Audience Response to British Reality Programming." In *From Grierson to the Docusoap*, edited by John Izod, Richard Kilborn and Matthew Hibbard. Luton: Luton University Press.

Kilborn, Richard. 1994. "How Real Can You Get: Recent Developments in Reality Television". *European Journal of Communication*, 9.4. 421-39.

Nichols, Bill. 1991. *Representing Reality*. Bloomington: Indiana University Press.

Pile, Stephen. 2001. "Radio Times View of the Nation Television Survey". *Radio Times*. 1-7 September: 30-34.

Willis, John. 2000. "Breaking the Boundaries". In *From Grierson to the Docusoap*, edited by John Izod, Richard Kilborn and Matthew Hibbard. Luton: Luton University Press.

Watson, Paul. 1998. "When I made "The Family", Viewers Were Shocked to see Real People on TV. Today, These Cheap Pernicious, "Fly-On-The-Wall" Shows Just Treat Us Like Fools". *Daily Mail*, February 17th: 9.

Winston, Brian. 2000. *Lies, Damn Lies and Documentaries*. London: British Film Institute.

Note: The meeting in Florence, November 1999 of Group One of the Changing Media/Changing Europe project of the European Science Foundation gave me the first opportunity for exploring these issues. The 'Documentary Seminar' of Nordic Television Days, Bergen, June 2000, gave further scope for discussion and development. I am grateful to the organisers of both events.

Ib Bondebjerg

The Mediation of Everyday Life.
Genre, Discourse, and Spectacle in Reality TV

The rise of reality TV genres in European and American television in the 90s is a phenomenon with a historical precedence in documentary television. However, the new key word for the new reality genres is entertainment, a fact that is especially true of some of the sub forms on commercial television where entertainment is combined with certain elements of information and documentary qualities. In fact, many of the aspects of modern reality TV can be traced back to the drama-documentaries and observational television of the 60s and to the early forms of, for instance, genres like *Hidden Camera* which were developed on American television and imported to Danish public service television in the 60s. But as a massive media trend reality TV belongs to the deregulated and globalized media-culture of the 90s and onwards. In many ways, reality TV combines a global format with a very 'glocalized' perspective: the global audience is all over the world looking into the real or staged events of everyday life at a very local level. The same global formats create very different programs and social reactions – such as the revolt of the Danish participants against the producers in the Danish version of *Big Brother* (see below). Reality TV formats are, in opposition to the export of TV-series, for example, nothing more than global program frameworks that can be adopted on a national level to fit into different cultures.[1]

Some of the programs are creating an almost obsessive public fervor, especially reality-shows like *Big Brother* which have turned reality TV into major media events where the popular and everyday representation of reality are met by severe elite criticism and moral rejection for its commercial infotainment version of reality. Therefore reality TV can be analyzed not just as a typical time bound hybrid form of factual entertainment, but also as a metaphor or a symptom of the development of a commercialized and globalized media-culture. It is an indicator of a new network society with changing relations between audience, reality, different media and media genres, between everyday life discourses and institutionalized discourses, and between popular discourses and elite discourses.

*Mediation and reflexive modernity: Reality TV
and the network society*

Analyzing the new forms of reality TV calls on the one hand, for a historical perspective on the aesthetics and rhetoric of reality TV, its forms and genres and their relationship to the fundamental documentary genres. On the other hand, it calls for a closer look at the context of these genres and their function in a new global and increasingly digitized media culture, where fundamental changes in the mediation of everyday life and the transformation of the public sphere are obvious. A large number of sociological and social psychological approaches to this new network society (Castells 1996/200, Giddens 1991 and 1999, Beck 1999, Meyrowitz 1985, Thompson 1995 and 2000, Held 1999, van Dijk 1999 and Appadurai 1996) have all dealt with the transformation of mass society into a network society. This transformation has already changed mass media communication into more interactive and hybrid forms of media and communication, representing the convergence of media (TV and internet) or genres (documentary forms, journalism, entertainment and fiction). Furthermore, they offer concepts to explain and analyze the transformation from a public sphere with well defined boundaries and rules, to a more complex public sphere with multiple groups and networks. In the process, the relationships between public and private, between the politics and discourses of the elite and the politics and discourses of everyday life are changing.

Meyrowitz (1985), with reference to Goffman (1974) talks about the multiplication of roles and stages. The simple division between front stage and back stage gives way to a whole new mediation of private and public life. Deep back stage is open for mediation of public figures in talk shows, news formats, observational documentaries and on reality TV. At the same time, the consciousness and awareness of 'mediation' and the staging of reality in media becomes part of the planning of communication for institutions and politicians and part of the media reception of ordinary viewers. Public and private merge and create new forms when politicians prioritize appearances on popular talk shows, displaying relaxed 'private' behavior, or when ordinary people suddenly become public stars and 'role models' after appearing in reality shows. Processes such as these cannot be dismissed as a result of the commercialization of media and the public debate, or with the cannibalization of everyday life. They are symptoms of deep-rooted changes in culture and society linked to globalization and thus the decline of traditional institutions, discourses, as well as frames of space, time and hierarchy. There is an interaction going on here between commercialization and democratization, between globalization and glocalization that has to be analyzed more carefully.

Beck et al. (1994) and John B. Thompson (1995) point to the importance of a new reflexive modernity, in which a more flexible identity building creates room to 'play' with roles and identities. Traditional institutions are loosing some of their power. As a result, reality mediated through media fills the void as a kind of advanced interactive para-social interaction, but also as a new social and symbolic resource. Where most public and private communication before the rise of television was either print based and depersonalized or a face-to-face interaction, modern network society offers an expansion of public-private communications beyond fixed time and space. With the rise of the personal computer and the global Internet, this process is expanded further, a fact directly reflected in the new reality-shows like *Big Brother*. This reality-show was launched not as a traditional TV-show but as a multiple media event through several media platforms.

In his discussion of self and experience in a mediated world, John B. Thompson (1995: 205ff) points to both the positive and potential negative results of this transformation of mediated communication:

By opening up the self to new forms of non-local knowledge and other kinds of mediated symbolic material, the development of the media both enriches and accentuates the reflexive organization of the self. It enriches this organization in the sense that, as individuals gain access to mediated forms of communication, they are able to draw on an expanding range of symbolic resources for the purposes of constructing the self. (...) it can provide individuals with a glimpse of alternatives, thereby enabling them to reflect critically on themselves and on the actual circumstances of their lives. (...) the growing role of media products can have negative consequences for self-formation (...) 1) the mediated intrusion of ideological messages; 2) the double bind of mediated dependency; 3) the disorienting affect of symbolic overload; and 4) the absorption of the self in mediated quasi-interactions (Thompson 1995: 212-13).

This reflexive modernity and the new awareness of the self in public and private life, as well as of the mediation of the self in a network society moving from a nation state to global frames which also interact with local levels, is the fuel of the new reality genres. When established forms of national identity, institutional foundations, and legitimating strategies of traditional societies are questioned, everyday life becomes political, and politics, culture and media have to form new alliances to adapt globalization to localization. Thus the term 'glocalization.' The explosion of reality TV formats began globally in the 1980s but did not become a major phenomenon until the mid-90s. The politics of globalization has created anxiety, aggressive anti-global movements, xenophobia as well as revived nationalism and local, regional identity-movements. Almost as if in response to this phenomenon, the 'politics of everyday life' has become a major theme in new factual TV-shows and in observational documentaries. Reality TV is a continuation of this media trend but takes TV one step further into the realm of staged and serialized realities dealing with everyday life. Identity politics, everyday culture and interaction boom and fascinate audiences in this new media culture. The rise of reality TV is not just the result of the need for cheap, popular infotainment formats, although it most certainly is that as well. It is also a reflection of the deep mediation of everyday life in a network society which creates a strong need for audiences to mirror and play with identities and the uncertainties of everyday life, thus intensifying our innate social curiosity. Reality genres are no more than the extension of our innate need for gossip and social interaction in a society and a world the complexity of which surpasses that of our old national and local communities. This development creates anxiety and uncertainty as well as fascination and a need for mediation.

The question of discourse in these genres also requires a closer look. Just as with the development of talk shows and observational documentaries, these reality genres represent a mediated form of everyday discourses on television. They are part of a move in factual genres towards "bottom up" journalistic discourses from below or based on a stronger populist notion of the expert, the elite and the ordinary citizen. This move has taken place in news journalism, too. The reality TV takes the discourses of everyday life even further towards the discourses of privacy and intimacy, thus completely transforming the public nature of television discourse. As in fiction, we are actually looking into a complete backstage world and discourse. Everyday discourses of a very different kind are represented in these programs, getting us close to social, cultural, generational and gender specific discourses. These discourses are mixed with journalistic discourses, expert discourses and media discourses, not just in the media in question, but also in other media. On the one hand, *Big Brother* has the very different discourses of the participants and the different forms of communication which take place for instance in the dining room, the bedroom and the confession room. On the other hand they invite a psychologist, family and friends to comment on the participants, and of course the media personal play an important role. In a more observational reality-show like *Fødegangen* (The Maternal Ward, Danish TV2, 2000) we move between the professional discourse among nurses, doctors and midwifes, the intimate discourses of the couples, the less intimate discourses between the couples and their families, and the more public discourses between the couple and the staff.

These tendencies in media discourses of the network society connect with a larger shift from a formal and public language to conversational and everyday language in factual and journalistic formats. In Fairclough's words (Fairclough 1995: 10ff.), this can be described as a tension between 'information and entertainment' and between 'public and private,' tensions which he describes as a media development towards 'conversionalization' and 'marketizing.' On the one hand, it is a move towards the conversational discourses and talk of everyday life in all TV genres, including the news, which is not in itself a sign of commercialization. On the other hand, this development is also a sign of commercialization and marketizing through entertainment and thus a move towards pleasing rather than challenging of the audience. The more demanding and sometimes paternalistic voice of public service TV has been transformed into the informal, relaxed conversational forms and into infotainment especially in the new commercial reality TV formats. However, it can be asked whether this is just a tension or whether we have in fact moved beyond tension into real interaction, or whether standards of quality have declined as a result of this development or if they have just changed. Certainly the development cannot just be described in the tradition of Habermas (Habermas 1984/1995-97) as the 'system world' taking over the 'life world'. It can also be described as a necessary mediation of everyday life that has taken place during a transformation from a traditional hierarchical mass society to a network society. At the same time it is clear that these formats contain a certain world perspective, which tends not only to exclude macro-structures but also themes related to both too mundane and too complicated, psychological or social cases. Reality TV seeks the spectacular and melodramatic aspects of everyday life or at least that which can be proliferated in a dramatized discourse. This is most obviously the case with reality magazines focusing on crime and accidents, and the reality shows (see for instance Fairclough 1995: 150 ff.), and to a lesser degree with docu-soaps or documentary series. This is less evident in public service versions of these genres than in the versions provided by commercialized stations (see Bondebjerg 1996/2000 and Dovey 2000: 78ff.).

The documentary tradition and reality TV genres

In his inspiring book *Freakshow: First Person Media and Factual Television* Jon Dovey discusses three positions in the academic and public debate on reality TV (Dovey 2000: 83):

- The *trash position* (considers these genres to be a product of an increasingly market-driven culture and thus as a low culture, or trash phenomenon)
- *The empowerment position* (considers these genres to be a challenge to and a democratic alternative to the paternalistic public service culture, creating an interactive social and communicative space for everyday discourses)
- *The simulacrum-nightmare position* (considers these genres to be a fake realism in an age where simulacrum has defeated the reference and reality doesn't really have value any more)

These positions are very clearly visible in the Danish debate on reality TV among others and especially the *Big Brother* phenomenon (see below). The trash position is readily at hand when intellectuals of almost all ideological positions simply react to programs like this with the projection of the high culture-low culture divide onto factual and documentary genres, or with the great divide between the tabloid press and the serious press. However, this fairly automatic and often unsubstantiated position is clearly not the whole answer since even the serious press has undergone significant generic and discursive changes. So unless one wants to hold back any development in social and textual discourses, reality TV also deserves a more nuanced and unprejudiced analysis. And this of course goes for the obviously philosophically insane theory of simulacrum as well. The fact that texts can be manipulated and staged and that visuality in a digital age is more complicated to read from a secured reference point doesn't make reference non-existent, but rather underlines the fact that no one to one ratio between any sign and reality is given.

In an article on documentary, John Corner speculates on the relevance of the word documentary in a culture he sees as potentially "post-documentary" (Corner 2000, and this volume, p. 149 ff.). His notion tends to lean towards the simulacrum position, but he is more sensible in his discussion, which is actually a discussion for and against the empowerment position. Identifying the three classic rhetoric functions of documentary forms as *exposition*, *testimony* and *observation*, Corner connects them to three social functions. First, there is *the project of democratic civics* or what might be called the great tradition of the radical enlightenment project carried by public service television, and the classic tradition of documentary films in the Grierson-tradition. The second is *the documentary as journalistic inquiry and exposition*, which Corner identifies with the central, and dominating genres on television from the 1950s to the 1980s and informed by a critical ethos towards the power and it institutions; a public watchdog on behalf of the public. A third function identified by Corner is called *documentary as radical interrogation and alternative*, and is defined with Nichols as his main reference (Nichols 1991), as the reflexive and self-referential documentary, mostly known from avant-garde documentaries, which question the referential and journalistic aesthetic and rhetoric of the other forms. As a fourth version he identifies *documentary as a diversive function*, simply defined as 'popular factual entertainment', to which he counts all the new forms of reality TV (high-intensity incidents, gossipy first-person accounts or snoopy sociability).

Corner's analysis has important insights and his concern for the status of more traditional documentaries is important. But he overlooks one of the important modern genres of documentaries, the observational form, and he seems to throw all reality TV into the diversion box. In fact, some of the reality TV forms continue the classical forms of observational documentaries from Wiseman to the present. This tradition is part of the civic and democratic tradition of documentary (see Bondebjerg 2001a and b in print) expanding the notion of the public and challenging the fine line between public, social and private. He also overlooks the traditions of staging reality in dramatized documentaries not just for the purpose of entertaining but of informing and educating. There is a crooked and complicated line aligning this tradition in the 70s with the reality-shows of today. Some of these reality-shows may be seen as commercialized perversions of the original, but others may be seen as direct remakes.

The difference is obvious if we compare for instance the 1969 Danish documentary by Poul Martinsen, *Broen* (The Bridge), where he challenges a group of hippies and a biker gang to build a bridge together promising them a monetary reward, if they succeeded, the *Big Brother* show which claims to be a social experiment and at the same time a game show, and the BBC-productions *The 1900 House* and *Cast Away* that are non-commercial documentaries with genuine historical and educational values. The same format can obviously be used for very different purposes and with very different intentions. *Big Brother* merely wants to entertain, using reality and everyday life as a popular framework. Poul Martinsen and the BBC-programs have a clearly social and educational goal where entertainment value is secondary. Corner himself mentions these BBC examples, but still his critical analysis only addresses part of the problem. It takes for granted that most reality TV is not founded in the documentary traditions, and that commercial tendencies will kill off the traditional forms of documentary. However, the evidence is not very convincing if we look at the American/European picture as a whole. Although the observational and journalistic forms may hold a weaker position in the American and European schedule they are certainly around and still get a big audience share on public service stations.[2]

Although I dismiss the simulacrum position as sheer nonsense this leaves both the trash position and the empowerment position on stage. As I have already indicated I don't see a principal difference between the documentary tradition and some of the new forms of reality. Most certainly there is a stronger commercialization going on and a tendency to focus on the more sensational spectacle or the unfocused and non-contextualized trivia in some forms of reality TV. Furthermore the very starting point of the reality shows like *Survivor*, *Big Brother* or *Temptation Island* are certainly heavily influenced by entertainment, more than the documentary tradition. They are first and foremost commercial entertainment formats created to insure a young and economically viable audience while documentary qualities, aesthetics and rhetorical strategies are secondary. But other reality TV forms are informed by the same informational, educational and democratic visions as the journalistic, observational and dramatized forms of documentary from the 60s and on. I believe there are four main genres in the main traditions of documentary television:[3]

- *The investigative and journalistic documentary* is dominated by 'epistemic authority' (Plantinga 1997), focuses on cases of vital public and political nature and considers the journalist to be the critical 'detective' or the public eye opposite the system. It is built using a rhetorical and narrative structure that unfolds its argument and very often also a story with more dramatic, narrative qualities. It is based on the posing of clear cut, critical questions, seeking answers and explanations through witnesses and experts, through visual and printed evidence, and aiming at a conclusive and complete clarification of the case in question. Aesthetically the use of symbolic, dramatic visual effects and reconstructions is not discouraged as long as they are controlled by the authoritative voice of a journalistic discourse and are clearly corroborated by the evidence. The case is made using the factual voice. The investigative, journalistic documentary has several sub-forms that can be placed on a line according to the dominance of arguments and a journalistic rhetoric and the amount of strong, dramatic elements and reconstructions.
- *The observational documentary* is based on a very weak epistemic authority. Instead it provides evidence not by explaining or telling, but by showing fragments and slices of an unfolding institutional world of every day life. Instead of the authoritative, journalistic voice of the journalistic documentary we find a more 'open voice' (Plantinga 1997). The rhetoric is based on voices from the public or private world and there is normally no specific case in focus. Instead the observational form takes up matters of general human interest with a social and human perspective from which problems and political and social issues can be drawn by the viewer as well as indirectly by the presenter/ director. Whereas the journalistic documentary is characterized by a linear structure in its argument, rhetoric and narrative, the observational documentary has an episodic, impressionistic and mosaic structure. Drama unfolds in real time and the structure most often follows time chronologically, although a thematic and contrasting montage is also a very common editing technique. Symbolic and visual effects are very subdued in this form and are often used to indicate a mood or function as 'chapter-breakers.'

- *The reflexive-poetic documentary* is a rare phenomenon on television while common in contemporary film documentaries. The main differences between this and the two more classical, documentary forms is its focus on form and style which is often tied to a very subjective point of view, and the questioning or framing of the referential dimension. The pre-production and production processes can use elements from fiction with casting of real people and even scripting of dialogue, or a strong element of symbolic visual 'inner landscaping'. Dreams, fantasies and inner thoughts are often woven into the visual narration or rhetoric, and calling into question the actual status of propositions on reality often lead to reiterative narrative structures with many versions contradicting each other. The Danish documentary director Jon Bang Carlsen (see Hjort & Bondebjerg 2001) calls his form 'staged documentary' and he feels free to produce visual and linguistic material based on research of the reality he is portraying. Here the actual footage is not always just the observed reality, but a reality staged in such a way that it reflects and expresses the reality of his characters both as he sees them and as they see themselves. So whole scenes can be constructed to express a particular feeling or dream to the camera. Another concrete example of the reflexive-poetic documentary is Earl Morris' already famous documentary *The Thin Blue Line* (see Bondebjerg 1994 and Williams 1998) in which several testimonies are confronted not just verbally but also through repetitive visual reconstructions. Visual quotations are also used to characterize the persons shown in the film.
- *The dramatized documentary* refers to those forms of documentary in which the story and characters are semi-fictional but based on authentic cases or problems. The docu-drama is the complete fictionalization of a true story with professional actors and traditional narrative structure. This form does not really belong to the documentary genre, but it is an extreme case of fictional realism. Other forms such as the early 60s and 70s productions by Ken Loach (*Cathy come Home* (1966) see Corner 1996: 90-108) or Peter Watkins (*The War Game*, 1970 and *Aftenlandet* (Evening Land) from Denmark 1977) represent highly dramatized stories based on journalistic research of real

social problems, often with a strong mix and montage of journalistic discourse and dramatic 'diegesis.' Other forms include the social experiment sub-form, where real people act out real social and psychological processes but in a constructed setting or outside their normal day-to day life. On Danish TV, a series of productions called 'spontan-spil' (spontaneous plays) by journalist Poul Trier Petersen involved people from schools, work places etc who performed typical situations from their life and combined them with debate and discussions. The same tendency can be seen in the already mentioned *Broen* (1969) by Poul Martinsen, and a similar experiment by Lise Roos *Familien Danmark* (The Family Denmark, 1994, 1-3) in which two very different Danish families switch homes for two weeks.

These four main prototypes of documentaries are all represented on national TV-schedules (the reflexive-poetic only sparsely) in at least Western and Northern Europe and can be found at least on public service stations, but also to a certain extent on national commercial stations. There is however a tendency to move away from dramatized documentaries in their classical form (from the 70s) which often created controversy and debate about the status of fiction and non-fiction. At least to a certain degree, the observational documentary has been the dominant form in the 80s and 90s. However, in the 90s reality TV became a new trend in those prime time slots where other documentary formats used to be. Furthermore this development was caused and fueled by the increased competition for viewers, and reality TV is now a documentary battle field between public service stations and commercial stations. Both docu-soaps and reality-magazines were developed by public service and commercial channels with BBC's *Crime Watch* (1984-), *Airport* and *Driving School* as the initiating successes, commanding around 30% of prime time viewers (Dovey 2000: 133).

It would be wrong to see the different forms of reality TV as completely new documentary prototypes. For instance docu-soaps carry on the observational genre in many ways and there is a clear line from the journalistic documentary to reality-magazines, although they lean towards tabloid, sensational and spectacular "soft" news stories. Even reality-(game)shows like *Big Brother* have roots in both the observational and the dramatized documentaries. But it is obvious that we can define at least three basic sub-forms of reality TV:

- *The docu-soap* is characterized by its link to reality through its characters and settings. They exhibit real spaces and real persons linked to a special locality, a special institution or a special common interest etc. Like in a serial or a series, the story of a group or a type of people unfolds in a chronological or otherwise time structured narrative. The narrative most often has one or two main-stories and several sub stories in each episode and the crosscutting follows the same patterns as in fictional soaps, although the dramatic potential is not as powerful and cannot be controlled since the stories came out of every day life. But the link to fictional realism and social melodrama is quite clear in most productions in this category. Most docu-soaps use documentary voice over, unlike most observational documentaries, but many sequences clearly follow 'fly on the wall' technique. Many docu-soaps have a much stronger casting element for the real people chosen as main characters. The so-called DR-Bible on docu-soaps, an internal document from the Everyday Life Section of the Non-fiction department of Danish Television 1 is clearly balanced between demands for authenticity and dramatic quality (see below).
- *The reality-magazine* is a regularly scheduled journalistic magazine presenting cases from real life, mostly about crime and accidents or other spectacular human interest stories. The program combines a journalistic, informative discourse with dramatic forms related to social melodrama and the crime and detective genres. The host commands the communicative structure of the program that has inserted interviews with victims of crime and accidents and the professionals, who take care of and protect our lives and welfare. Interviews take place on location or in the studio. An important part of these programs are either real footage from crime or accidents or reconstructions based on real events. These mini-dramas often have a classical melodramatic storyline. The idyllic situation or scenes from a daily

routine suddenly broken by fate, disaster, panic and maybe death or near death. The heroic powers intervene, either by the miraculous effort of an ordinary person or the extraordinary action of a professional, and afterwards we have re-established order and are given a moral and a lesson taught by the story (see Bondebjerg 1996 and 2001b and Dovey 2000: 78ff.).

- *The reality-show* is a serialized form of game show where ordinary people are put in extraordinary situations in order both to cooperate with and compete against one another. Normally there is a price at stake for individuals who win the game and also for groups during the program who compete against other groups. For instance in *Big Brother* the contestants are given weekly competitions and special tasks, in *The Robinson Expedition* (the Danish version of *Survivor*) programs start out with group competitions that gradually become a fight between individuals. The format is based on specifically formulated rules, but the real rules being tested are the social and psychological rules and conventions of our everyday life. All the norms of the family, love relations, work relations and the cultural gender games and identity games become visible and can be discussed and scrutinized by the participants and the viewers at home. The shows mirror the identity and role playing games of our daily lives but are put under pressure by extraordinary circumstances. The deep back stage behavior and the often invisible and intimate aspects of interpersonal relations are played out and staged for dramatic purposes but also with informative and pedagogic potentials. In many of the commercial station formats, the competition dominates the social experiment aspect, while other forms concentrate more on the social experiment. Again, the difference between *Big Brother* and *The 1900 House* is illuminating.

The melodrama of everyday life: Docu-soaps

In the new dominant forms of docu-soaps, which are essentially a new form of reality-serials, the classical form of the observational documentary merges with elements of the fictional soap-genre and thus with the melodrama of everyday life and the ordinary. Just as British serials like *Coronation Street* or American serials like *Dallas* in their own very different and culturally specific way have commented on and mirrored British and American family life, the docu-soaps have started a search for stories in social and cultural spheres covering national everyday life, both in its trivial routine form and in its melodramatic and ritual moments. Docu-soaps then, are not just the result of a search for cheap TV that can fill the growing need for more and more programs as a means of filling the many channels. Nor are they the result of the larger audience's discovery of some of the same qualities here as those found in the much more expensive fiction and the more researched, observational documentary program. This is certainly the drive for at least the more commercial versions of this genre and possibly also for the public service channels. However, unlike the Reality-show, which is basically developed on commercial channels, the docu-soap genre exists in many variations on both commercial and public service channels.

At the same time, the docu-soap can be compared to tendencies within the 90s independent documentary cinema in which subjectivity and privacy have been dominant, although in contrast to the docu-soap, these films often have a reflexive dimension. In films by Ross McElwere, Roger Moore, Alan Berliner, Nick Bloomfield, Robert Gibson (Dovey 2000: 28ff.) and Richard Billingham to mention a few, the traditional observational focus on others has changed to a focus on the subjective sides of the filmmaker and his family. This shift in documentary film is probably a reaction to the long dominance of observational documentaries. The 'fly on the wall' social observation of a social reality with a very subdued 'auteur' seem to be met by a shift towards both a subjective and a meta-textual approach to reality. But even in this tradition parallels can be found to the observation and penetration of the deep back stage in soap opera and reality shows. As Dovey has demonstrated in his analysis of Robert Gibson's *Video Fool for Love* (1995), this film is inspired by the popular formats of amateur camcorder programs which can be seen as the direct forerunners of use of cameras to focus on reality in docu-soaps, on everyday life, or to peep into a staged reality as in *Big Brother*.

Docu-soaps did not appear out of nowhere in the 90s, but were preceded by several long running documentaries in the USA and the UK in the 70s and 80s. The first reality/documentary serial was probably Craig Gilbert's *An American Family* (PBS, 1973), and as Jeffrey Ruoff has pointed out in his analysis of this serial (Ruoff 1998), it could never have been developed at that time by commercial networks that had downplayed documentary forms in order to expand entertainment and fiction. So this 12 hour long serial, following an upper middle class American family for a year, although it was an example of a very long observational documentary, is also clearly, as Rouff points out, the first documentary form in which the gap between the daytime fictional soap and the prime time factual program is bridged. The serial has the classical open, episodic form of the observational documentary, but it also has stronger elements of dramatic narrative. It is a documentary serial announcing "the breakdown of fixed distinctions between reality and spectacle, public and private, serial narrative and nonfiction film and television" (Ruoff 1998: 288-89). In contrast to the classical observational documentary it not only uses a first person voice over, but it also uses a third person voice over. In this sense, it points directly to the same characteristic mixture of observation, continuity and presentational comments found in the new docu-soap of the 90s. Furthermore, the focus is not on social problems as is mostly the case in the observational tradition, but it is rather on the more ordinary everyday life of ordinary people which again links this program to the docu-soap.

In the UK, the same kind of documentary serial was made by BBC. *The Family* (1974), which was also in twelve parts, followed the life of an ordinary family in Reading. As Dovey has pointed out (Dovey 2000: 134-35), John Willis at Yorkshire TV in 1986 also produced a series called *Jimmies* based on life at a hospital in Leeds and *Animal Squad* based on an animal rescue team also in Leeds. These documentary serials clearly indicate the diversity of the later docu-soaps in which focus is often placed on a specific group of people united by a special interest or ritual (for instance weddings, horse races, wishing to be a pop-star, stripping). An example of this would be the British docu-soap *Babewatch* about girls seeking to be models. The focus might also be a special institution and its employees and clients (for instance a police station, an airport, a driving school, a newspaper, a department store, a hospital etc), such as *Driving School*, *Airport* and *Children's Hospital*.

At least in a Danish context, there is a clear difference between the themes, groups and institutions taken up on commercial channels and public service channels. The commercial channels often pick police/crime or sex as themes or the more spectacular parts of everyday life in general where the public service channels try to focus on more ordinary aspects of everyday life and institutions of some public and general interest. However, what all these docu-soaps have in common is the combination of observational, documentary elements, casting and narrative forms and storylines normally dominating in fictional forms. Furthermore the soaps often swing between strong, emotional and melodramatic moods and more trivial aspects of everyday routines. There is a common trait here which unites almost all reality-formats, namely the intention of lifting the ordinary and the trivial to a more intense and emotional level of experience, just as melodrama in classical films bring ordinary existence to extremes but always restores normalcy in the end.

In the afore-mentioned internal DR document *The Docu-soap Bible*, the format is defined as "stories with human depth and identification" and the casting of the characters move along the same line as casting of a fictional film. But at the same time, it is pointed out that the film crew must not manipulate characters, action or dialogue. The narrative format is defined as a multiple story line with one or two main stories with a linear structure and a set of smaller narrative sub-stories and sequences – just like the fictional soap. Speak should not be too dominant, but on the other hand it is accepted in order to connect and introduce characters and story lines and to secure continuity in space and time. Interestingly enough, this is combined with clear indications of how to get the characters to "think out aloud" and act out emotions so that a speak is not necessary at all times. What we see in this TV- station's internal bible is a very clear merging of a documentary, rhetorical form with a narrative format, in which the usual keywords are used: intro and conflict, set-up, pay off etc.

The Danish TV2 docu-soap[1] *Fødegangen* (The Maternity Ward) is one of the most watched quality programs on the Danish public service channels, and a short analysis of the structure and aesthetic in the first episode can illustrate the general tendencies of the program. The program starts with a montage of live images and short statements from the main characters (in some programs, albeit not in this one, characters are immediately identified by name). The montage carefully catches both the staff at the maternity ward in characteristic work situations and a number of parents and babies during or after birth. The montage is very dynamic and has an emotional structure with a strong impact on the viewer. Soon after the first sequence the staff is introduced at a morning session, and a third person narrator explains where we are, who the persons are and we get the set-up for the main stories in the episode, seen from the staff's point of view and underlined by interview sequences (without the questions inserted) with both staff and clients. A new member of the staff is in focus, together with one of the more experienced nurses.

In the following sequences we have cross cuts between several story lines: a birth, introduction of a group of pregnant women and their husbands to the hospital, a doctor's long talk with a couple now pregnant again, but with a severe trauma after having lost their former child. Small lyrical breakers and shots of the hospital from the outside, seasonal shots of the snow or from hospital details inside interrupt these storylines from time to time. Through the whole course of events, the third person narrator and interview sequences with the involved characters comment on the observational scenes. Both the traumatic story with the pregnant couple and the birth, which is very complicated and only seconds form a caesarean and disaster create a melodramatic tension and dramatic conflict in the two main story lines. But they both have a happy ending and in this sense completely follow the canonical, narrative structure of fictional melodrama. However, at the same time the whole set-up combined with an instructional voice over putting events in human and clinical perspective as well as the insights into the doctors' professional work and their conversation with the couples gives the series a very documentary, educational and informative dimension.

It is an example of how docu-soaps can combine narrative and rhetorical qualities, melodramatic and emotional intensity with factual authenticity. In this case the fact that casting and planning has taken place doesn't influence the documentary quality of the program. This qualitative mixture is certainly not always present in docu-soaps. Often the melodramatic or sensational focus overshadows both the documentary value and the informative dimensions of the program where spectacle and staging of reality for entertainment purposes dominates.

Life as a stage: The reality-show

Big Brother, the global format which is now produced in 18 national formats and has a total of more than 2 billion viewers, is always launched under the shared slogan: "10 contestants, 100 days, 24 cameras, 30 microphones, 1 house, 24 hours a day." The slogan indicates that the name, taken from Orwell's dystopic novel *1984* (1949) has the intensive surveillance of a group of people with no privacy whatsoever as its main feature. The format plays on our deeply imbedded curiosity about and fascination with privacy and the lives of our neighbors. Here privacy and life behind the curtains are put on a stage as a real life drama, but edited and manipulated through casting and games within the game. The stage is not a simple front stage with a curtain between the viewer and the scene as in the traditional theatre, but a stage with several layers including a front stage, a back stage and a deep back stage. This is indicated in the house structure and the use of daylight, infra-red night vision in the bedroom or the special staging of the isolated confession chair. In the English version (sent on Channel Four) they even published a book on the series shortly after the end of the program, called *Big Brother. The Official Unseen Story*, where selected aspects of the pre-production process and the production process are revealed. As if the national obsession with the participants and all angles of the program were not covered enough during the 100 days, this book promises to reveal the last uncovered part of the deep back stage. Not one aspect seems to be ignored by the ever curious, public eye.

Unlike Orwell's novel then, this Big Brother is not the incarnation of an authoritarian political or ideological power, not a sign of a dystopian future, but an ironic, self-reflexive entertainment format that seems to underline Neil Postman's critique of American television culture as the age of show business (Postman 1985), a culture where surveillance is not the problem, but the fact that we seem to be amusing ourselves and any serious public discourse to death. But whereas Postman bases his very general rejection of television on the notion of the audience as passive, this reality-show is based on interactivity between viewer and program, not just in a concrete sense as in the 24-hour live Internet-version and the voting procedure, but in the very reflexivity of a modern TV-audience. Part of the staging of reality is the fact that the audience is rather used to TV and the way reality is staged and edited. The modern audience has a meta-consciousness of media, and part of the fascination of a reality-show like *Big Brother* is to play upon this meta-consciousness and at the same time mirror the conflicts, emotions and everyday life situations of the audience in the staged reality of the show. The audience (mostly a very young audience) is aware of the role-playing, but still identify themselves with the real persons and the roles they play.

The construction of the program seems to invite at least 3 different but interwoven audience positions:

- *The life style and role model position* in which the audience looks at the different characters in relation to their symbolic, cultural qualities: their sexual roles, their gender role, style of clothing, ways of speaking, body appearance and language, what is in and out of fashion etc. In a society in which roles are often mediated and not based on firm and predictable social functions and norms, the lifestyle signs are important guidelines especially for a younger teenage audience. The possibility of moving from the anonymous crowd to media fame is part of this fascination with signs of lifestyle and symbolic and cultural capital as one of the gateways.
- *The emotional and psychological view* in which the focus is more on the psychological and emotional relationships and conflicts and the processes of intimacy, bonding, friendship,

love and 'pseudo-family' roles with sisters, brothers, fathers and mothers. The strong fascination with intimate, emotional and psychological dimensions, usually satisfied through fictional forms, is transferred to reality-forms thus reflecting the changing of private life and socialization in a highly modern insecure and high risk society in which roles and socialization are transformed and challenged all the time (Giddens 1991).

- *The cult position* in which the focus is on the game and role playing as a mediated event. Where an obsessive fascination with the program and perhaps special characters in the program is combined with a distanciated, meta-reflexive fascination with the show as a show and often with the show as part of a collective viewing culture. Part of this position is definitely enhanced by the interactive possibilities on the Internet and through the voting procedure in which a cult audience can participate in the reality show as a media event.

It is too easy just to reject the documentary aspects and qualities of *Big Brother* and other reality programs by referring to the commercial entertainment frame, the game element, and the staging, editing and casting processes. Of course the framework is a fictional construction and we know that the real persons have been cast as a team to allow certain conflicts, character roles and story lines to develop. The competitions and assignments given during the program as well as the whole semi-fictional framework all underline the fact that the program is about spectacle, drama and narrative more than it is about factual discourse and straightforward everyday reality. However as one of the producers in the Dutch company Endemol has phrased it: "it is all true, it is all real, nothing in this show is fake or unreal, it is merely controlled." One can dispute this, but at least there is an element of reality that is difficult to control, even though the producers try to set up rules and frames meant to control it. It is difficult to foresee the stories and conflicts that will develop, and it is difficult for most people to play a role for 100 days. The intensity of 24 hour surveillance and the competitive atmosphere forces their real personalities to appear and the surface to crack. This is perhaps the ultimate appeal of the show. We know that the television version is a very edited version of 100 hours of unedited material seen from the perspective of 24 cameras and 30 microphones, and we know that the persons are characters cast to a certain degree involved in a strategic game with each other. But every now and again, a "live" and authentic conflict and emotion breaks through the surface and the emotional layers, and the unpredictability of reality makes itself visible. For instance, it is emotionally and psychologically difficult to have to eliminate persons that you have come to like, because the game demands it. However, this aspect is not terribly far removed from those situations in real life or at a work place where people compete for jobs and money. So in spite of the program's fictional entertainment elements, it reflects true aspects of reality. The live emotional quality of the program is underlined in its editing technique, camera movements and shot-selections by selecting emotional highlights and conflicts, and cutting away the dead time which accompanies everyday life (see also Jerslev 2000).

There is no doubt what so ever that the editors behind the shows, normally four editors and one producer, have developed a script based on several possible storylines and conflicts as soon as the casting is done. At a seminar in Århus, Denmark in September 2001, the Dutch producer Paul Römer, clearly admitted that they had a virtual script with several attractive conflicts, personal development possibilities and relationships between the characters. He also admitted that the games in the program were selected to steer the show in specific directions and that the editing of course could change the whole viewpoint on the characters and the story lines by focusing more on some aspects of discourse, some aspects of action and on some characters more than others. But he also stated that they were never really able to control or develop the story and that the time pressure alone made it difficult to control and steer. On the other hand, as the show develops and material from previous shows can be used for other sub-programs, like the talk show, other editing procedures become available. But the chronological narrative is usually followed in the daily 30 minutes updates of the last day's events. It is too dangerous, according to Paul Römer, for the producers to try to manipulate chronological time, since at least some of the audience has knowledge of the 24-hour uncut version on the Internet.

The editing and casting of reality is one part of the staging of the show, another is the role-playing of the participants. It is, as already indicated, difficult to maintain a role for 100 days in front of the whole nation, and generally the voting procedure seems to indicate that authenticity on a personal and emotional level is valued more than extreme role-playing. The winner of the first Danish *Big Brother*, Jill, was very outspoken and honest in her revelation of a traumatic past with incest. Her direct emotional reactions were valued in the same way as Pil, the most popular person on the show until she left the show in protest, who was completely natural and direct. Examples of strategic emotional behavior and dishonesty can be found in many of the global shows, but are instantly punished. For instance in the English version, one of the persons (publicly known as Bad Nick) broke the rules and tried to influence the voting by sending written messages around. But this was revealed and he was publicly exposed. In the Spanish version, one of the girls falsely claimed to be the lonely mother of a handicapped baby, and the audience, after having supported her strongly and collected money for her, of course found out and sent her home. Role-playing and unethical behavior is risky and immediately punished, but still role-playing within limits is accepted, just as role-playing is part of our everyday lives. We behave differently at work, at home, in the family and in more intimate situations. So role-playing is not a constructed phenomenon in reality TV, but an important part of our social and cultural reality as well.

The original framework of *Big Brother* was based on a 'bible' with seven very basic rules:

- The 10 contestants must never have met each other before the program starts.
- The group is completely shut off from any information from the outside world.
- The house is defined by a back to basics lifestyle. This means that only the bare necessities are available and that participants have no real personal belongings brought with them. The weekly games can provide extra luxuries or the opposite.
- There is constant surveillance via cameras and sound and every participant has a body microphone.

- In the so-called Big Brother room, every participant has to give a personal report every day, which only the viewers but not the other participants will hear. The voice of Big Brother can summon anybody to the chair at any time to give instructions or ask questions.
- Every second week one of the participants must leave the house. The participants themselves vote for which two must meet the decision and vote of the audience. Thus the audience ultimately decides who of the two must leave.
- Any participant can decide to leave the house of his own free will and can then be replaced by a new participant. However, only the ten participants selected in the first place can win the price.

These basic rules are followed by all the national producers, but some of the rules may be interpreted differently. For instance the Dutch producers decided to tell the participants about the September 11 terror action on New York, whereas the Danish producers decided not to. Studying the different national versions also supports the concept of glocalization in that the individual national versions are very different in the way the show unfolds and the focus and casting of the participants. In both the Dutch, the Norwegian and most of the Southern European versions, sex was very much at the center of life in the house and subsequently in the press and in public discussions. The participants had sex on screen (but tried to hide it under blankets etc) and the public discussed and focused on sexual relations among the contestants. In the first Danish version there was sex, but no sexual relations ever developed, whereas the second version was cast much more with singles from whom sexual desires could be expected. All national versions tried to cast not just according to the specific social and cultural structure of that nation but also in regards to ethnic balance.

In different countries different social problems and norms created different internal conflicts and public reactions. For instance in the Portuguese version a big public debate was started when one of the couples (a man and a woman) got into a physical fight and the man hit the woman because she had insulted his mother. The domestic violence on the show and the following discussions created debate in a society where gender roles are still very traditional and domestic violence quite common. In the Danish version on the other hand, the almost successful collective rebellion against the program, led by Pil, who ended up leaving the house with the most intellectual and outspoken participants, sparked a huge debate on communication ethics and freedom of speech as the program producers, according to the deal signed by the participants, insisted on having first publication rights to anything they wanted to say and denied them free access to other media.

The national versions thus reflect national cultures although they also conform to an overall global format. *Big Brother* is in fact many different national *Big Brothers* and in the same way it is fair to say that *Big Brother* as a text is many programs in one and at least two different media converge into a large and very differentiated *reception text* created by the *media event Big Brother*. The Dutch producers are currently in the process of developing completely new versions of the same format. *Big Brother: the Battle* running as *Big Brother 3* on Dutch television in fall 2001 is based on class struggle between rich and poor where rules and games makes it possible for the participants to be transferred from one world to another. So the class struggle is not dead, but recreated as entertainment on commercial TV!

Looking at the original version, the program also contains several sub-programs within itself. In the Danish program listing we are confronted with the following separately named sub-programs: Big Brother Disputable, Big Brother Up-date, Big Brother, Big Brother Live, Big Brother – The Hot Chair, Big Brother Weekend, Big Brother Xtra, Big Brother – The Contest and Big Brother – The Talkshow. The reason for this multitude of sub-forms is of course partly to create logical commercial breaks, but it is also a genuine sign of the *hybridization* of modern reality TV. I think we can fruitfully discuss at least three different forms of hybridization.

- *Genre hybridization*, which is the direct use of several genres, creates formats within the overall format of the reality-show. There are clearly elements of the docu-soap and observational documentary genres in the edited or live versions of Big

Brother's daily updates and recaps. The casting, the use of storylines and the sometimes uncommented, sometimes commented bits of uncut everyday life which form a mosaic structure clearly look like docu-soap and observational documentary. The different sub forms listed in the program indicate some of these genre mixings: Big Brother (the main daily prime time slot), Big Brother Update, Big Brother Live and Big Brother Weekend are the forms that most clearly use docu-soap and observational style and aesthetic. However, within these forms the element of game and competition brings us close to the quiz show. On the other hand journalistic elements are mixed with entertainment in *Big Brother the Talk show* where the host and hostess guide us through interviews with former participants, relatives, friends and viewer representatives.

- *Discursive hybridization* refers to the existence of very different forms of discourse in one and the same genre. Mixing is already obvious in the house itself, where living room, kitchen, bathroom, bedroom and garden normally indicate different levels of talk and a different form of relationship between intimate/private/semi-public discourses. We go through most of the levels of everyday talk in families and groups including very sexual, competitive, gender related, aggressive or inclusive forms of couple- or group discourses. The discourse of confession is also present in the hot chair and the Big Brother room where the anonymous Big Brother voice is mixed with very sensitive, intimate, and private revelations. We also have expert interviews and comments, for instance from psychologists, from the talk show hosts and from the voices of relatives and friends. The Internet version has its own discursive universe with chat and other forms of interventions from the outside.

- *Aesthetic meta-hybridization* stems from the fact that Big Brother is a staged reality, which the participants, the producers and the audience are all very aware of. In the German publications on the German *Big Brother*, the reference – when talking about this meta-level – is partly Goffmann's notion of life as a series of imbedded stages with different forms of role-playing, stages that we are familiar with and move across without difficulties when the frame and perspective changes (Mikos et al.

2000). It also and partly refers to Foucault's concept of the Panoptikon (Bleicher 2000) as a metaphor for life in modernity. According to Mikos et al. (2000: 75ff.) the editing principles and camera-work are based on contrast and parallel-montage between different persons, storylines and spaces in the house, and a very intense mix of long distance shots of the whole interior, medium shots of couples and groups. and close ups and extreme close ups of body parts and faces. The camera work is certainly not invisible and the participants are very aware of the camera. They comment on it, act for it, try to look through the two way mirrors to get a glimpse of it or show playful disrespect for the camera with gestures and verbal comments. So the participants show examples of a meta-textual role-consciousness and deliberately play on the different frames and the knowledge of cameras and an invisible audience. In much the same way the audience is presented with a system of frames inside frames (Mikos et al. 2000: 113): a game containing other games which are part of a reality show, which is a combination of several genres like soap and other forms, which ultimately reflect, mirror and comment on a wider social reality. This play between a staged reality with several frames and the overall interactive dimension with the audience ensures a well-informed play between authenticity/reality and staged role-playing/ staged reality.

The *Big Brother* format is so far the most successful reality-show globally, but although it is clearly a very commercialized entertainment product with no psychological or social intention other than commercial drive, it is nevertheless symptomatic of the blurring of boundaries between public and private, between entertainment and documentary and between authentic moments and a totally staged frame. However, the moral panic reflected in the reaction seen in many countries, seems just as much of an over reaction as the media hype and hysterical cult is. Entertainment formats will always follow mainstream tendencies in society and media culture as such – perhaps pushing it a little further. But commercial programs and new genres like this could not exist, were they not compatible with mainstream norms and ethical boundaries. Reality-shows flourish at the moment because of changes following a transformation from a traditional modern mass society to a new network society in which identity, social and cultural roles and norms have become more fluid and dynamic. Just as more serious journalistic documentaries to a larger degree investigate everyday life and the more private spheres of life, reality-shows turn role-playing, identity-work and symbolic and cultural forms of everyday life and interaction into entertainment.

Mediation, commercialization and the audience

"Forget Goethe, forget Schiller, Beethoven, Kant and this guy Peter Sloderdijk. They are of no importance. The cultural place known as Germany is in ruins. Today it is figures like Jenny Elvers (German *Big Brother* participant) who dominate prime time – and a large part of the society around it" (*Information*, Torsten Weper, January 20-21, 2001). These were the words written in a small intellectual, Danish quality journal just a few months before the Danish *Big Brother* was aired for the first time. And true enough, at least for a couple of months as elsewhere in the world *Big Brother* in Denmark seemed to be a media event overshadowing every other cultural and media phenomenon. The serious morning news papers and TV-stations took a purely moral decline position calling it trash TV while the rest of the press, especially the tabloids, greedily tried to capitalize on the hot information and fuel audience interest by going behind the scene, thus extending the public voyeurism even further and finishing the job of making media stars out of completely ordinary people. The themes in the public debate in the serious press were generally very critical, although few papers went to the extreme of anticipating the decline of a whole culture. The triviality of the show, the fact that nothing important really happened and the fact that several psychologists criticized the un-ethical and potential for personal damage on participants was very dominant. At the same time the show was symbolically read and understood as a sign of the decline of media culture in general. Others, like for instance the Danish art historian Rune Gade, talked not just about Big Brother, but also about the new subjective documentary films as a sign of a traumatic realism, or a desperate search for reality in a time, where media has torn privacy to shreds and left the individual open and vulnerable (Rune Gade, *Information*, October, 21-22, 2001, see also Jerslev 2001).

Two incidents in particular in the first Danish version of the show made headlines and led to a broader discussion about the show's way of dealing with reality. In the first incident Jill, the later winner confessed to one of the other girls that she had been traumatized because of incest experiences in her childhood. The general reaction, even in the tabloids, that also put the story on the front page, was that this was going too far in direct transmission from a traumatic deep back stage. The other case came in the form of the rebellion against the show where three of the most popular participants left the house and tried to get the rest of the participants to follow, which lead to a closing of the transmission for several hours. In other words, as soon as something critical against the program occurred, reality became too dangerous and the line to the audience was cut, whereas the more private, ethical problem was aired. This showed the intention of commercial entertainment in a nutshell: sex and tragedy sells every time, but not media criticism.

The commercial entertainment discourse is obvious in the program itself and in the tabloid press coverage: they cater to the same audience and have the same advertisers. In the public reactions otherwise the trash-position and the simulacrum-nightmare positions are also very obvious and dominant. However, in connection with *Big Brother* and reality-shows like it the empowerment position was also present, although in a rather weak form. One example was, when the Danish politician Naser Khader in an essay in the central Danish Newspaper *Politiken* (Khader 2001) defended the program as a social experiment, which could teach young people with immigrant backgrounds something about the rules of interactions in the Danish society while referring to a couple of persons in the program with an immigrant background. Khader said that the *Big Brother* house "is multi-cultural and yet void of ethnicity as a negative factor, it is 'de-ethnified'."

The strong and contradictory reactions to reality-shows are not repeated to the same degree in connection with docu-soaps, although some of the docu-soaps with nothing but sexually oriented and hot tabloid-themes mostly on commercial channels, have been met by the same criticism. But all in all, the docu-soap has also developed as a public service genre and very much as a new sub-form of the already established observational tradition. This difference in the public debate on reality TV is also visible in the different audience to different reality-forms.

Figures on both the Danish and the German *Big Brother* (Mikos 2000) indicate that there is a high overrepresentation among young viewers between 14-29 (25% between 14-19, 22% between 20-29) while 34% of viewers were between 30-49. This is not just a teenage-audience. But at the same time, the audience profile indicates that it is a young (post) modern group either very much oriented toward material goods and career, a lifestyle avantgarde testing borders or a more playful hedonistic group. And it is certainly not the lowest educated among the young but a rather well educated group. It is entertainment TV for a large group of young people but mostly for the modern, city-oriented mainstream group of young people on their way up in an educational and material sense. The Danish figures point in the same direction and in terms of the Danish Gallup Institute's segmentation of audiences according to life style, the modern individuality oriented and also to a certain degree the traditionally individuality-oriented are the core viewers of the program, again with a very young profile[5]. Programs like *Maternity Ward* have a much broader and traditional audience profile and also a higher rating and share. The audience here is more like the traditional audience of documentary programs on the two public service channels.

From an audience point of view, reality TV covers very different formats and tendencies and cannot just be dismissed as commercial trash-TV. Entertainment has entered deeply into the classical formats of documentary television as it has entered the whole global media culture. But it is not as bad that we watch *Big Brother* as having *Big Brother* watching us. After all, entertainment is just entertainment, and solid documentaries of all sorts still have a strong place on public service channels and a good hold on a large audience.

Notes

1 At a seminar in Århus, Denmark in September 2001, in connection with the Nordic Panorama Festival, the Endemol producer of *Big Brother* said that most decisions concerning the national versions of BB are taken by local producers. However, on certain general aspects of the program Endemol has the right to intervene and give instructions.

2 Programs from both TV2 and DR in Denmark of the journalistic investigative type or the observational type are normally placed in prime time around 8 pm and normally get a rating around 20-30%, only slightly behind the best national fiction series. Even in UK documentaries the figures for documentaries and the overall evaluation of them by the audience is very high, according to John Corners latest article (Corner 2001). Corner writes in a note: "In a listing of 'best programs' on television, documentary came top with a 42% vote. Soaps managed 27% while 'Reality TV' was tenth (and bottom) with just 8%. When it came to the 'like to watch' category, documentaries came top with the over 35's and second (behind comedy) with the under 35's. Once again, 'Reality TV' came bottom, scoring only 2% with the under 35's. Whilst these figures certainly cannot be seen as a reliable guide to viewing behavior, they still indicate a significant durability in the public presence of the category."

3 The categories here are in many ways inspired by both Nichols' (1991) four main categories for film documentaries: expository, observational, interactive and reflexive, and Plantinga's (1997) more simple division in three 'voices' of documentary films: formal voice, open voice and poetic voice. I use categories and concepts from both these works. However my categorization is made from the perspective of documentary forms on *television* and thus a much stronger connection to differences and connections between journalistic and other factual forms and fictional and dramatized forms in the institutional forms of both public service and commercial TV. Therefore the genre categories are different from the film genres in several ways.

4 In Denmark the public service channels have quite obviously been negative towards the generic term docu-soap. TV2 in the beginning used this term, but very soon the term 'everyday drama' replaced it and by now there is a general agreement to use the term 'documentary series.'

5 The figures on the Danish *Big Brother* and other reality programs are taken from Stig Hjarvard (2001) and *Mediawatch* (nos. 3 and 6, 2001).

References

Appadurai, Arjun. 1996. *Modernity at Large: Cultural Globalisation.* Minneapolis: University of Minnesota Press.

Beck, Ulrich, et al. 1994. *Reflexive Modernization.* London: Polity Press.

Beck, Ulrich. 1999. *What is Globalization?* London: Polity Press.

Bleicher, Joan Kristin. 2000. "Zwischen Menschenzoo, Panoptikon und Dauertheater. Inszenierungsstrategien im "Big Brother"-container und ihre gesellschaftlichen Funktionen". *Medien und Kommunikation.* Jahrgang 48, no. 4: 518-536.

Bondebjerg, Ib. 1994. "Narratives of Reality. Documentary Film and Television in a Cognitive and Pragmatic Perspective". *Nordicom Review* no. 1: 65-87.

Bondebjerg, Ib. 1996. "Public Discourse – Private Fascination. The Hybridization of True-Life-Story Genres in Television". In *Television the Critical View*, 6th. ed, edited by Horace Newcomb. Oxford & New York: Oxford University Press.

Bondebjerg, Ib. 2000. "I dialog med den danske virkelighed – TV2's dokumentariske profil". In *TV2 på skærmen*, edited by Henrik Søndergaard et. al. København: Samfundsfagslitteratur.

Bondebjerg, Ib. 2001. "Verden ifølge Lars Engels". In *Analyser af tv 1-2*, edited by Jens F. Jensen, in print. København: Medusa.

Bondebjerg, Ib. 2001a. "Med politiet i 'virkeligheden': reality TV og kriminalitet". *Mediekultur* (in print).

Bondebjerg, Ib. 2001b. "Den medialiserede virkelighed". *Ekko* no. 8: 20-25.

Castells, Manuel. 1996/2000. *The rise of the network society.* 2nd ed. London: Blackwell.

Corner, John. 2000. "Documentary in a Post-Documentary Culture. A note on Forms and their Functions". Webpublication: *http://www.lboro.ac.uk/research/changing.media/index.html*

Corner, John. 2001. "Documentary Values". In *Realism and Reality in Film and TV. Northern Lights. Film and Media Studies Yearbook. 2002*, edited by Anne Jerslev. Copenhagen: Museum Tusculanum Press.

Dauncy, Hugh. 1996. "French Reality Television – More than a Matter of Taste". *European Journal of Communication*, vol. 11, no. 1: p. 83-106.

Dijk, Jan van. 1999. *The Network Society.* London: Sage.

Dovey, Jon. 2000. *Freakshow: First Person Media and Factual Television.* London: Pluto Press.

Ekstrom, Mats. 2000. "Information, storytelling and attractions". *Media, Culture & Society*, vol. 22, no. 4: 465-492.

Engels, Lars. 2000. "Station 1 Danmark". *Politiken*, October 14, interview by Niels Steensgaard.

Fishman, Mark & Gray Cavendar (eds.). 1998. *Entertaining Crime: Tele vision Reality Programmes*. New York: Aldine de Gruyter.

Giddens, Anthony. 1991. *Modernity and Self-Identity*. London: Polity Press.

Giddens, Anthony, 1999. *Runaway World: How Globalization is Reshaping Our Lives*. London: Profile Books.

Goffmann, Erving. 1974/1986. *Frame Analysis*. Boston, Mass.: Northeastern University Press.

Habermas, Jürgen. 1984/1995-97. *The Theory of Communicative Action 1-2*. London: Beacon Press.

Held, David. (ed.) 2000. *The Global Transformation Reader*. London: Blackwell.

Hill, Annette. 2000. "Crime and Crisis: British Reality TV in Action". In *British Television. A Reader*, edited by Edward Buscombe. Oxford: Oxford University Press.

Hill, Annette. 2000. "Fearful and safe: Audience response to British Reality Programming". In *From Grierson to Docu-Soap*, edited by John Izod, Richard Kilborn and Matthew Hibberd. Luton: University of Luton Press.

Hippels, Klemens. 1993. "Parasoziale Interaktion als Spiel. Bermerkungen zu einer interaktionistischen Fernsehtheorie". *Montage/AV*, vol 9 no. 1: 135-150.

Hjarvard, Stig. 2001. "Virkelighedens teater". *Tid og Tendenser*, no. 4, August.

Hjort, Mette & Ib Bondebjerg (eds). 2001. *The Danish Directors. Dialogues on a Contemporary National Cinema*. London: Intellect Press.

Imhof, Kurt & Peter Schultz (eds.). 1998. *Die Veröffentlichung des Privaten – Die Privatisierung des Öffentlichen*. Opladen: Westdeutscher Verlag.

Jerslev, Anne. 2000. "Nuets affekt. Virkelighed, liveness og katastrofisk intensitet i reality TV". *Working paper*. Århus: Århus Universitet.

Jerslev, Anne. 2001. "Jeg er desparat. Desparate mennesker onanerer for åben skærm". *Ekko* no. 8: 26-29.

Kilborn, Richard. 1994. "How real can you get". Recent Developments in "Reality" Television". *European Journal of Communication* 9: 421-39.

Khader, Naser. 2001. "Big Brother med andre briller". In *Politiken*, March 22.

Langer, John. 1998. *Tabloid Television*. London: Routledge.

Mikos, Lothar et al. 2000. *Im Auge der Kamera. Das Fernsehereignis Big Brother*. Potsdam-Babelsberg: Vistas Verlag.

MediaWatch 2001: 9/2, 23/3 and 6/4: Articles and statistics on reality TV.

Nichols, Bill. 1991. *Representing Reality*. Bloomington and Indianapolis: Indiana University Press.

Nichols, Bill. 1994. *Blurred Boundaries*. Indiana University Press.

Plantinga, Carl R. 1997. *Rhetoric and Representation in Nonfiction Film*. Cambridge: Cambridge University Press.

Postman, Neil. 1985. *Amusing Ourselves to Death*. New York: Viking.

Ritchie, Jean. 2000. *Big Brother. The Official Unseen Story*. London: Channel Four Books.

Robins, Kevin. 1997. "The City lost from View". In *Into the Image*, 137-146. London: Routledge.

Ruoff, Jeffrey K. 1998. "A Bastard Union of Several Forms. Style and Narrative in An American Family". In *Documenting the Documentary*, edited by Barry Keith Grant & Jeannette Sloniowski. Detroit: Wayne State University Press.

Schlesinger, Philip & Tumber, Howard. 1994. *Reporting Crime: The Media Politics of Criminal Justice*. Oxford: Clarendon Press.

Søndergaard, Henrik. 2001. "Reality TV". In *Analyser af tv 1-2*, edited by Jens F. Jensen. København: Medusa (in print).

Thompson, John B. 1995. *Media and Modernity*. London: Polity Press.

Thompson, John B. 2000. *Political Scandal*. London: Polity Press.

Wieten, Jan. 1998. "Reality Television and Social Responsibility Theory". In *The Media in Question. Popular Cultures and Popular Interests*, edited by Kees Brandts, Joke Hermes & Liesbet van Zoonen. London: Sage.

Weber, Frank. (ed.) 2000. *Big Brother. Inszenierte Banalität zur Prime Time*. Münster: Münster Verlag.

Williams, Linda. 1998. "Mirrors without Memories". In *Documenting the Documentary,* edited by Barry Keith Grant and Jeannette Sloniowski. Detroit: Wayne State University Press.

Zoonen, Lisbet. 1998. "The Ethics of Making private Life Public". In *The Media in Question. Popular Cultures and Popular Interests*, edited by Kees Brandts, Joke Hermes & Liesbet van Zoonen. London: Sage.

John Ellis

A Minister is About to Resign: On the Interpretation of Television Footage

Here is the news

A minister is about to resign. A not uncommon scenario in European politics, and one that suits television news as it provides a mixture of serious politics and speculative gossip. The bulletin's headline menu will contain a brief shot of the minister snatched as they leave their house or office: a moment spent in public space before they disappear into conclave again. After the news menu, the item begins. It repeats the shot of the minister, but run at its full length, with newsreader commentary introducing the story of the "embattled minister" and including the line "seen here earlier today leaving his home"[1]. The footage is signalled as highly specific: this is the minister as they appear at the almost-present moment in the crisis. Often a forlorn reporter will call out "Minister, will you be resigning today?", not in the hope of a sudden confession but more that an involuntary reaction should cross the minister's face, betraying the hidden truth of their feelings. The viewer can therefore, as the commentary almost invites, scan the footage for what Carol J. Clover calls 'demeanour evidence'[2]: signs of stress, of regret, of defiance, of intention to resign or tough it out, of bewilderment or malevolence towards the press or fellow ministers. We read the footage in an attempt to predict the story for ourselves. It is offered as a privileged moment of witness[3], anchoring the speculation of commentators and correspondents, allowing the viewer a direct engagement with the unfolding crisis.

The news story then unfolds with more details and an increasing level of speculation and commentary from observers and actors alike. At some point, the news team's political correspondent offers an overview, and the snatched footage of the minister returns once more. But this time it has a very different status. It forms the background to a graphic which lists the key events leading up to the crisis, or the principal actors in it, or the issues at stake. This time in slow motion, the minister walks the few yards (or metres) between doorway and waiting car. The image is treated in a monochrome wash or texturised or solarised; it is framed in some way to incorporate a title 'The Minister Scandal'; written bullet points begin to appear over the processed footage in synch with the correspondent's recorded commentary. At the beginning of the item, the footage had an evidential status, attesting to the demeanour of an individual. Now it has suddenly acquired another status: that of standing for or gesturing towards the whole political crisis. At the start we are to understand the image as indexical. A few moments later we are to see it as far more iconic. What makes possible this rapid shift in interpretation?

This is an unexceptional visual event in contemporary television news. Modern videographic practices provide many examples: title sequences grab passing gestures of public figures (politicians, presenters, actors) from the indexical flow of their performances and endow them with a designation of typicality. The above example is remarkable only for demonstrating the speed with which the change in status can take place. Such an activity of meaning, though accepted and commonplace, does challenge many conceptions about the nature of the photographic image. For how can an image change its status in a matter of moments, from 'real' at one moment to 'generalising' at the next? Many proponents of 'the photographic as real' theories have to resort to references to 'postmodernism' to explain such a phenomenon. I believe that there is no need to resort to such ramshackle theoretical life-rafts. More productive concepts can account for the phenomenon and place it within a wider evolution of visual meaning into a post-naïve rather than a post-modern process.

Index and icon

Images are, in C.S. Peirce's terms, indexical with iconic aspects. The indexicality lies in the physical connection between the image as sign and its object[4]. It is the imprint of a moment, filled with the potential of meaning. Indexicality brings with it the sense of witness common to all photographic processes: the insistence that the moment of capture of the image still bears down on its potential meanings. The moment leaves its imprint, but, importantly, this is not an imprint of its totality as a moment. So the photographic image is also iconic: it abstracts the visual and the auditory from the range of possible sense impressions of the moment; it conducts a process of foregrounding and backgrounding of elements through the selectivity of focus and microphone directionality that are built into the recording equipment. The photograph, film and the video recording, constitute a particular class of signs. They are instantly recognisable as carrying the imprint of the moment, yet involve significant abstraction.

Equally, they are complex signs, full of potential meanings. These potential meanings are realised through processes of interpretation. The footage of the minister harbours the potential of many meanings: it could be part of an examination of fashion and class (the doorway, the business clothes, the car), an example of weather and human response to it (is it raining? What are the people in the shot wearing and how do they respond to the rain? etc.) or an exposé of press harassment (the flashbulbs, the insistent questioning). Photographic images carry the weight of witness through their indexical qualities: they are the mute witnesses of something, but we are not sure what. Images are concrete but unspecified, holding a surplus of meaning which in practice means an indeterminacy of meaning. An image without a context of some kind is liable to provoke the response "what am I supposed to be looking at?"

So the work of understanding these images begins immediately. The image always already specifies to some degree what we are meant to be looking at. Its very construction implies certain avenues of understanding. It frames and focusses on its ostensible subject, implying a hierarchy of reading. At the same time it sets in motion the interplay between in-frame and out-of-frame which arguably has become a significant part of the aesthetic of modern television with its taste for mobile hand-held shooting. The shot moves to reframe a subject. Its scale of foreground and background, the selection of a particular sound perspective, even its use of colour, all bring forward some potential meanings and fade out others. In other words, the photographic image is more than a result of the accident of the shutter-click: it contains its own 'instructions for use'.

The extent of these instructions varies from photo to photo, from shot to shot. But they inevitably initiate a process whereby the mute witnessing function of the image is given voice. The shot is placed within a sequence; the sequence is made for a particular purpose, as an item in a particular kind of programme which has an anticipated range of uses within already defined channels of distribution. These powerful determinants on the activity of interpretation all exist beyond the shot itself, but are essential to its interpretation. This is almost a truism nowadays, but it is essential here to stress that these determinants are not simply textual functions, readable from the image flow within which the particular shots are placed. They are properly generic considerations, determined in arenas that stretch far beyond the specific textual practices of the medium itself. The first point may be obvious, but its consequence is often overlooked in studies of broadcast texts, and, I will argue, lead to a re-evaluation of ideas of genre.

So how are we to understand this activity of interpretation which intervenes in the very activity of creating the image itself, at the very moment of photographic witness and the formation of a predominantly indexical image? The activity of interpretation sets up what could be called a drift towards the iconic. The fullness and flux of the witnessed moment with all its ambiguity is moulded by a movement towards generality: from an 'only-this-ness' to a 'like-these-ness'.

This drift towards the iconic seems to be implied within Peirce's typology of signs[5]. In one of his many scattered definitions, he sees every sign as determined by its object, with an Index "being really and in its individual existence connected with the individual object" and an Icon "by partaking in the characters of the object". Clearly there is a potential of interpenetration here. These are not mutually exclusive categories. Rather they explain (with the category of the Symbol[6]) three tendencies that can be found within within a particular sign. He shows this when discussing the status of diagrams:

196

A Diagram is mainly an Icon, and an Icon of intelligible relations. […] Now since a diagram, though it will ordinarily have Symbolide Features, as well as features approaching the nature of Indices, is nevertheless in the main an Icon of the form of relations in the constitution of its Object, the appropriateness of it for the representation of necessary inference is easily seen … (Pierce in Hoopes ed. 1991: 252)

A sign, and particularly a complex sign like a diagram, a photographic image or moving image shot, will have tendencies which link it to the indexical, the iconic and even the symbolic. The diagram is meaningful to the extent that it shows the relations between objects, and it may contain little information about those objects themselves. In the case of a diagram, instructions for use are always relatively explicit and can extend to the totally explicit (hence the 'Symbolide features', which are labels and so on). In the case of the shot or the photographic image, however, the instructions are generally less explicit, depending on institutional and personal practices of interpretation. The plethora of possible meanings can be great, as is shown by the example of the minister's brief walk from door to vehicle.

Interpretation is an activity of selection and placing of potential meanings. It relies on the indexical witnessing power of the shot, but it necessarily reduces that which is witnessed to manageable and intelligible proportions. In doing so, it relativises the indexical aspects and emphasises the iconic.

This is precisely the movement that is pushed to its extreme within the hypothetical news item about the minister's resignation. The shot is offered in as an indexical item, but the context has already screened out many potential avenues of meaning. The minister's suit is only of interest if its crumpled state might betray his state of being, not as an example of contemporary business fashion. The witnessed moment itself is already grasped by an iconic function. Further processing of the shot, its insertion into the news bulletin's particular graphic style, accentuates the drift towards the iconic. The shot was already beginning to stand for more than itself through the very activity of interpretation that gave it any point, and solicited our attention to begin with. The further processing within the graphical regime of the programme seals that drift towards the iconic. It ceases to be a sign of the present (or almost contemporaneous) state of mind of the minister and becomes a sign of the whole news story in which the minister is the principal actor. The image has become properly iconic, an abstraction that stands for more than a fleeting moment and begins to stand for a class of events.

Communities of understanding

The 'instructions for use' govern the process which determines the iconic drift of any seemingly indexical image. But, unlike diagrams, the instructions for use are nowhere explicit. Instead, they exist within the network of assumptions and competencies that make up the community of understanding within the televisual audience. In Peirce's terms, this is the level of 'thirdness', another level of intellective activity to that of 'secondariness' to which the familiar designations of index, icon and symbol belong. Thirdness is the level of generality, of theories, of deductive thought, hypothesis and accepted knowledge. For Peirce this is not the real of 'ideas' so much as of grounded thought: thought not in isolation but within the real institutions of understanding that shape our culture[7]. The ambition of Peirce's semiotic seems to extend further than Saussure's[8] not only in its attention to the visual, but above all in Peirce's overall philosophical ambition, which seems to have been to try to define the nature of thought itself as a physical activity with concrete embodiments and consequences[9].

It is easy enough to ignore the existence of such concrete institutions when we open our mouths to speak. The years of induction through school, home and social networks into particular discursive regimes makes itself prudently invisible. Speech in the abstract, however, is never possible. We always speak in different ways and in different modes, and these define the meaning and salience of our words as well as the context of the particular interaction. Behind every utterance lie concrete institutions to ensure that a community of understanding exists enabling the adequate interpretation of that utterance. Behind the particular utterance that you are reading lies the institution of higher education, its push to define concepts and its ability to create the material circumstances whereby I can fashion such an utterance and it can then be disseminated and understood. In the normal course of events, such utterances necessarily do not reflect on their conditions of existence; nor will this one.

The key point here is that meaning requires communities of understanding, and that these communities cannot exist without concrete organisations. Sometimes these ensure the equality of exchange whereby all listeners can become speakers; more often they ensure that there exists an inequality of exchange. The electronic media represent an interesting case whereby 'listeners' do not normally become 'speakers' and do not possess the competences or the wherewithal necessary to create their own utterances. Nevertheless they are absolutely able to understand the utterances of others. To put it plainly, almost everyone in contemporary Western society will routinely understand the transformation of the shot of the minister, but would be unable to effect such a transformation even if they had the necessary equipment and could operate it. By the same token, the news personnel capable of producing such an utterance would need further training to produce an effective piece of fiction. In the electronic media there exists a production community and a community of understanding. The community of understanding does not itself produce utterances in the normal course of events; and producers of utterances in one area of production tend to be members of the community of understanding in other areas.

Genres as institutions

So how does audio-visual communication take place so easily and rapidly when such disparities exist between the production community and the community of understanding? The mechanism of genre seems to be what ties the two communities together. Genres are properly institutions of meaning, in that they comprise common sets of assumptions and practices which underpin the creation and understanding of particular texts. Genres here should be understood as informal institutions of meaning that exist in the circulation of texts rather than within those texts. They have physical embodiments in the planning and execution of production activity; in censorship and regulation; in labelling, promotion and public debate; in fan clubs and professional organisations; in memory of past instances and future expectations; in habitual patterns of understanding. Yet genres are hardly ever codified outside academic study. They are very often not explicit, but they are spontaneously recognised by audiences and makers and are inscribed in the channels of distribution and practices of production. The 'instructions for use' that exist within complex media utterances invoke ideas of genre.

Genre definitions are therefore invoked within texts but it cannot be understood by looking at texts alone. No one text could possibly exemplify the whole of one genre, and neither should any one text should be seen as belonging to just one genre. Even a genre as specific and narrow as 'The Western' has its variants, its historically specific tendencies, and even conflicting characteristics. Genres are defined in textual circulation, within a triangular relationship with creators, audience and industry as its three points. The relationship is dynamic, as Steve Neale points out:

The process-like nature of genres manifests itself as an interaction between three levels: the level of expectation, the level of the generic corpus, and the level of 'rules' or 'norms' that govern both. [...] The elements and conventions of a genre are always *in* play rather than being, simply, *re*-played; any generic corpus is always being expanded" (Neale 1990:56).

Generic meanings are 'in play' not only because every example of a genre brings something new, but also, and more importantly, the activity of defining genres goes on far beyond the texts which are destined to be understood within those genres.

Grounded discourses on genre permeate the institutions of meaning. From the implicit evocation of genre in cinema publicity materials to television's recourse to explicit generic labelling, genre definitions surround and organise particular texts. Key in this process are the informal (i.e. non-analytic) discourses of genre. Newspapers discuss 'outrageous' television programmes; radio

DJs and phone-ins discuss the behaviour of a star or the plotline of a soap. These are essentially discourses which discuss the appropriateness of particular representational strategies within the context of shared generic understandings. Indeed such informal discourses are crucial in maintaining and refreshing informal social genre definitions. They are concerned with competence (how to understand sequences, whether they 'worked') and appropriateness (whether such material 'should be shown' or 'is true or not') Such discussions are crucial in maintaining the connection between producing communities and communities of understanding or interpretation.

Generic systems provide the implicit instructions for use that, for example, enable a contemporary viewer to read the footage of the minister in two different ways within the space of a couple of minutes. The news context is now 'generally known' to use images in this way, but such a manipulation of images would have been outside the available competences for news teams in television of the 1970s and before. This is not so much because the technological capacity was unavailable, but because news images were not generically defined as having such iconic possibilities at that time. News images were, during television's initial period of scarcity, held towards the indexical end of their potential, and generalisation was regarded as solely a matter for (written or spoken) words.

Genre and appropriateness

Generic systems are concerned with the appropriateness of meanings, defining many different spectrums of what is suitable, usual or even permissable. Generic regimes of appropriateness range from character behaviours to graphic styles[10]. Such is their complexity that it is quite possible to defy the conventions in one area, for reasons of innovation for instance, whilst maintaining the conventions in other areas. One example can be found in situation comedy, where characters are meant to have little or no memory of their previous on-screen exploits; soap opera characters by contrast carry an increasing freight of accumulated experiences. Yet recent sitcoms have begun to use soap-style character development and the awareness of history to ensure continuing audience loyalty and even to mark first run shows from repeats. In the American sitcom Friends, the relationships between the core characters have evolved over time, with Ross and Rachel forming and dissolving a partnership, and Monica and Chandler having a 'secret' affair. Nevertheless, there are limits to this new access to memory in sitcom characters. When Ross remarked "Do you remember when I had that monkey?" (a feature of the first series regarded by some fans as a mark of the show's initial uncertainty of tone), all he can say is "weird wasn't it?", clearly uncomfortable with this very specific act of remembering. Whilst character development has begun to make an appearance in sitcoms like Friends, otherwise such shows remain within the generic conventions of sitcom.

Generic appropriatenesses extend to visual regimes as well. Had the shot of the minister been sped up, looped and overlaid with graphics which strobed between orange and mauve, then the context of understanding would not have been that of news but of MTV or satire. It is possible, though, that the attempt to make news 'relevant' or 'engaging' to an MTV audience might lead to such an experimentation, just as the pressure to hold audiences has introduced elements of character memory to sitcoms. This shows that both competence and appropriateness are historically specific, and also leads to a further important point.

The graphic styles of news and of MTV are both recognisable, but have different kinds of institutional existence. The genre of television news develops within an increasingly global television culture. News material and news services cross national television boundaries. Television news-making is a specialised profession which looks to its global television peer group for discursive innovation rather more than it does to other national news producers. The expensive process of graphic design of news formats is equally highly specialised, with design sometimes contracted out to the major global centres of computer-driven design like London. This closed culture produces a remarkable uniformity of 'news look' around the world. MTV however is a specialised channel whose name has become synonymous with a generic style. MTV is the name of a single commercial operation, but it has an open culture in that its material emerges from the innovation-driven, low-cost culture of music videos, and its in-house presentational graphics respond to this stimulus. The MTV style is of showy novelty and eagerness to impress.

Both genres belong to television, though MTV is permeated by wider culture which is that of video usage, particularly of replay, reuse and large screen exhibition. Indeed it is more useful here to regard this 'culture of video usage' itself as a genre, since it displays all the features of a genre: a dynamic relationship of expectations and appropriatenesses shared between creators and users, inscribed within concrete and virtual institutions of marketing, venues and social habits.

Are media themselves genres?

If this is the case, then broadcast television itself should also be regarded as an overarching genre with its own (pervasive) community of understanding requiring particular competences so that utterances can be adequately understood. This is the logical consequence of the expansion of audio-visual media since the 1970s. Broadcast television has long since ceased to be co-extensive with the idea of 'television' let alone with the range of uses of the video image. The more that consumers are faced with the multiplication of technologies, commodities and systems (e.g. video/film; game machines/phones; linear narratives/interactivity), the more it becomes clear that generic systems are multiplying around them.

It is not possible to 'pick up' a video game and be able to play it. Games systems assume a level of skills in their users, both in the physical use of controls and in the design of the games and their graphical universes. These can be acquired by peer group induction or by individual trial and error, but acquired they must be, and they form part of a system of habits, expectations and institutions which surely deserve analysis as generic relations. Generic practices such as these cannot be read from a particular text, rather they provide the conditions of existence for any text. Nor are they to be found principally in 'subsidiary' means of circulation (movie posters etc) like the indicators of fictional genres such as the Western or melodrama. Instead they are assumed in whole basis of circulation including textual criticism and analysis.

For instance, one element in the genre of the filmic narrative is its creation and assumption of audience behaviour. The filmic narrative assumes that audiences will pay it a great deal of concentrated attention, and the institution of cinema is formed so that this will take place. In cinemas across the world, rows of seats face a screen. Sitting down and keeping quiet are a key part of the interpretive act[11]. Audience members have to be aware of what behaviours are tolerated, within overall limits that admit variations from cinema to cinema, from locale to locale, as well as over time. This is the interpretive community in a very concrete form, sometimes involving the physical eviction of those who are "spoiling the enjoyment of others" by their inappropriate behaviour.

The generic relations of specific media might be called 'big genre' in the prescient term coined by Alan Williams (1984) in writing of filmic genres:

For the phrase 'genre films', referring to a general category, we can frequently, though not always, substitute 'film narrative'. Perhaps *that* is the real genre. Certainly there is much more difference between 'Prelude to Dog Star Man' and 'Star Wars' than there is between the latter and 'Body Heat'. It's mainly a question of terminology, of course, but I wonder if we ought to consider the principal genres as being narrative film, experimental/avant-garde film, and documentary. Surely these are the categories in film studies that have among themselves the sorts of significant differences that one can find between, say, epic and lyric poetry. … What we presently call film genres would then be *sub-genres*.[12]

Williams here is pointing to the fundamental problem associated with most genre studies, particularly those undertaken within film studies. They remain blind to the fact that, once genre is seen as an institution of understanding rather than a set of conventions, generic relations must be seen to exist at a number of levels. Film narrative (distinct from television narrative or games narrative) underpins filmic genres such as melodrama and the western. In turn, however, both these genres have existences or relevancies beyond the institution of cinema and filmic narrative. Melodrama exists, for instance, in theatre (Blood Brothers), in television (Dynasty) and in the novel (Thomas Hardy). This makes it difficult to rest with Williams' notion of 'sub-genre' because it implies that sub-genres are merely variants of the 'big' genre of filmic narrative. Instead we should see each text as criss-crossed by generic relations which exist at different levels. Some of which are rather more taken for granted than others. Hence no text can be seen as 'belonging' to a single genre, neither as being an example of a single genre.

Genre remains an underused term in critical studies because it still struggles under weight of inherited definitions. In literary studies it has been used since the Romantic era to differentiate the mass of what was seen as repetitive and meretricious work from 'real literature': genre was associated with mass production, and high culture was seen as transcending specific generic concerns. Now it can be seen that high culture itself is a genre. It has its own rules and common understandings, and its own very concrete institutions. The rules of understanding have to be learned every bit as much as those of a video game, and can render its individual texts as opaque to outsiders as a video game is to the uninitiated. The genre of high culture, of serious literature and art, determines the status of the textual system, its representational register and even its ethical stance, this being understood as both its rules of behaviour and its prevalent tone.

The institutions of the high culture genre privilege attention to formal concerns: matters of style and construction. They do so every bit as much as the genre of television news at another level determines the nature and degree of indexicality that should be found in the image of the minister at various points in its discourse. The genre of high culture privileges attention to morality and its dilemmas just as much as the generic system of documentary. And the concerns of this genre are readily borrowed by critics to empower audiences and creators alike within new forms, creating the possibility of a 'high culture' reading of the filmic narrative or of 'melodrama' by a simple transfer of skills. Institutions to enable and expand a high cultural appreciation of media have been set up explicitly modelled on those of high culture in other media: academies, festivals, art cinemas and cinema museums, canonical lists of 'great' films.

Such reinterpretations are common. Since generic relations vary across time and between cultures, images and textual systems can (but do not necessarily) become detached from them in the process of circulation. Some become 'classics', swept up by the generic system of high culture. Others can be opened to fresh forms of interpretation. The image of the minister retains the ghost of witness, and therefore the potential for its resurrection and re-reading. This can happen in a number of ways. Viewers can 'go against the instructions' and read this news footage as an artistic event. A future researcher might identify someone in the background, an unimportant figure at the time who later becomes crucial in events. Their image can be brought forward in the footage by being circled and highlighted. Or again, an archival history programme can push the footage towards the iconic in a different way by using it in the vaguely illustrative way that such programmes use: no longer attached to any one event, it simply shows "what things were like at the time". Or even, with the more or less comic digital insertion of a character, our hapless minister could encounter Zelig or Forrest Gump, combining the relics of the indexical (footage of important event) with the addition of the iconic (visible trickery).

A new definition of genre?

Genre is therefore a matter of communities and of common understandings, of protocols and ideas of appropriate behaviour which are sustained by concrete institutions and common practices. Genre's common understandings therefore imply more than protocols of reading. They are concerned with values, with epistemology and ethics. Genre analysis encounters the big words of life: belief, ethics, reality, acceptability, limits of tolerance. The nature of these beliefs cannot be determined from within texts but exists in the relationships that surround them, on which they float, often so elegantly. Such relationships are not accessible to textual analysis, except insofar as textual systems are symptomatic of the generic relationships that buoy them up.

Documentary (one of Williams' 'super-genres' alongside 'narrative film') is a clear example. The documentary genre depends on a series of assertions of the truthfulness of its material, and the criteria of truthfulness differ between cultures and historical periods.

Reconstructions were common and accepted in the 1930s (in the studio-shot *Night Mail* for example), but became anathema in the 1970s and 1980s in European television. They retained a currency in cinema in films like *The Thin Blue Line* (1988), and the influence of this film lead to a resurgence of stylised reconstructions in certain forms of documentary. Documentary as genre depends on emphasising the indexical nature of its images, by limiting the extent of iconic drift in their interpretation. Documentary makes the appeal "look at this, it really happened". The more iconic stance of "well, something like this happened" is regarded as having a lesser value within the genre, and is often therefore marked with the caption: 'Reconstruction'.

The documentary genre therefore makes related epistemological and ethical claims. The epistemological claims concern the relationship between its images and a reality that they seek to address. These claims are endlessly debated, not only by academics but also by viewers on an everyday basis. Scepticism about the implied truth-claims of documentary footage can become a matter of public debate when those claims are thrown into crisis[13]. Such debates. which take place in everyday talk and the ephemeral media of radio talk and newspaper gossip and comment, are vital for the maintenance of generic relations between the producing and interpretive communities. These everyday epistemological debates interact with an ethics of documentary. Filmmakers and broadcasting organisations, the producing community, set limits on their interactions with the subjects of documentaries, and these are often codified. Issues include the 'exploitation' of those who appear in documentaries (which is to be avoided) and the belief that filmmakers are to be trusted that that what they say happened did happen, within the prevailing generic practices of truthfulness. Questions of exploitation and trust are equally the subject of general debate, and can – perhaps as a result of their explicit and public nature – change relatively quickly. Documentary is not alone amongst genres in having an ethical dimension. Many of the public controversies around representations of violence or sexuality involve generic assumptions.

All of this is to draw a wide definition of 'genre', which may need revision. But the essentials are clear. Audio-visual material is routinely subject to very different uses within the very confined space of a single news item. Yet this poses no particular problems of interpretation. We therefore need some means of definition of the institutions which sustain the community of understanding and link it with the specialised producing community. A definition of genre which acknowledges its very material existence and incorporates an understanding of its double level (fundamentals of reading and major variants) seems to offer such a means of definition[14].

Notes

1 At this point the gender of the minister has to become clear as the language is straining to breaking point. I have chosen to designate the hypothetical minister in this instance as male, mainly because in Britain at least the ministers who are forced or choose to resign are overwhelmingly male.

2 Carol J. Clover, in a paper at the 'Law's Moving Image' conference, Birbeck College/Tate Britain Gallery, London January 2001.

3 For a discussion of this concept see Ellis 2000, pp. 6-38.

4 "[…] There should be three classes of *signs*; for there is a triple connection of *sign, thing signified, cognition produced in the mind*. There may be a mere relation of reason between the sign and the thing signified; in which case the sign is an *icon*. Or there may be a direct physical connection; in which case the sign is an *index*. Or there may be a relation which consists in the fact that the mind associates the sign with its object; in which case the sign is a *name*" (Peirce in Hoopes ed. 1991: 183).

5 Curiously, Umberto Eco (2000) in a recent discussion of Peirce's work ignores the term 'index' completely, preferring to substitute the term 'hypoicon'. This may account for the somewhat surprising discussion on pp. 371-5 of "the trusting attitude we have towards television, as well as our tendency to receive most programs as though they were closed-circuit live broadcasts."

6 "Every sign is determined by its object, either first, by partaking in the characters of the object, when I call the sign an *Icon*; secondly, by being really and in its individual existence connected with the individual object, when I call the sign an *Index*; thirdly, by more or less approximate certainty that it will be interpreted as denoting the object, in consequence of a habit [which term I use as including a natural dispo-

sition], when I call the sign *Symbol*" (Peirce in Hoopes ed. 1991: 251).

7 "By adopting the viewpoint of Peirce's semiotic, it is possible to avoid either gnawing the old bone of the relation of thought to behaviour or else isolating intellectual behaviour from society. Once intellectual activity is understood to be "real" behaviour, its possible importance can be weighed fairly against other "real" elements in society. Conversely, social institutions such as government, political parties, corporations, labour unions, voluntary associations, and so on may be regarded as thought, once a thought is understood to be, not an idea known immediately within a mind, but rather, an interpretive relation. Once thought is understood as a process of sign interpretation, a great range of social phenomena too large to be comprehended within any individual mind may nevertheless be best understood as the result of a process of intelligence. Institutions are semiotic syntheses, so to speak, of the thoughts of a great many people" (Introduction in Hoopes ed. 1991: 12).

8 This is in no way to disparage Saussure. Both his work and Peirce's are expressed in less than satisfactory forms. Saussure's *Course in General Linguistics*, though a completed text, is, as its title implies, the synthesis of his students' notes from his lectures, which probably eliminate both prevarications and asides which might have pointed to extensions of his basic theory. Peirce's work consists of multiple drafts and fragments, where he often seems to be arguing from within a perspective that he has established to his own satisfaction, rather than setting out that perspective in any systematic way.

9 Peirce seems unaware of the Marx's critiques of Hegel's idealist system, but writes with an American bluntness that Hegel "has committed the trifling oversight of forgetting that there is a real world with real actions and reactions. Rather a serious oversight that" (Peirce in Hoopes ed. 1991: 197).

10 See for instance the recent discussion of digital image manipulation by Arild Fetveit: "These changes require us to place a greater emphasis on the differences between photographic practices, and less upon the technical features that unite them. Such an idea, moving from the idea of trust as linked to the technology itself and towards placing it in a larger techno-institutional context, largely resolves our initial paradox originating from the simultaneous proliferation of digital imagery and visual evidence" (Fetveit 1999: 799-800).

11 I have examined this in relation to British entertainment movies of the 1930s in Ellis 2000a.

12 Alan Williams 1984 (cited in Neale 2000: 20). Neale, however, does not go on to examine this question to any great degree.

13 For accounts of a recent such instance in British television see Brian Winston 2000, pp. 9-35 and Stella Bruzzi 2000, pp. 90-4.

14 I am grateful to Jostein Gripsrud for this helpful comments on an earlier draft of this article.

References

Bruzzi, Stella. 2000. *New Documentary: A Critical Introduction*. London & New York: Routledge.

Eco, Umberto. 2000. *Kant and the Platypus*. London: Vintage.

Ellis, John. 2000. *Seeing Things. Television in the Age of Uncertainty*. London: I. B. Tauris.

Ellis, John. 2000a. "British Cinema as Performance Art: Brief Encounter, Radio Parade of 1935 and the circumstances of film exhibition", in *British Cinema, Past and Present*, edited by Justine Ashby and Andrew Higson. London & New York: Routledge.

Fetveit, Arild. 1999. "Reality TV in the ditigal era: a paradox in visual culture?" *Media, Culture and Society*, vol 21, no. 6: 787-804.

Hoopes, James (ed.). 1991. *Peirce on Signs: Writing on Semiotic by Charles Sanders Peirce*. Chapel Hill: University of North Carolina Press.

Neale, Steve. 2000. *Genre and Hollywood*. London & New York: Routledge.

Peirce, Charles Sanders. 1991. *Peirce on Signs: Writing on Semiotic by Charles Sanders Peirce*, edited by James Hoopes. Chapel Hill: University of North Carolina Press.

Williams. Alan. 1984. "Is a Radical Genre Criticism Possible?" *Quarterly Review of Film Studies*, vol 9 no 2. 121-5.

Winston, Brian. 2000. *Lies, Damn Lies and Documentaries*. London: British Film Institute.

Arine Kirstein

Decentering the Subject: The Current Documentary Critique of Realism

Post-colonial critique of the notion of realism

Lexicographer Émile Littré writes in *Dictionnaire de la langue française* (completed 1873) that the term realism has been known since the Middle Ages, but "as a new coinage, realism is applied to art and literature to delineate the endeavor to reproduce nature without ideal." In the middle of the 19th century, artists and writers were enthusiastic about this new possibility of depicting man without any preconceived notions, symbolic superstructures or theological determinations. Almost 150 years and several realism-critiques later, post-colonial theorist and film director Trinh T. Minh-ha dissociates herself from realism of the exact same reasons that made the artist in the nineteenth century subscribe to it. To Trinh, the notion of depicting the individual as it is rather than it should be is in and of itself an idealization of human life. For Trinh, contemporary realism professes a naturalized ideology, thus representing the dominating discourse, white, Anglo-American and male. This discourse is based on the notion of a stable world and subjects which can be categorized once and for all according to race, geography, culture, and gender.

The history of the critique of realism is also the story of how the 'self' has gradually been perceived as ever more complex, fragmented and disjunctive. Ann Kaplan (1988) notes that the first decisive step towards a critique of realism occurs with semiology's argument that subjectivity is always discursively constructed and not preexisting discourse. But the break with the Cartesian subject was commenced much earlier by thinkers such as Rousseau, Nietzsche, Darwin, Marx and Freud (Kaplan 1988: 82). Consequently, theoretical efforts to decentralize the autonomous and individualist 'I' in realism are not new. Robert Stam and Louise

Spence note that many suppressed groups have fought realism as an integrated part of the battle against hegemonic representations: "Women and third-world filmmakers have attempted to counterpose the objectifying discourse of patriarchy and colonialism with a vision of themselves and their reality as seen 'from within'" (Stam & Spence1985: 639). Representations of the subject cease to be simple and straightforward when created from positions such as these.

This article will discuss two documentaries as examples of a new representation of the subject. *Tongues Untied* by Marlon Riggs (1989) and *Looking for Langston* by Isaac Julien (1989) both deconstruct the assumption that there is a unified and coherent self at the heart of human behavior from which personal and social change originate. Instead they tell us that it is no longer possible to represent a true self. Films such as these suspend realism thereby challenging the documentary genre as a "discourse of sobriety" (Nichols 1991). I will argue that this occurs in accord with a project of identity politics. The films employ strategies that decenter the documentary subject suggesting new forms of documentary aesthetics and new forms of spectatorship. Trinh T. Minh-ha's discussion of a new subjectivity beyond the stereotype is central to my argument. It is of no coincidence that *Looking for Langston* and *Tongues Untied* have been made in the United Kingdom and the US, respectively. These countries both exhibit a cultural and ethnic diversity and much of the seminal work in postcolonial art and theory has been produced there. Both films address black homosexuality, while dealing with the process of identity formation itself.

Looking for Langston – in search of a political subjectivity

Isaac Julien calls his film *Looking for Langston* (1989) "a meditation" on the Afro-American poet Langston Hughes. Hughes artistic breakthrough coincided with the "Black Renaissance" of the 1920s in New York. The film is a meditation because it does not restrict itself to the protagonist's life and work as in conventional portraits. Instead, Langston Hughes becomes the point of departure for a far-reaching investigation. By way of associative links to his biography, issues of race, nation, the formation of a black homosexual identity, past and present, are raised. *Looking for Langston* can be considered an homage to a pioneer of identity political art. On the film's soundtrack several artists and theorists recite poetry and make statements, among them Stuart Hall, Toni Morrison and Essex Hemphill. "A revolutionary does not *choose* to be against society," as one voice in the film informs us. As a black homosexual, Hughes was twice stigmatized by the cultural elite in New York, and ironically, he was also adored for the exact same reasons.

The strongest feature of *Looking for Langston* is the way in which the film unfolds its fictionalized sequences in black and white, occasionally then interlaced with archival footage. A 1920s nightclub clouded by smoke from slim cigarettes establishes the ambiance of the era. It also functions as the locus for a sexual fantasy, evoking a nascent ideal of black and male beauty. Furthermore, the nightclub takes us to the present, where skinheads kick in the front door and remind us that harassment of blacks and homosexuals still exists. The imaginary converges with the real, fictional scenes blend with archival footage of Harlem and with television clips of Hughes reciting his poetry. In *Looking for Langston* the portrayed character is named but the depicted identity is not restricted to one person. Instead, Langston Hughes' bitter experiences of being black and homosexual in New York City in the 1920s and 1930s are "absorbed" into a contemporary setting. The protagonist's identity and experience becomes a collective one by bringing together different positions and projections of Langston Hughes as a black, homosexual public figure. The title *Looking for Langston* indicates that the recovery of this black political identity is a creative pursuit that does not end with definite answers.

Tongues Untied – creating a collective experience and going beyond authenticity

When *Tongues Untied* was launched in 1989, black homosexuality was a rarely described cultural phenomenon in the US. This hole in the visual archive is thematisized in the film by extensively focusing on emergence and physical disclosure.

In the film, the subjects dance, make love, rehearse gender political poems and snap their fingers as part of a 'Snaptology.' The film is complex in its construction as it is assembled with different kinds of visual and aural material. Archive footage of gay marches, confrontations between police and black men, and still photos combine with highly staged scenes on the street or in studios not to mention the many different voices weaving into each another without comments being fixed to any particular individuals. The collage of voices provides the elaborate texture of the film. *Tongues Untied* incorporates both the condescending, oppressive and marginalizing representations of black homosexuality, while also soliciting experiences of anger, loneliness and pain caused by misrepresentation, persecution and invisibility imposed on them by the Black Church and the gay community. These experiences and emotional states are not conveyed as testimonies through the traditional documentary method of 'giving voice.' They are rather performed as poetry in highly stylized spaces.

Perhaps the title *Tongues Untied* refers to the most important statement in the film namely the untying of muted tongues. This may seem to be concurrent with "giving voice" as in the documentary tradition mentioned above; but the theme of untying tongues and depicting the invisible is dealt with without resorting to realist notions of 'life as it is lived.' Marlon Riggs is obviously not interested in the simple authenticity emanating from 'a real person testifying his real problem.' Instead, he animates the themes of the film with the many kinds of visual and aural material that converge in a collective tale founded by physical expression. Thus Riggs avoids atomizing the message into individual statements.

Both *Looking for Langston* and *Tongues Untied* are decentralized and subjective but simultaneously non-individualized representations. They are highly stylized, aesthetisized, self-conscious and emotional films. Both are concerned with what could be called "Cultural Apartheid," in the way they address the dominant cultures' segregation of other cultural phenomena. A policy of which leads to a situation where certain groups in society hardly figure in the visual archive and are consequently absent from official memory (Marks 1994).

Looking for Langston and *Tongues Untied* both belong to a large group of films, which are created in what Bill Nichols (1994) calls the performative mode. This mode is the fifth, added to the four existing modes of representation in the documentary film, which Nichols introduced in 1991 in *Representing Reality*. Nichols defines modes as historical and analytic tools to systematize fundamental ways of representing reality in the documentary genre. The fifth mode is designated as performative in *Blurred Boundaries* (1994), to attach importance to the staged and mediated in films. Performing documentary material implies a separation from traditional documentary methods, but it does not necessarily entail an outright rejection. As Nichols points out, in recent years there has been a blurring of boundaries in the field of documentary. It is becoming more and more difficult to distinguish documentaries from experimental films, art films and feature films. As such performative documentaries are films that stage and fictionalize and put personal experience, often physical and visceral, at the center.

In *Representing Reality* Nichols stated that it is difficult to avoid the term realism when trying to define the documentary genre. "Along with the more specific matters of perspective and commentary, personal style and rhetoric, realism is the set of conventions and norms for visual representation which virtually every documentary text addresses" (Nichols 1991: 165). Whereas four years later, in *Blurred Boundaries*, when delineating the new mode, he suggests that

Performative documentary suspends realist representation. Performative documentary puts the referential aspect of the message in brackets, under suspension. Realism finds itself deferred, dispersed, interrupted, and postponed. These films take the proposition that it is possible to know difference differently. Realist epistemology comes under question and under siege (Nichols 1994: 97).

But why this paradoxical duality between disrupting the documentary genre and at the same time paying tribute to it? Nichols traces this move to a need to disrupt and disturb the discourse of knowledge to which the documentary film belongs. The performative poses questions about the possibility for knowledge, and displays how we construct it. What counts as sufficient or necessary knowledge? Such questioning defies the close links that documentary filmmakers have traditionally sought with "the discourses of sobriety."

Documentary film has a kinship with other non-fictional systems that together make up what we may call the discourses of sobriety. Science, economics, politics, foreign policy, education, religion, welfare (...) Discourses of sobriety are sobering because they regard their relation to the 6real as direct, immediate, transparent. Through them power exerts itself. Through them things are made to happen (Nichols 1991: 4).

And when the organizing backbone of documentary, like other discourses of sobriety, is to present an argument about the historical world, it is very disturbing to have films that not only thematicize the production of knowledge but also challenge and hinder the possibility of serving as providers of knowledge qua their formal expression. Thus, performance is exactly what characterizes the enunciation of *Tongues Untied* and *Looking for Langston* which are difficult to understand from a traditional documentary audience's perspective. "They seem comprehensible more as fictions or formal experiments than as documentaries" (Nichols1994: 97). At the same time, they do not represent a denial of the real at all.

Although many current films defy realist representation without disclaiming access to the real, Nichols does not suggest what may be common ground for these critiques. The reason for this could be that his selection of films delineating the performative mode also includes films that have well-known styles of enunciation but touch on alternative, anthropological themes such as *Forest of Bliss* by Robert Gardner and *Cannibal Tours* by Dennis O'Rourke. These filmmakers subscribe to the documentary genre rather than the art film in order to place their films in a discourse of knowledge about the real world. Their goal is to call attention to the filmed world and to unsettle and disturb our need to understand what we see. These mechanisms are also at stake in the films

I am discussing here, though they do not represent the most pressing issues. I think that the underlying motivation for the change in documentary practice found in Riggs' and Julien's films is closely related to a different notion of representation of subjectivity. The critique of realism in my argument can subsequently be traced to a new perception of subjectivity.

Beyond essentialism

The American-Vietnamese director and theorist Trinh T. Minh-ha's theoretical work can point to important steps in understanding this new kind of subjectivity. The critique of the essentializing language of realism figures prominently in most of Trinh's work. In the following quote, she outlines the history of her line of thoughts while touching on a key issue in her work, namely the practice of leaving unfilled spaces in representation, thereby allowing the unrepresentable and the transient to manifest itself.

The belief that there can exist such a thing as an outside foreign to the inside, an objective, unmediated reality about which one can have knowledge once and for all, has been repeatedly challenged by feminist critics. For centuries, this belief has perniciously served to reduce the world to the dominant's own image, and the fight against "realism" is, in fact, not a denial of reality and of meaning, but rather, a determination to keep meaning creative, hence to challenge the fixity of realism as a style and an arrested form of representation (Trinh 1991:164).

Trinh refers to Claire Johnston's seminal article "Women's Cinema as Counter-Cinema" from 1973, where Johnston describes the goal of a counter-cinema as creating a consciousness of the gender ideology hidden in cinematic realism. The spectator must realize that what the camera grasps is not a phenomenal world but the "natural world" of a dominant ideology. It is the same act of making the otherwise hidden line of thought come out from behind the conventions of realism, which concerns Trinh in representations of cultural difference.

Realism as a form of representation defined by a specific attitude toward reality is widely validated to perpetuate the illusion of a stable world (even when it depicts sickness, poverty, and war), in which the same "how to do's" are confidently standardized and prescribed for different realities (Trinh 1994: 164).

This kind of representation contains a series of dangers, because as Trinh explains; "the stereotype is not a simplification because it is a false representation of a given reality. It is a simplification because it is an arrested, fixated form of representation" (Trinh 1991:163). The gap between the good intentions of giving voice and discriminating representation is not very wide if the filmmaker does not take into account that the style of realism contains an outlook on life, where the world is seen as stable and unchangeable.

Realism and the stereotype

How does one create a cinematic language that goes beyond the stereotype? Trinh suggests a cinematic method containing both a poetic documentary dimension and a deconstructive approach. Poetry is not understood as a site for constituting the subject or an aestheticizing practice of language.

Rather I am referring to the fact that language is fundamentally reflexive, and only in poetic language can one deal with meaning in a revolutionary way. For the nature of poetry is to offer meaning in such a way that it can never end with what is said or what is shown, destabilizing thereby the speaking subject and exposing the fiction of all rationalization. Roland Barthes astutely summed up this situation when he remarked that 'the real antonym of the 'poetic' is not the prosaic, but the stereotyped' (Trinh 1999: 216).

To be able to go beyond the fixed meaning of the stereotype, Trinh suggests a reflexive approach to the cinematic medium. First and foremost, one must not mistake the cinematic reality for phenomenal reality. Instead, one should uncover the techniques of production described as "ostranenie" techniques in Russian formalism. In this way she refers to a method where the unique texture and materiality of the cinematic reality is made apparent. Belief in the transparency of the form is "to stay in ideology." "Meaning can therefore be political only when it does not let itself be easily stabilized, and, when it does not rely on any single source of authority, but rather empties it, or decentralizes it" (Trinh 1991: 41). Trinh does not think that it is possible to either construct or exclude meaning. Instead she inserts *intervals* in her own films, creating an intermittent space in which the escaped meaning can be thematisized (Trinh 1991: 49).

The experiences of minorities who are repeatedly stereotypically represented often give rise to the wish to become visible in a personalized way and do so in the form of autobiographical expression. But as Trinh argues, the autobiographical is not the key to going beyond the stereotype, because the autobiography as a genre may easily isolate questions of gender and race to one person. The political message is hindered by this style of individualization, unless the autobiography expresses a singularity as well as a collectivity. "It's diverse forms can favor the emergence of new forms of subjectivity: the subjectivity of a non-I/plural I, which is different from the sovereign I (subjectivism) or the non-subjectivity of the all-knowing I (objectivism)" (Trinh 1991: 192).

The *interval* highlights the relationship between the personal and the political, the public and private, in line with the politicizing of the personal in feminism. The interval activates the field of tension between otherwise rigid categories such as fiction and documentary, the collective and the individual. According to Trinh the alternatives to the fixity of documentary realism, are films at the boundary between documentary and fiction that demand a constructive effort of the spectator and do not claim to represent reality exhaustively. The identity of the depicted remains in flux between several positions.

Creating the spectator

Even though Nichols is not preoccupied with political identity, as mentioned above, he has a very interesting discussion of the role of the spectator in the performative mode. In his argument he employs theoretical perspectives drawn from feminist film theory represented by Teresa de Lauretis as well as from Frederic Jameson's discussion of political representation.

A characteristic of the performative mode is the importance of raising consciousness in the spectator. Nichols compares this effort to the consciousness-raising strategies in the reflexive mode, which he traces back to documentary films from the 1960s and 1970s. In both types of representation, messages are created by a series of textual strategies rather than emerging from the historical world, and their consciousness-raising aspect is grounded in an attempt to develop a political aesthetics. As in Russian formalism, the reflexive and performative modes employ defamiliarizing techniques, as also suggested above by Trinh T. Minh-ha. This points to aesthetic strategies that aim at removing the automated in the spectator's perception of reality, for instance by making the familiar seem strange and the strange familiar. Whereas the reflexive mode is preoccupied with displaying any referential message as being constructed, the performative mode directs our attention to the documentary epistemology. This effort is not employed to alienate us from the film, but rather to offer a different kind of spectatorial sensibility than normally experienced when watching documentaries. Performative films seem to suggest and evoke rather than explain and argue, whereby consciousness-raising works through the senses and identification. To explain this change of documentary practice, Nichols points out a paradox in the performative mode. At first glance these films are not referential while at the same time they pursue referential aims. "The referential aspect of the message that turns us toward the historical world is not abandoned (…) the indexical bond, which can also prove an indexical bind for the documentary form, remains operative but in a subordinated manner" (Nichols 1994: 98). It seems the historical world is pushed aside to make room for another matter. This matter would seem to be the importance of addressing the spectator in a different way.

Creating a social subjectivity

The spectator is called upon to be the anchor of the fabricated and stylized diegesis in the historical world. Nichols describes this invitation as the effort to give shape to a *social subjectivity* hereby drawing on Teresa de Lauretis' 1987 book *Technologies of Gender*. In line with the central position of spectatorship in feminist film theory de Lauretis discusses the possibility of a feminist subjectivity being created cross-genderly. Her book has very strong points, however Nichols only uses de Lauretis' ideas sporadically to delineate the political positioning of the spectator in the performative mode. First of all de Lauretis makes a clear distinction between feminine films and feministic films. The attempt to construct a new kind of subjectivity lies in the endeavor to create "femini-*stic*" films, meaning gender-political films rather than films documenting women's activities and lives.

The effort and challenge … is how to effect another vision: to construct other objects and subjects of vision, and to formulate the conditions of representability of another social subjectivity [...] The idea that *a film may address the spectator as female* (de Lauretis 1987: 137).

The gender political project lies in this idea of addressing the spectator as feminine regardless of sex. In other words, in the attempt to create a feminine position with a distinct cross-gender social subjectivity. In a discussion of *Looking for Langston* and *Tongues Untied* one might expand this point to include other differences than gender such as sexual and racial difference. The creation of a social subjectivity should then be considered to work cross-sexually and racially as well.

Nichols combines the idea of a social subjectivity with Jameson's notion of *figuration* which he uses to conceptualize a political representation that is not based on an unchangeable definition of class. Instead, figuration emerges when class-conflict "can be grasped imaginatively as well as conceptually" (Jameson 1977: 716). The term conceptualizes the notion of letting a political structure come into view by means of aesthetic strategies, rather than succumbing to an abstract definition of underlying structures. According to Nichols the precondition for a concrete representation of any political message is that the films create an existential situation. A concept that points to the ability to place the combination of personal and collective conditions of life in a concrete and tangible form: "[…] the possibility of giving figuration to a social subjectivity that joins the abstract to the concrete, the general to the particular, the individual to the collective, and the political to the personal, in a dialectic, transformative way" (Nichols1994: 94). Nichols is here pointing to two dimensions – one found in the textuality of the films and the other extra-diegetic, namely in relation to the spectator.

Tongues Untied addresses and affects the spectator directly, in an extremely musical and rhythmic formalist style. In the film we "experience" what the participants must have experienced numerous times – being named condescendingly by their surroundings a misfit and abject. In a close-up a man looks us straight in the eye and raps a story about recognizing his own sexuality. Rapping how he as a teenager learned how to kiss from a friend, until the brother of the friend found out and called them "homo." The man (Marlon Riggs himself) asks, "What's a homo?" and the brother answers, "faggot, freak, punk." In a rhythmical montage the rap is intercut with faces framed without eyes, and anonymous mouths and voices of the majority shouting sneering remarks such as, "Niggers go home" and "Uncle Tom." The individual becomes collective, just as the personal story harbors the political issues of being discriminated because of race and sexual observation. By means of the editing, the spectator is deeply affected by the insults shouted at the characters, which seem to be shouted at us, too. The anger generated by the montage makes the theme of untying the tongues even more pressing.

Looking for Langston uses a more indirect approach of affecting the spectator. Less activist and more suggestive, it invites us into an erotic, sensual and melancholic experience. The spectator is involved in a fantasy of Langston Hughes' search for the ideal of a black male beauty via conventions of fictional storytelling. When an actor looking like the young Langston Hughes spots an attractive man in a nightclub they exchange flirting glances. Through eyeline matches we come to identify with the man falling in love. He fantasizes of windswept beaches and secluded bedrooms but the images of dream and desire are interrupted by images of scary alleyways where men making love show the seedy reality of illegal sexuality. As the contemporary poet Essex Hemphill puts it "we are the hunger of shadows […] in the dark we don't have to say I love you." The fantasy sequences make us experience how love becomes brutal when it is forbidden. We experience this without the film ever resorting to explanations.

Both films address our feelings through different aesthetic strategies. Both film seem to try to encompass the gulf between discriminating surroundings and suppressed erotic and romantic fantasies. Focusing on black homosexuality now and then the films not only represent a phenomenal world but also inner experiences and emotional states caused by political conditions.

The idea of the performative mode as the proper strategy to create a social subjectivity via a figuration of racial and sexual identity is a rewarding approach to the sensual and suggestive appearance of *Tongues Untied* and *Looking for Langston,* and it provides us with good tools to understand the identity politics of both films. In this view, the consciousness of the spectator is the real object of the films, more so than phenomena in the historical world. The films address the historical world and the spectator in a process that simultaneously attempts to go beyond stereotyping and distanciating explanations in relation to the spectator as well as to the social world.

The construction of a social subjectivity is concerned with the creation of a spectatorial sensibility/susceptibility towards issues that would otherwise seem to be abstractions and beyond known experiences. *Tongues Untied* and *Looking for Langston* are both concerned with the processes of identification while sharpening our sense of social conditions and political issues. The decentered subjects in *Tongues Untied* and *Looking for Langston* are part and parcel of the endeavors to address the spectator. The subject is never exhaustively or ultimately defined just as there is not one single message in the films. The spectator cannot limit the course of the film or statements to a single individual, but must make connections between the many positions which will inevitably demand an investigation of the spectators own experiences.

Consequently we must localize the suspension of the documentary realism diegetically as well as extra-diegetically. Teresa de Lauretis' emphatic differentiation between the "femini-stic" and the feminine film seems to me to facilitate an understanding of the change in documentary practice I have been preoccupied with in dealing with the performative mode and *Tongues Untied* and *Looking for Langston*. The feministic film moves the question of gender differences from the level of meaning to that of form, representational strategies. The decentering of the subject within a discourse of realism can be viewed as an attempt to create a new social vision dealing with racial and sexual differences.

References

de Lauretis, Teresa. 1987. *Technologies of Gender*. Bloomington and Indianapolis: Indiana University Press.

Kaplan, Ann. 1988. "Theories and Strategies of Feminist Documentary". In *New Challenges for Documentary Film*, edited by Alan Rosenthal. Berkeley, Los Angeles & London: University of California Press.

Marks, Laura U. 2000. *The Skin of the Film: Intercultural Cinema, Embodiment, and the Senses*. Durham and London: Duke University Press.

Nichols, Bill. 1991. *Representing Reality*. Bloomington and Indianapolis: Indiana University Press.

Nichols, Bill. 1994. *Blurred Boundaries. Questions of Meaning in Contempoary Culture*. Bloomington and Indianapolis: Indiana University Press.

Jameson, Frederic. 1985. "Class and Allegory in Comtempoary Mass Culture: *Dog Day Afternoon* as a Political Film". In *Movies and Methods vol.II, An Anthology*, edited by Bill Nichols. Berkeley, Los Angeles & London: University of California Press.

Stam, Robert et al. 1985. "Colonialism, Racism, and Representation: An Introduction". In *Movies and Methods. vol II, An Anthology*, edited by Bill Nichols. Berkeley, Los Angeles & London: University of California Press.

Trinh T. Minh-ha. 1991. *Framer Framed*. New York and London: Routledge.

Trinh T. Minh-ha. 1994. *When the Moon waxes Red, Representation, Gender and Cultural Politics*. New York and London: Routledge.

Trinh T. Minh-ha. 1999. *Cinema Interval*. New York and London: Routledge.

Stig Hjarvard

Simulated Conversations.
The Simulation of Interpersonal
Communication in Electronic Media

> *Man is an organism with a wonderful and extraordinary past.*
> *He is distinguished from the other animals by virtue of the fact*
> *that he has elaborated what I have termed extensions of his or-*
> *ganism. By developing his extensions, man has been able to im-*
> *prove or specialize various functions. The computer is an exten-*
> *sion or part of the brain, the telephone extends the voice, the*
> *wheel extends the legs and feet. Language extends experience in*
> *time and space while writing extends language. Man has elab-*
> *orated his extensions to such a degree that we are apt to forget*
> *that his humanness is rooted in his animal nature* (Edward T.
> Hall, 1969: 3).

The history of technological means of communication and of the
mass media can be seen as a continuous development during which
physical and biological limits on man's communicative capabilities
are steadily and increasingly overcome. In this sense, the media are
extensions or enhancements of the sensory system on the one
hand, and of spoken language and non-verbal communication on
the other.

As discussed in the above quotation by American anthropologist Edward T. Hall, our excitement over the transgression or lib-
eration from physical limitations causes us to forget that we still
have physical and biological roots. To a certain extent, these roots
make up the foundation and influence the design of our man-made
(i.e. social and technological) extensions of body, senses and communicative abilities. The types of communication that permit us to
transgress the limits of time and place are marked by non-extended
communication: interpersonal communication.

Against this backdrop, this article will put forward the follow-

227

ing argument. That interpersonal communication can be said to constitute a particularly important analogy, a fundamental form or matrix, for the development of technologically mediated forms of communication. On the one hand, the development of the media can be described as an attempt to overcome the limits of interpersonal communication. On the other hand new media also attempt to re-establish the characteristics of interpersonal communication in new forms. In each their own particular way, telephone, radio, television and computers provide an opportunity for users to take part in a kind of face-to-face communication over great distances.

The development of the media can also be described as an on-going innovation that builds on similarities between the various media and communicative formats. One medium serves as a model for the next and new media often contain old media, etc (Bolter and Grusin 1999, Carey 1989, McLuhan 1964). The telegraph was modeled on physical transportation, first and foremost the railway network. Film was modeled on theatre. TV was modeled on radio. New techniques are socially and culturally marked by their predecessors, institutionally as well as in terms of content and form. However, each of the new media also draws upon features of interpersonal communication.

Interpersonal communication (here taken to mean face-to-face, verbal or non-verbal communication between two or more people localized in the same time and space) is a kind of fundamental communicative form, the main features of which are mastered by the members of a given language community. Non-verbal communication is in some ways universally intelligible. Of course this does not mean, that communication is not also culturally determined and variable within a given language community. However, it is true of all people that interpersonal communication comes first in terms of socialization and that forms of communication based on media presuppose the mastery of interpersonal communication.

Technologically mediated communication frequently consists of various partial elements of this fundamental form, the subcomponents of which undergo varying degrees of modification in relation to the point of departure. For instance, the introductory greetings in a radio program resemble the opening of conversation

228

in face-to-face interactions, but the sentence structure, intonation etc are often changed to accommodate specific radio talk formats. Another example is the oralization of language in email messages. Because of the immediate, on-line nature of the medium, email messages are typically written using spoken language in contrast to the tone of a traditional letter. However, it is nevertheless a written message without aural cues, only resembling some features of oral speech. Technology also allows for the manipulation of subcomponents of interpersonal communication. For instance, the volume control on a telephone allows the user to change the voice level in the receiver, thereby manipulating the user's sense of proximity in telephone conversations.

The view of media history presented here may conjure recollections of McLuhan's history of media development in *Understanding Media. The Extensions of Man* (1964). According to McLuhan, the media can be seen as extensions or enhancements of senses and speech, the logic of which leads to the re-establishment of an original, pre-modern "interpersonal" state: the global village. Although thought provoking, McLuhan's presentation is misleading in many ways. In spite of its technological optimism (or perhaps precisely because of it), McLuhan's presentation shares the same romanticism that characterizes some of today's postmodern celebrations of the Internet's potential for new forms of community building. Robins (1999) has rightly argued that "for the most part, the new techno-communitarianism is conservative and nostalgic: it is about the imagined recovery and restoration of some original bond" (Robins 1999: 45). The fact that modern media adopt various forms of interpersonal communication does not imply that the fundamental form of interpersonal communication is recreated. Technological means of communication do not return us to the small talk and well-known world of the village. Instead they help us to participate in the enormously widespread – and mediated – social networks of a highly urbanized society.

Another problem with McLuhan's theory is the level of abstraction at which he suggests media influence society. It is the medium as such that changes society. The inherent characteristics of a new medium force themselves upon society. However, these characteristics may, at least to some extent, be a result of the ways in which technology has adapted to society and not the other way around. In other words, McLuhan overlooks the fact that the historical development of the media must be seen, to a large extent, against the backdrop of the influences of institutional, cultural, psychological, and technological factors.

Contrary to McLuhan's grand scale theorizing, the present study tries to discuss the relationship between interpersonal and mediated communication at a more detailed level that focuses on the ways in which communicative features of electronic media have accomodated to the social and psychological usage of media in everyday life. As such, the present study is inspired by Horton and Wohl's (1986) seminal study of the media's potential for creating "para-social interaction." If the media are capable of creating such a sense of interpersonal co-existence across time and space, what are the communicative features of media that makes such phenomena possible?

Simulating communicative forms

If there is indeed a significant difference between interpersonal communication and technologically mediated forms of communication, how can we claim that media communication has interpersonal communication as a fundamental base or source of inspiration? The connection should be sought at the level of *form*. It is characteristic of modern media that they simulate the components of interpersonal communication in various ways in terms of communicative forms of expression and forms of interaction with users or the audience, i.e., in terms of the user interface.

When the development of media technologies and the design of software and interfaces draw on forms of interpersonal communication, it is because this fundamental form is recognizable, understandable and familiar to a larger audience. As such, simulation of face-to-face communication serves several interrelated purposes in mediated communication. First, recognizability serves cognitive purposes. *Comprehensibility* is aided by a similarity to the fundamental communicative form. Second, it contributes to a general feeling of *ontological security* on the part of the user (Giddens

1991), because relatively abstract communication systems such as radio, television or the computer appear to be recognizable and similar to the forms of "immediate" and natural interpersonal communication. Third, it provides the media with a *"transparent immediacy"* (Bolter and Grusin 1999). In the same way that new media remodel older media forms through representational strategies that tend to make the medium invisible, mass media use aspects of interpersonal communication in order to make the media interface transparent. Fourth, it enhances the sense of *embodied presence* in a mediated encounter (Biocca 1997, Lombard and Ditton 1997), thereby intensifying the feeling of being a real participant in the communicative exchange. Fifth, it invites *social and natural responses* to the media (Reeves and Nass 1996), allowing media to be integrated into the *habitual practices* of everyday life supplying media usage with an element of *sociability* (Scannell 1996).

The media contribute to, and are themselves a result of, the technological and institutional transformation of modern society and therefore do not in any way bring us back to a more "original" communicative state. But in order to ensure comprehensibility and create trust and sociability across time and space (Hjarvard 2000) that are crucial tasks in highly complex societies, mediated communication must draw on the characteristics of interpersonal communication. Increasingly this also becomes apparent in media *contents.* Television especially seems to have become increasingly dominated by certain genres (soaps, talk shows, etc), the main content of which is not so much socially relevant information as it is the display of face-to-face interaction. Other media have also adopted for these contents, such as chat lines on the telephone or the Internet and various phone-in programs on the radio, in which there is a constant flux between music and casual conversation.

Since mediated communication has a number of similarities with interpersonal communication, we can use several theories and analytical methods from the area of interpersonal communication in order to shed light on mediated communication. This is the case, for example, with non-verbal communication theories and related analysis methods which, with some modification, can be used in the analysis of visual communication in film and on TV. Likewise, methods for analyzing conversation can also be used in order to understand for example radio, TV, and the telephone.

This kind of transfer of theory and method obviously requires careful consideration of the apparent differences between interpersonal and mediated communication. In some cases the transfer of theory and method will primarily serve to illuminate differences rather than similarities. For example, the study of turn-taking in conversational analysis will require modification before it can be used in mass communication analysis. In return, turn-taking analysis will be able to contribute heuristically to clarifying the differences between social conversation in the living room, on the telephone, and through a computer (Hutchby 2001).

The point of the present argument is not to deny or downplay the differences between interpersonal and mediated communication. However, the central argument is that we are *not* dealing with radically different forms of communication. Differences are primarily empirical-analytical problems. In the following I will discuss some of these. None of the media has its own unique language that requires translation in order to be understood and interpreted. When someone whispers, shouts or weeps on the radio, it should typically be understood in the same way as in non-mediated interpersonal communication. Therefore we are not talking about a specific TV, computer or radio semiotics marked by radical differences in expression as compared to other types of human communication or perception.

Although there are differences between the interpersonal and medial expression systems, the differences reflect an inner continuity. Several forms of expression in the media are to be understood as modifications, abstractions and formalizations, in short, *artificial versions* of interpersonal forms of expression. As such, mediated communication can be considered a *partial simulation* of interpersonal communication. However, before pursuing this analysis, it will be useful to consider how better to understand the concept of simulation.

Simulation

From an etymological point of view, it can be noted that simulation stems from the Latin verb "simulo," meaning "I imitate" or "I pretend." Related to this is the Latin noun "simulacrum," which has the positive meaning "image" or "work of art" as well as the more negative meaning "shadow" or "reflection."

When looking at language history, an old work of reference like *Salomonsen's Encyclopedia* [Salomonsens Konversationsleksikon 1926] defines simulation as being associated with deceit, malingering and the like, in relation to sickness. More recent encyclopedias emphasize a somewhat different meaning, i.e., the scientific or pedagogical use of simulations. For example, *The Great Nordic Encyclopedia* [Store Nordiske Leksikon 1980] states that simulation is "purposeful modeling of complex processes in order to study their effects" (445). In recent post-modern (media) theory, simulation is included in the characterization of a particular post-modern cultural state, in which traditional time and space relations are detached from one another, and in which the referential relationship between symbolic representation and social and physical reality have disappeared. In the post-modern context, meanings of simulation such as malingering, synthetic, pseudo-reality, fiction, etc, are particularly common. In such theories, the mass media is often referred to as an exponent of or even the cause of the emergence of a state of simulacrum.

On the whole, the different meanings of simulation can be placed along a line of negative vs. positive. The negative meanings emphasize the synthetic, the reduced and the insincere. The more positive or neutral meanings interpret simulation as emulation under artificial circumstances, a partial modeling or recreation that may be useful and productive in varying ways. In the present discussion of mediated communication as partial simulation, I take my point of departure from the latter meaning of simulation. In this sense, simulation has nothing to do with being insincere or creating fiction. I will argue that simulation, along with analogy and metaphorical projection, is an indispensable cognitive and psychological creative mechanism that we constantly use in order to make meaning. In this sense, a simulation is not a faint reflection of the real world, but instead a mechanism through which we can achieve an adequate understanding of the world.

Simulation is also a psycho-social mechanism through which we can develop and test adequate mental schemata or repertoires for social action in new interactive contexts. New communication technologies form the basis for changed patterns of interaction. If technology is to facilitate meaningful interaction, relevant action schemata must be developed. The interplay between technology, interactive patterns and action schemata is of course a mutual process in that both the development and the more specific design of technology are marked by the models and schemata that researchers and other communities work with in defining the meaning of the concrete developmental activity.

I have already mentioned analogy, metaphor and simulation as mechanisms for development, use and understanding of mediated communication. Let me now attempt to specify the main thread connecting these three concepts. Traditionally, analogy is a (logical) conclusion made on the basis of similarity. When two elements are similar to one another in one way, they are similar in other ways as well. The formation of analogy is a universal as well as efficient mechanism for creating new rules and meanings. For example, in the institutionalization of the media, with the advent of audio cassettes, legislators looked to the laws applying to gramophone records, and this was typically extended to cover audio cassettes due to the close resemblance of these media.

Like analogy, metaphor is also based on an element of similarity, albeit indirectly. The metaphor describes a subject matter using words or concepts from another subject matter: Life is described as a journey, argumentation as a battle, beauty as a field of flowers, etc. It is typical of the metaphor that something more abstract or general is interpreted through words and concepts representing something more concrete or specific (Lakoff and Johnson 1980). The rhetorical and poetic power of the metaphor originates in difference. A particular state is perceived from the point of view of some other very different context. But the basis for a meaningful coupling of two very different domains of reality is the existence

234

of a similarity between them. This may be a similarity of structure, process, surface characteristics, etc.

Seen in this light, the difference between analogy and metaphor is a matter of degree rather than of principle. In analogy, one particular state is understood in light of another particular state. In metaphor, one thing is understood in terms of the premises of the other, from the point of view of simple similarity, even if the two are very different at the outset.

Research on analogy and metaphor has typically been reserved for rhetoric, linguistic and literary analysis, and has often been limited to questions about the stylistic functions of analogy and metaphor. However, Lakoff and Johnson have argued that metaphor plays a much larger role. They view metaphor as a fundamental cognitive mechanism through which we understand the world by way of language. Metaphor is not only a linguistic exterior or a poetic "as if" exercise. On the contrary, it is the very way in which we understand a phenomenon. When reading in the newspaper that the economy has come to a standstill, that there is a risk of overheating in the building sector, or that politicians will adjust public expenses, the economy is metaphorically understood as a machine. But this is not only a phrase. Our actual understanding of the phenomenon of economy is governed by this machine metaphor. Moreover, Lakoff and Johnson point out that the way we speak about specific phenomena within the various fields of human experience has its origin in a finite set of central metaphors.

Johnson (1987) continues his efforts to discover the basic metaphors of language use and thus for comprehension. He argues that there are several non-propositional schemata that form the basis of linguistic and more complex metaphorical formations of meaning. On the one hand, these schemata can be referred to as abstractions of specific core structures in meaning and the formation of meaning. On the other hand, the point is also that they are based on fundamental experiences of space and motion. The primary starting-point of these so-called *image schemata* is man's sensory orientation and motion in a physical space. Examples of such schemata are "path-goal," "blocking of motion," "the body is a container," etc. In contrast to linguistic expressions, these schemata have a non-propositional character, and they have an analogous and figurative form.

Having a non-propositional character means that these schemata are not in themselves sufficient or substantial enough to form the basis of meaningful statements. Thus, Johnson calls them Gestalts, that contain sufficient inner coherence to support meaning and play a delimited role in relation to semantic fields. Image schemata are basic metaphors that are projected onto a given subject matter. Therefore, they have a structuring effect and contribute to the production of a higher, true propositional meaning.

Lakoff's and Johnson's work with metaphor and cognition is interesting in this context because they make plausible the notion that metaphor (and analogy) are fundamental mechanisms of meaning. Therefore, this provides a more scientific basis for the claim that the development of technologically mediated forms of communication is a question of constantly transferring cognitive frameworks from one medium to another, as basic perceptions and experiences of older media are projected onto the understanding of new media.

Moreover, Johnson's work with pre-propositional conceptual schemata is interesting in relation to visual media, in that it largely consists of pictures of people's motion in space and of their non-verbal communication. A number of elements in non-verbal communication are characterized by their pre-propositional character such as gestures, distance between actors and objects that rarely have an unambiguous and propositional meaning. It is only in connection to linguistic statements that they become truly meaningful or more specifically that they support meaning. We can see certain aspects of gestures, facial expressions as well as the positions of people and objects in space as being based on a few basic, in some cases innate, conceptual schemata, that both help to structure higher linguistic meanings and act to support them.

Both analogy and metaphor denote a transfer of meaning from one semantic domain or field of experience to another. However, these concepts can also be taken to describe some pragmatic aspects of communication, such as the communicative framework through which communication is considered to be meaningful to the receiver. The concept of simulation can then be used to move the notion of analogy and metaphor into the domain of pragmatism. Interaction that is simulated through a medium can be construed as being a way to define *a specific social interaction through analogy*. A simulation is a realized or performed analogy, an analogy in action.

The simulation of presence created when a TV studio host turns directly to the viewer helps to define the specific act of communication for the viewer. This is a personalized interaction in which the studio host's facial expressions, gestures, diction, etc, in combination with picture framing, lighting and the speech itself, help to specify for the viewer what she should expect from the current program. In order to understand a program, the viewer must accept this simulation as meaningful, since it expresses and establishes the direct intention of the program.

The return of interpersonal communication

As mentioned, media development is also characterized by analogy on an internal level, i.e., in relation to form and content. The analogy to interpersonal communication can be found on the one hand, on a higher level where media communication as a whole resembles interpersonal communication, as when the TV host turns directly to the viewer. On the other hand it can be found on a more detailed level, where components of interpersonal communication have taken over. One interesting aspect of the history of technologically mediated communication is that it makes apparent the fact that interpersonal communication consists of a number of separate components that are transferred to the media and manipulated in particular ways.

To create an overview of this development, table 1 presents an outline of the characteristics of central, technologically mediated forms of communication in relation to aspects of interpersonal communication. Forms of communication are considered in terms of the following four criteria:

Table 1. Characteristics of central forms of communication.

	Mutual exchange	Inter-active	Time: displacement	Time: simultaneity	Point to point	Mass medium	Non-verbal expression
Face-to-face	x	x		x			x
Hand writing	x		x		x		
Printed book			x			x	
Telegraph	x			x	x		
Telephone	x	x		x	x		x
Gramophone			x			x	x
Film			x			x	x
Radio			x	x		x	x
Television			x	x		x	x
Computer	x	x	x	x	x	x	x

Forms of communication are considered in terms of the following four criteria:

1. *Mutual exchange* of communication, including *interactivity*. Mutuality means that the communication, as with non-mediated communication, allows for an exchange on the part of the participants. The *interactive* possibility allows for continuous, mutual exchange in which a participant can intervene and change the flow of communication. Thus, writing letters involves mutuality but not interactivity, since each letter must be written and mailed before the other party is able to respond. However, telephoning comprises both mutuality and interactivity where constant interventions in the process of communication are possible.
2. The *time* of communication: Do the sending and receiving of messages coincide in time as in interpersonal communication, or is there typically a delay between sending and receiving?
3. The network structure of the communication: There are two different basic models here: *point-to-point* communication, which requires a network system in which all points can potentially be linked to one another, as in the case of the telephone. The other model is the *mass media network*, in which one point is linked to all other points in a one-way transmission.

238

4. The presence of *non-verbal* elements in the communication. Non-verbal elements are understood as visually accessible expressions such as gestures, facial expressions, distance markings, and bodily contact. Auditory elements are also included to the extent that they have a non-propositional or pre-propositional character, for example acoustics, tone, and loudness of voice.

When a broad outline of media history is considered, two main phases can be discerned. In the first phase, handwriting and later letterpress printing and the media resulting from them (books, newspapers, magazines, etc) were used to transgress distances and maintain communication across time. By virtue of being written, these media are characterized in a number of ways by their movement away from the sensory characteristics of interpersonal communication. Although the invention of the telegraph portended a new epoch of mass media, the telegraph was in certain respects more similar to written media. The telegraph allowed for a mutual but non-interactive point-to-point communication that did not contain non-verbal expressions. The subsequent sound and picture media, from the photograph to the computer, all have in common that they through sounds and pictures bring back a number of non-verbal aspects to communication. If we disregard film and the gramophone, there is also the possibility of temporal simultaneity in communication, i.e., a characteristic of interpersonal communication. The printed media (newspaper, books etc) attempt to adapt to this development, in particular through visualizations that make places and people more concrete, as in interpersonal communication, but also through a change in writing style that makes written text resemble spoken language (e.g. "oral" headlines in tabloid newspapers (Barnhurst 1994)). The media of the second phase, thus, come closer to the characteristics of interpersonal communication.

It is also characteristic of newer media such as radio and TV, that they are *flexible* in permitting more manipulation of individual factors such as the possibility of both time shifts and simultaneity. In this regard, the computer can be said to represent the essence of this development, since it permits all aspects of communication to appear in many different combinations. The computer is developing into a kind of super or universal medium that integrates the functions of all other media, permits manipulation of the single components and characteristics of other media, and of interpersonal communication as well.

Framework for interaction

In communication and media theory, the difference between point-to-point communication and mass communication is often emphasized as a crucial dividing line, as these two forms of communication have quite different features and possibilities. The lack of individual adjustment and feedback characterizing the mass media does, of course, make a difference. However, it should be pointed out that the institutions responsible for mass communication constantly make efforts to compensate for the lack of feedback by anticipating the processes of reception. For example, Scannell (1994, 1996) has worked with the concept of communicative intentionality. He describes the forms of expression on radio and TV as being governed by a desire to show consideration for the audience, the same consideration that is shown between actors in interpersonal communication in regards to saving face. According to Scannell, mass communications show consideration and indeed care for the audience both in the sense that the external aspects of communication (e.g. program scheduling, degree of complexity) are adjusted to fit the receivers' disparate needs and conditions, and in the sense that the spirit of communication is marked by politeness and compliance.

One of the ways in which mass communication compensates for the lack of feed-back is by organizing the contents in terms of genre. In order to ensure an understanding of and correct expectations for TV's broadcasts for example, such broadcasts are produced within the framework of fixed genres. Goffman (1959) has pointed out that in the context of interpersonal encounters, negotiating and establishing the definition of the situation is decisive if the interaction is to be performed in a meaningful way. According to Palmer (1990) *genre* serves a similar function in mass communication as negotiation and establishment of the *situational definition* does in interpersonal communication, since the objective of both is to establish the communicative framework. I would like to pursue this notion using a somewhat more detailed comparison of genre and situational definition, as outlined in table 2.

Table 2. Comparison of genre in mass communication to definition of situation in interpersonal encounter.

Definition of situation in interpersonal encounter	Genre in mass communication
Typical roles and expectations as to actors' intentions and behavior	Typical roles and expectations as to actors' intentions and behavior
Set of conventions for actors' style of behavior	Set of conventions for narrating style and representations of reality
Typical themes, conflicts and courses of interaction	Typical themes, conflicts and courses of events in the represented universe
Often a specific institution in which the type of interaction takes place	Communication often takes place in a specific institution and thematisizes specific institutions
Negotiation of situation between actors along the way	Continuous cueing of the receiver's expectations as to development of communication and represented universe

A media genre and a situational definition both serve the purpose of indicating what kind of communicative interaction we are dealing with. This involves specification of the typical distribution of roles and expectations in regards to intentions, behavior and particular style of behavior. This typically also involves a demarcation of themes, conflicts and courses of events that can be expected to occur during the interaction. These characteristics are usually organized institutionally, for example as particular types of behavior, themes, courses of events, etc and belong to specific institutional frameworks.

The clearest difference between genre and situational definition as seen through Goffman, is the absence of an actual negotiation surrounding the establishment of the framework. However, like the situational definition, the establishment of genre is not static or permanently established at the beginning of, e.g., a radio broadcast. It also constitutes a process in the form of a continuous cueing of the receiver's expectations throughout the entire broadcast.

This lack of opportunities for feedback is not just absent from mass communication, but it also constitutes a *relief* for the viewer. The receiver is not responsible in the same way as the sender for the course of the communication. On the one hand this relief means that the receiver can enter and exit the communication as he pleases. On the other hand, it means that there is a greater possibility for him to *concentrate* on the media message. As opposed to the situation in interpersonal communication, the receiver is not supposed to come up with responses in the right places or at the right times, but can instead devote himself to the sender's message. In this light, we might hypothesize that this feeling of relief is very important in attracting people to mass media – across specific media and genres. By using the mass media, people are able to participate in social communication without having any responsibility for the outcome.

The lack of responsibility can also involve an *aesthetization* of the communication. This absence of a chance to respond and thus to act linguistically, creates the foundation for an aesthetic attitude towards mediated communication that is not permitted in an interpersonal encounter. It is important for the sender of the message to be aware of this aesthetic attitude and the increased attention it brings because it requires a modification of the sender's message in relation to customary interpersonal standards. For example, in visual mass media, gestures and facial expressions must be highly formalized and moderated in order not to appear exaggerated or to completely distract the receiver's attention from the intended message. In an interpersonal meeting, none of the participants in the situation itself are able to scrutinize another party's gestures and facial expressions or view them according to more aesthetic criteria. In a TV broadcast, gestures and facial expressions must be moderated because the receiver is able to attentively follow every gesture or muscle contraction in the face.

The importance of body distance

In the following, I will try to show more specifically how forms of expression from interpersonal communication are transferred to mediated communication. I will focus on how body placement in interpersonal communication forms a point of departure for portrayals of people in visual communication, particularly how it forms a basis for conventions used when framing pictures.

The anthropologist Edward T. Hall (1959, 1969) is the pioneer in the area of "proxemics", which deals with the use of physical space in social interaction. Based on observations of human behavior, he points out that the varying distances between people are associated with different basic meanings. He identifies four distances, referred to as intimate, personal, social-consultive and public distance. Each of these can be further subdivided into a close and a half-close distance, resulting in a total of eight different distance types. Each of the four fundamental types is associated with a particular set of sensory, motor and communicative possibilities that together form a whole and provide character to the interaction taking place at the distance in question.

Table 3 provides a simplified presentation of Hall's own, more detailed scheme (Hall 1969: 126-127). As can be seen, each of the four fundamental types is characterized by a specific kinetics, tone of voice/audition/form of speech, body heat and odor, and sight. Note that access to a particular type of information *per se*, particularly the amount of detail, provides information about the type of relationship and the interaction between the people involved. If you are talking to someone and can see the finer details of her or his eyelashes, you not only get information about the eyelashes but you also understand that the interaction has an intimate character. The particular types of distance are not only determined by the degree of detail in the information they provide, but they are also a result of the opportunities for action that they naturally open up. This does not imply, for example, that touching will occur just because there is a personal or intimate interaction; but the possibility for touching is in and of itself enough to signal a particular interactional characteristic.

The different distances are, as mentioned, associated with meaning. But even if it is possible to give them specific names (intimate, personal, etc), the distances must be said to have a nonpropositional character, thereby correlating Johnson's image schemata. A given distance is rarely enough to define a situation on its own, since among other things, each of the single distances may mean something very different during a concrete interaction. An intimate distance can thus be used for both pleasurable contact (such as sex) and hostile behavior (such as aggression). A social or public distance can be used to express a low degree of involvement as well as to pay someone a high degree of respect.

Table 3. Simplified presentation of Hall's typology of distance in interpersonal interaction based on Edward T. Hall: *The Hidden Dimension: 126-127.*

Type of distance (meters)	Intimate (0 – 0,5)		Personal (0,5 – 1,2)		Social-consultive (1,2 – 3,0)		Public (3,0 –)	
	Close	Not close	Close	Not close	Close	Not close	Close	Not close
Kinetics	Touch is easy and hard to avoid	Occasional touch can be avoided	Two people barely have enough elbow room	Touch is possible by stretching out hands	Possible to pass objects by stretching out hand	Physical contact through objects not possible		
Tone of voice, audition, form of speech	Whispers are clearly heard	Soft voice Intimate speaking style	Conventional modified voice Casual or consultive style of speech			Normal conversation not possible	Loud voice when talking to a group	Strong tone of voice. Frozen speaking style
Body heat and odor	Heat and odor sensed	Heat seldom noticed	Body odor noticed	Body odor presents a social problem				
Sight	Vision blurred or distorted	Details fully visible and enlarged	Half of face fills central field of vision	Gaze must be moved to see other body parts	Peripheral vision includes whole body	Peripheral vision includes others present	Peripheral vision includes several people present	Accommodative convergence ends; objects and people appear "flat"

244

Visual mass media (film, TV, photography) consist of images of the locations of people and objects and movements through space. These pictures may be so-called objective shots, i.e., neutral pictures in which people and objects can be seen in a physical environment. Here, the viewer is able to use the distance typology very directly. Interpreting meaning by observing the distances between two or more people and objects on the screen is basically similar to how it is done in real world encounters.

In so-called subjective shots, where the distance between camera and objects and picture framing in one way or another express a point of view, we see Hall's distance typology integrated into picture framing conventions. As both Tuchman (1980) and Meyrowitz (1986) have suggested, the choice of frame in a photograph, film or TV picture can be seen as a choice of distance that at the same time signals a particular relationship between the depicted object-person and the subject, whom the camera eye represents. Parallel to the range of interpersonal distances (intimate/close to public/non-close) there is thus the range of possible picture frames (ultra-close, close-up, medium close-up, medium and long shot). It is interesting to note that in this regard, the typologization of picture frames in instruction manuals for TV or film production is often built up around how many people and which parts of the body are visible in the picture (e.g.Thorsen and Møller 1990).

Thus, against the background of Hall's typology, choice of frame makes a difference. Going from medium-close to close changes the nature of the receiver's relationship to the depicted person from social to personal. The receiver is brought so close to the depicted person that they would be able to touch one another in the real world. Moreover, being close enough to touch is an important threshold that changes how we can express sympathy or exercise authority. Likewise, close-ups and ultra-close ups pictures bring the receiver into intimate visual contact with the depicted person. In the real world, this would normally imply certain rules for behavior and emotions, such as a high degree of empathy, intimacy, etc. Lombard (1995) has substantiated these assumptions through a series of experiments with variable TV screen sizes showing that the receiver's emotional response to people depicted in images is changed by the screen size itself and, thus, by the size of the person depicted and the degree of detail in the image. Just as with choice of picture frame we can see choice of angle and perspective, from low angle to normal perspective to bird's-eye view, as a means of transferring particular experiences from real perception and cognition to a set of conventions for visual representation. It is possible to go much further in comparisons between real perception and cognition modalities and conventions for representation in visual communication. Along these lines, Grodal (1997) has given an account of the representation of emotional relationships in feature films, and Messaris (1997) has shed light on aspects of mechanisms of persuasion found in images used in advertisements.

Converging media – converging spaces

The spatial structures of interpersonal communication are not only reflected in the conventions of image framing but they also affect the patterns of media use and the development of new media. A concrete case – the convergence between various screen media – can illustrate this argument.

The convergence of various electronic media is to a great extent made possible by the spread of digital technology. However, the social and communicative forms that new media acquire as a result of media convergence are also based on the social and physical characteristics of media consumption and in particular, the interpersonal interaction which takes place in the home. In the past, when a typical home had only one telephone, one radio, one TV and one computer, each individual medium was able to define the social situation of reception. As a consequence, media reception was lifted out of other daily routines and became an independent activity concentrated on specific media such as listening to radio, watching television etc. Today, almost all rooms in a typical home are equipped with several media and different media are integrated into media "platforms" (radio, CD and tape recorder in one audio box; TV, teletext and playstation in a moving picture box; telephone, wap-service and videogame in a mobile phone, etc), and the structure of daily life has regained some authority over the various media. In the flow of life each individual uses media as part of ongoing social practices, including social interactions with other people. Media serve as the tools to the individual as a means of creating and specifying social situations such as waking up, relaxing with friends, being intimate with your lover, doing housework alone etc (Larsen 1998). Media use has perhaps always served to define social situations for the viewer, but the sheer increase in availability of media in every social setting has increased their flexibility as tools for individuals as a means of defining social situations for their own purposes.

Accordingly, media tend to converge with forms of communication that support such a flexible usage. In the case of screen media, a convergence of different media according to specific screen sizes seems to emerge. The screen size of the desktop computer is now similar to the size of a small TV, and the display of some mobile phones tends to grow towards the screen size of PDA's, Personal Digital Assistants. As such, different screen media increasingly adjust to physical and social characteristics of interpersonal interaction, i.e. the number of people involved in a typical interaction, the physical distances related to the kinds of social situations in which media use is embedded and so on. Once again, Edward T. Hall's typology of interactional distances has explanatory value. The ongoing convergence of screen media tends to favor four different screen sizes which correlate with Hall's distinctions between intimate, personal, social-consultive and public distance. Table 4 provides an overview of the characteristic features related to the use of different screen sizes. An important factor in choice of screen size is the question of interactivity, either with the screen itself or between users via the screen. Thus, practical and social rules of interaction between people (including appropriate distances) are transferred to the interaction between people and screen. As a general rule, smaller screens invite more interaction, and larger screens invite a usage that is more "passive."

Table 4. Screen size and characteristics of typical media usage.

Interaction			Reception
Intimate distance	Personal distance	Social distance	Public distance
The micro screen < 10"	The small screen 10 – 19"	The big screen 20 – 35"	The silver screen > 35"
Work and leisure. Small practical tasks, pastime, inter- personal communi- cation. For 1-2 persons. (Calendar, wap, SMS, email, telephony, chat, simple games, calculations)	Work and leisure. Alone or with others Larger tasks and small events. For 1-3 persons. (Internet, word processing, radio, TV, video advanced games, email)	Leisure. Shared experience and entertainment, major events. For 2-6 persons. (Feature films, rented videos, weekend enter- tainment, concerts, football games- matches)	Leisure. Shared and big experiences outside home and on weekday. For large groups of people without personal connec- tions. (Premiere movies, IMAX theatre).

The different screen sizes encourage specific kinds of communication practices, but human beings are flexible. Thus, due to practical circumstances like availability, people will use a micro screen for tasks that are better performed on a small screen and vice-versa. As such, the typology in table 4 is a proto-typical one and is not based on mutually exclusive definitions of social activities. However, the important point is that the development of media technologies and media platforms tends to take structural features of interpersonal communication into consideration. Interaction between media screen and media user thus come to resemble some of the physical and social characteristics of interpersonal communication.

Changes in interpersonal communication

Media develop in such a way that they are more and more able to use elements from interpersonal communication. However, the question is whether interpersonal communication itself is unchanged by the current development. In an interesting but brief essay, Schudson (1978) points out that interpersonal communication is typically made synonymous with a conversational ideal characterized by continuous feedback and equality, and by contents that are spontaneous and unique to a given situation. This conversational ideal is used as a yardstick for media communication, which rarely measures up.

However, according to Schudson, even if this conversational ideal has not been created by the mass media, they have at least helped it on its way. Much interpersonal communication, now as well as in the past, does not live up to this ideal but is instead based on various power relationships. It is unidirectional and extremely stereotypical. By virtue of their widespread democratic accessibility, the mass media have contributed to the notion that communication must be equal for everybody. Through their extensive treatment of every possible topic, the media have provided themes for interpersonal communication and made it richer and more diversified, in terms of contents as well as form, an argument that has been further developed by Meyrowitz (1986). Schudson concludes that "we should pay more attention to the irony of blaming the mass media for not living up to a standard, i.e., the conversational ideal, that they have themselves helped to make possible" (Schudson 1978: 328). The ideals and values that are associated with interpersonal communication are, in other words, themselves changeable. It is therefore more fruitful to think of communication forms as mutually dependent. As such, interpersonal communication and mediated communication are in constant development and under mutual influence.

Avery and McCain (1986) regard the conversational ideal as totally misleading in our attempts to understand mass communication. Instead, they recommend a new communication ideal for understanding the relationship between media and the receiver. Through such an ideal, "based on the technological and functional realities of the mass media, we can begin to understand mass communication against the background of these media's own norms and standards" (Avery and McCain 1986: 128). The point of view expressed by Avery and McCain is at first glance a reasonable one, since they reject the implicit nostalgia and romanticism associated with the interpersonal ideal. However, in their effort to de-nounce this idealistic notion of communication, they overlook the fact that the mass media themselves draw on a number of forms of interpersonal communication and in some cases, they build their entire mode of address around a simulation of interpersonal con-versations. Part of the attraction of some mass media and genres is in fact this simulation. Thus, even if a (utopian) conversational ideal is not to be taken as a standard for work produced by the mass media, analysis of this work should take into account the so-cial and psychological reality constituted by the conversational ideal and manifested through the media's continuous simulation of conversations.

For the receivers, it is clear that a simulation is taking place. When the TV host addresses the viewer, this simulation is not ful-ly associated, in a cognitive sense, with addressing someone face-to-face. But the simulated character of the communication does not render it less authentic or of a lesser rank; the receiver's reac-tions to these addresses, which are socially and psychologically real and integrated with the rest of communication, are not unlike reactions in interpersonal communication (Horton and Wohl 1986). In understanding mass media, it is necessary to maintain a double perspective of a new technological, social and psychologi-cal reality on the one hand, and a constant simulation first and foremost of the forms of interpersonal communication as well as of older forms of communication on the other.

References

Aschehoug og Gyldendals Store Nordiske Leksikon. 1980. Oslo: Kunn-skapsforlaget.
Avery, Robert K. and McCain, Thomas A. 1986. "Interpersonal and Mediated Encounters. Reorientation to the Mass Communication Process". In *Inter/Media. Interpersonal Communication in a Media World,* 3rd edition, edited by Gary Gumpert and Robert Cathcart. New York: Oxford University Press.
Barnhurst, Kevin G. 1994. *Seeing the Newspaper.* New York: St. Martin's Press.

Biocca, Frank 1997. "The Cyborg's Dilemma: Progressive Embodiment in Virtual Environments". *Journal on Computer-Mediated Communication*, vol. 3, no. 2, September.

Bolter, Jay D. and Grusin, Richard. 1999. *Remediation. Understanding New Media*. Cambridge, Mass.: MIT Press.

Carey, James. 1989. *Communication as Culture*. Boston: Unwin Hyman.

Giddens, Anthony. 1991. *The Consequences of Modernity*. Oxford: Polity Press.

Goffman, Erving. 1959. *The Presentation of Self in Everyday Life*. New York: Doubleday.

Grodal, Torben. 1997. *Moving Pictures*. Oxford: Oxford University Press.

Hall, Edward T. 1959. *The Silent Language*. Garden City, New York: Doubleday & Company.

Hall, Edward T. 1969. *The Hidden Dimension*. Garden City, New York: Anchor Books.

Hjarvard, Stig. 2000. *Mediated Encounters*. Global Media Cultures, Working Paper no. 2. University of Copenhagen.

Horton, Donald and Wohl, Richard R. 1986. "Mass Communication and Para-social Interaction: Observation on Intimacy at a Distance". In *Inter/Media. Interpersonal Communication in a Media World*, 3rd edition, edited by Gary Gumpert and Robert Cathcart. New York: Oxford University Press.

Hutchby, Ian. 2001. *Conversation and Technology*. Cambridge: Polity Press.

Johnson, Mark. 1987. *The Body in the Mind*. Chicago: The University of Chicago Press.

Lakoff, George and Johnson, Mark. 1980. *Metaphors We Live By*. Chicago: The University of Chicago Press.

Larsen, Bent Steeg. 1998. "Media Situations – a Situational View on Media Use and Everyday Life". *Sekvens 98*. Copenhagen: Dept. of Film and Media Studies.

Lombard, Matthew. 1995. "Direct Responses to People on the Screen: Television and Personal Space". *Communication Research*, vol. 22, no. 3, June.

Lombard, Matthew and Ditton, Theresa. 1997. "At the Heart of It All: The Concept of Presence". *Journal on Computer-Mediated Communication*, vol. 3, no. 2, September.

McLuhan, Marshall. 1964. *Understanding Media. The Extensions of Man*. London: Routledge & Kegan Paul Ltd.

Messaris, Paul 1997. *Visual Persuasion*. Thousand Oaks, CA: Sage.

Meyrowitz, Joshua. 1986a. *No Sense of Place*. New York: Oxford University Press.

Meyrowitz, Joshua. 1986b. "Television and Interpersonal Behaviour: Codes of Perception and Response". In *Inter/Media. Interpersonal Communication in a Media World*, 3rd edition, edited by Gary Gumpert and Robert Cathcart. New York: Oxford University Press.

Palmer, Jerry. 1990. "Genrer og medier – et kort overblik" [Genres and Media – a Brief Overview]. *MedieKultur* 14. Aalborg: SMID.

Reeves, Byron and Nass, Clifford. 1996. *The Media Equation. How People Treat Computers, Television, and New Media Like Real People and Places*. New York: GSLI Publications / Cambridge University Press.

Robins, Kevin. 1999. "Foreclosing on the City? The Bad Idea of Virtual Urbanism". In *Technocities*, edited by John Downey and Jim McGuigan. London: Sage.

Salomonsens Konversationsleksikon. 1926. Copenhagen: J. H. Shultz Forlagsboghandel.

Scannell, Paddy. 1994. "Kommunikativ intentionalitet i radio og fjernsyn" [Communicative intentionality in radio and television]. *MedieKultur* 22, August.

Scannell, Paddy. 1996. *Radio, Television & Modern Life*. Oxford: Blackwell.

Schudson, Michael. 1978. "The Ideal of Conversation in the Study of Mass Media". *Communication Research*, vol. 5, no. 3, July.

Thorsen, Michael and Møller, Hans-Georg. 1990. *TV Journalistik [Television Journalism]*. Aarhus: Forlaget Ajour.

Tuchman, Gaye. 1980. *Making News. A Study in the Construction of Reality*. New York: The Free Press.

John Caldwell

New Media/Old Augmentations: Television, the Internet, and Interactivity

Old media strategies after the dot-com crash

Many evangelists of digital media in the 1980s and 1990s built their theoretical predictions about the imminent arrival and near-term dominance of a global, interactive, networked, cyberspace on two fundamental and unfortunate flaws. First, proponents erred in their model of technological change – assuming naively that technological change is revolutionary, is marked by discontinuities with the past, and forces new kinds of cultural practice and radical social alignments. Technological change is marked as much by continuities as discontinuities, is more evolutionary than revolutionary, and is managed by existing social and cultural formations rather than replacing and eclipsing them. Second, cyber-theorists erred in promoting their visionary models of the future by dramatizing them in a rigid binary model as the antithesis of "old media" (film and television). Events of even the two short years that have passed since the world-wide, dot-com/high-tech collapse of Spring 2000 suggest two important correctives to the cyber-theorists: that "new media" technologies will depend for survival on more traditional "old economics" (involving real revenues rather than virtual ones); and that "old media" (film and television in particular) may well prove to be the "trigger application" that the cyber-prophets speculated about but looked elsewhere for.

In this article I hope to provide a cross-section of the kinds of activities that are currently being deployed in the digital, interactive, and new media realms by the ostensibly more traditional television networks and film studios. Although many of my examples will come from Hollywood studios and the American context, it is increasingly clear to almost everyone involved that film, television, and digital media today are inevitably global in character. International mergers (Vivendi/Canal+/Universal Studios) and multi-national conglomerations (AOL/Time-Warner/Turner) provide an inter-continental reach that is far beyond what either national governmental regulators or critics of media could imagine two decades ago. Both the aesthetic forms and business strategies from Sony/Columbia or Newscorp/StarNetwork/Fox that I describe are as operative and accessible world-wide today, as they are in the Japanese, American, British, or Australian boardrooms that launch and oversee such schemes. The account that follows examines four interrelated areas. I begin by surveying the institutional playing field (and institutional competitors) of the Darwinian marketplace that has emerged since the dot-com crash, paying particular attention to the difference between "technology-centered" and "content-centered" strategies for succeeding at interactivity. The second section offers the close description and analysis of the actual textual and interactive forms that several successful TV/dot-com websites employ to entertain and build audiences on-line. The third section attempts to situate these kinds of old media/online practices within a broader understanding of the flexible forms of capital, labor, and consumption that characterize current post-Fordist business practices in entertainment media. The final section concludes by offering suggestions about the prospects and cultural impact of the kinds of old media/new media augmentations I have examined here.

Technologically, the competition to launch and secure profitable and on-going forms of interactive entertainment is being waged by at least four broad groups: Cable ITV (Interactive Television), DBS ITV, Broadcast ITV, and Hollywood/online studios. Of course, for the decade up to the dot-com/high-tech crash many analysts imagined that the internet and world-wide web (by themselves) would somehow enable universal interactivity. What the web has been less successful at establishing, however, is e-entertainment; the traditional province of film and television. This failure of motion-picture entertainment on the web has as much to do with the severe shortage of enough "bandwidth" on the net as with anything else. For this reason, surviving dot-coms today regularly seek "synergies" with established media firms. The rhetoric of "convergence" a few years back used to mean the conflation of all sorts of activities and digital channels of information onto and through a single, personalized portal: the pc. As often as not today convergence signifies corporate mergers and technological alliances between internet companies and entertainment studios who can adequately capitalize them and provide "content."

In countries like the United States, the historic wiring of much of the country for cable television provided de-facto and formidable challenges to the Internet companies. Cable TV, after all, had achieved tremendous "reach" as regulated monopolies in cities nationwide. In addition to almost universal access in some cities cable TV had something the dot-coms could not get their hands on: an extensive, pre-wired system comprised of "coaxial" cable with more than enough bandwidth for both "two-way" interactivity *and* hi-resolution streaming/cablecasting of image and sound. Historically, in the American context, he who controlled the "wire" controlled the profits—as the telephone companies like AT&T had proven for decades before the 90s. Now TCI, Century Cable, and Time-Warner Cable are picking up the post-dot-com slack as formidable "off-web" players who now offer "real-time" interactivity alongside the screening of films and television programs. As a technology newer than cable TV, DBS (direct broadcast satellite) ITV companies have demonstrated sophisticated, but proprietary, systems of interactivity for their subscribers. Because DBS was digital from the start, two-way interactivity could be an integral part of its expanding service. DirectTV, for example, has formed an alliance with ShopNBC to provide two-way e-commerce alongside and related to its DBS entertainment content. Because "analog" broadcast television, a third industry, had none of the technological advantages for interactivity that Cable ITV (coaxial) or DBS (digital technology) had, many would see it as the least likely of the competitors to successfully weather the shift to digital media. Yet (as I hope to show in the section that follows) this has not been the case. Terrestrial, analog broadcasters do have and regularly utilize a "back-channel" two-way path for communication to the network after all: via the telephone line. Unlike some resilient dot-coms still trying to "stream" both hi-res image/sound on the Internet *and* interactive data-streams (a frustrating goal in a world of incompatible streaming protocols and 56K telephone modems),

TV tends to segregate the two task: hi-res image/sound flows to the television set, while real-time interactivity occurs back and forth through a simultaneous internet hook-up. From a technological point-of-view, those market-winners able to establish a dominant form of ITV will have to confront and master three factors: 1) control of technical infrastructure (coaxial Cable ITV currently dominates here); 2) market penetration or reach (analog terrestrial Broadcast ITV dominates here); and 3) "middle-ware" standardization (DBS is competitive in this regard). Middle-ware refers to the "set-top" decoding box that will be used in countless homes to deliver and process the ITV. Microsoft, Motorola, Phillips, and Sony cannot control either the reach and penetration of a system, or the infrastructure, or the lucrative "final mile" of cable to the home. Hence these corporations enter the market to intending to control market-share on the black-box middle-ware needed in any domestic set-up (with everything from WebTV to HD-Decoders to PlayStation2).

Yet, as the financial markets have dramatically shown, any investor, venture-capitalist, or corporation that places its bets on technology alone faces sobering risks. Stated quite simply: *technology does not fuel technological change; "content" does.* Audiences/users will not learn technology just to be technological, but they will learn technology to get to some unique and compelling screen-experience not otherwise available. In some ways, and despite their many activities in new media for over a decade (CDs, video-games, music, new media merchandizing) the old media studios and networks have maintained relatively conservative digital media positions: largely holding back on the sidelines as the brutal technological, infrastructural, and bankruptcy "shake-down" takes its toll on the other players. Warner Bros., Paramount, Columbia, Universal, Fox, Disney, and NBC all imagine that they control the "fuel" for the shift to digital—Hollywood's creative and intellectual "property"; the films and programs stockpiled in studio vaults (Caldwell 1995a, 1995b). As they continually experiment with interactive configurations, Hollywood and its trade organizations for the past two years have been repeating the mantra: "content is king; content is king." All of the major film studios and networks have substantial online activities, yet none of those operations are making profits in predictable ways. The much anticipated Sony Studios/Warner Bros. launch of its comprehensive, joint interactive "MovieFly" project has been delayed four times. NewCorps' much publicized interactive, downloadable service "Movies.com" has stalled in its launch, even as Miramax Studios and Comedy Central found ways to allow its users to download feature films on the net through "Sight-Sound Technologies." Yet, unfazed, these same studios intend to do with these sorts of Napster-like (for a fee) downloading schemes what the same studios have increasingly done in the home video market. The dramatic success of sales of DVD's by the studios ($3.5 billion in sales in 2000), shows the tremendous potential of "after-market" sales of films in digital form. Shifting to online downloading schemes would in effect cut out the retailers and middle-men even more-so, and provide far greater profits than the TV networks and video retailers would provide or license to the film studios.

While the Hollywood film studios' many digital activities have stuttered in their attempts to profit from online interactivity (expenditures which they typically justify as R&D), the Los Angeles-based television networks, by contrast, have pursued much broader-based forms of TV/dot-com convergence. All of the six major American networks ABC/Disney, NBC, CBS, Fox, UPN, and the WB also produce proprietary content, distributable world-wide, and all of them utilize more ubiquitous forms of online engagement with audiences. These ITV forms include: "electronic program guides (EPGs), video-on-demand (VOD), the means to access related to on-screen programming, the means to interact with advertisements, chat functions, e-mail, and personal video recorder functionality, like pause, fast-forward, and storage" (Grotticelli and Kerschbaumer 2001: 34). The strategies and focus of each network brand have different emphases. NBC is the only one of the six networks to emulate AOL and Yahoo in its attempt to be a one-stop web "portal" (NBCi). CBS has emphasized online financial services ("CBS *Marketwatch*") tied to its programs, from both the news division and new hit reality series imported from Europe, like *Survivor*. ABC has emphasized what it terms "Enhanced Content" and original off-air reporting to augment is broadcast news shows and cablecast sports shows (on ESPN). Both the WB and

Fox have authored intricate sites to cultivate fan cultures for their hit and cult series *Buffy the Vampire Slayer* and *Dawson's Creek* (WB), and the *X-Files* and *the Simpsons* (Fox) on the other. Each of these enterprises has publicly rejected the current rhetoric that the "internet is bust", by developing complex and extensive TV/dot-com texts. A closer look at several of these sites shows how television, far more than film, has succeeded at converging fandom activities, e-commerce, and on-line merchandizing as an intricate part of their television shows.

Forms of new media/old media augmentations

TV websites operative on the Net demonstrate the complicated strategies by which television in the digital age continues to extend its historical niche as a form of entertainment commerce. The most effective TV-websites succeed by keeping viewer-users engaged long after a series episode is aired, and this requires greatly expanding the notion of what a TV text is. Shows accomplish this through at least six on-line strategies: "characterized" proliferations of the text; "narrativized" elaborations of the text; "backstory" augmentations; "meta-critical" commentary; technological augmentations; and merchandizing augmentations. Although only one of these approaches may appear explicitly like a business practice (merchandizing augmentations), I will argue in the section that follows that on-line interactivity and temporality in and of themselves on sites like this embody economic exchange. They are all integral parts of the site's "branding strategy" even if the narrative and formal augmentations do not sell specific online products. "Dawson-screek.com," for example, offers to its web fans numerous possibilities to interact by utilizing each of the above mentioned six modes. The site makes special efforts, for example, to benefit from characterized proliferations, by providing users web access to the "personal lives" of its many characters and actors. The wind-swept icon of one character, Joey, seductively entices users to "click here" to delve more into her personal life. At the same time the site also enables visitors to explore all of the show's four main characters through *their* "computers" (which appear as convincing simula-

tions of Microsoft Windows icons and layout). To convince viewers that they are actually in the position to access the television
characters' computers, the site's design graphically mimics "real"
computer environments. Each week one of four different desktops
is featured so that visitors can voyeuristically peak into a range of
digital artifacts from the characters: "private" emails, AOL-style
"instant messaging" chats, journals, and even (faux) trash-cans.
Through this interchange, visitors to "Dawson's Desktop" are set-
up and positioned as unseen "hackers," secretly surveilling not just
the characters' personal computers, but the characters' "real-time"
web-chat as well, scripted and naturalized to mimic the kinds of
dialogue viewers have experienced on the televised show proper.

The website also sets up access opportunities for "intimacy."
Users can find out, for example, who's on Joey's Christmas list or
what she has written in her "college essay." This kind of back-sto-
ry elaboration fleshes out character biographies in far more detail
than a broadcast episode ever could – and makes the users better
narrative decoders of the series as well. Users are thus sutured into
the world of the characters throughout the week through variously coded internet activities. Having in one episode fictionally de-
parted from the series town of Capeside, Andie has ostensibly
been sending her friends post-cards "from Europe" (Tuscany,
Milan, Florence). The show then allows real users to sign-up to
receive an e-mailed "post-card" each time Andie reaches an additional city or location in Europe. This kind of narrativized elaboration of the text works by allowing the narrative arc of the show
(and the narrative reception of the show) to "continue" outside of
the show itself. In further linking the electronic, virtual fiction
with the user's real electronic activity, the website then allows
those same recipients to "forward" Andie's post-cards to their
own friends by using real email addresses. This device is an effective mechanism that allows the producers to further aggregate fans
of the show – with virtual email triggering a proliferation of "real"
emails through the fan-base.

The show's website also utilizes technological augmentations of
the text to secure an on-going relationship with viewers in "off-
air" time. By downloading or utilizing "Quick-time" or "Real
Video" motion-image protocols, the site invites viewers to take a

360 degree "virtual tour" of the show's "Potter's Bed and Break-fast" (a real set in the production, but a fictional building on the show). This augmentation thereby enables viewers to live vicariously in a constructed diegetic world and space outside of the show. They do so, furthermore, in a "place" that allows them to "book reservations" and to "read the guest book" in order to discern the identities of other guests that have stayed at the B&B. Technical augmentations also include another "fictional" website that users can access through links -"capesidehigh.com"- which lets the visitor read a "real" newspaper printed at the show's fictional high-school. After listening to the show's theme song on Real Audio (another downloadable extension) users can then purchase the music on-line (crossing yet another technical format). Merchandizing augmentations on the site most fully betray the centrality of e-commerce in website design and operational practice. In the early years of the web, television and film producers were publicly content to justify their expensive website initiatives as loss-leaders, or as a form of "value-added" to their existing entertainment properties or content. With the growing ubiquity of on-line shopping, however, TV-websites now almost always exploit one of the few proven methods of returning capital on the Net. The dawsoncreek.com online "store," for example, features sale items for the high-school bound user: student planners, key chains, buttons, and locker magnets are sold in a way that extends the show's text into fans' very real spaces – spaces far from either Hollywood's Capeside or the user's home and internet connection. Users on the site are encouraged to "shop the creek" for novels, collector's books, and posters to pin-up on bedroom walls. With improved streaming technologies and software links now embedded during video post-production, many shows now go a step further, by allowing viewers to immediately click on a sweater, garment, or prop worn or used by an actor. Doing so allows the user to purchase, ship, and import a show artifact to the very non-diegetic world of the audience. In this way, convergent merchandizing augmentations work to narrativize the world of the user rather than vice-versa.

If merchandized augmentations smack of complete viewer cooptation by the producing entity, another mode counterposes commerce with a mode that is in many ways more critical: meta-critical augmentations. "TVGuide.com" and "E!" ("eonline.com") are among the most popular television websites, offering as they do scheduling information, critical reviews, news items, and bits of backstory. Many successful websites have learned valuable lesson from composite print-broadcast-online entities like these. Such sites suggest that criticism, deconstruction, and analysis – even when negative and internalized – help fuel the entertainment machine. In this way, Dawsonscreek.com is like the official *X-Files* and MTV sites. All allow the viewer-user to weigh-in with critical analysis and dialogue on the given series. These critical reflections on the series are solicited both through fan chatrooms, and with contests and polls that allow viewers to vote (in Dawsonscreek.com) on such anti-official-PR spins as "the worst part of season four."

As I have argued elsewhere, any interactivity (good, bad, or indifferent) is economically valuable to producers and has been a defining goal of broadcast television since its inception in the 1940s (Caldwell 1995b: 258-262). These six recurrent forms of online textual elaboration, proliferation and augmentation – all simultaneously operative in successful TV-websites like dawsonscreek.com and thexfiles.com – also provide producers, studios and advertisers with an expansive text that dwarfs the traditional 30 and 60 minute time-slots of traditional shows. Convergent TV-websites, therefore, represent a kind of model for the mutating, migrating and aggregating textual ideals that branding, pitching, stunting, syndication, and repurposing have all aspired to in contemporary industrial practice. The story of Go.com is revealing in this regard. Disney/ABC was bound and determined to take on Internet success stories like Yahoo.com by building their own portal. Launched to great fanfare, and monitored closely by analysts seeking to underscore Disney's route to success, by January 2001 the portal was lauded as a dot-com winner by observers who marveled at the apparently immense numbers of users that frequented the site. With over 20 million discrete users in one month alone, this media/dot-com site was now approximating the scale of audience that made traditional broadcast doable. A few weeks later, however, Disney CEO Michael Eisner, pulled the plug on Go.com. He claimed that advertisers were not rushing or willing to support the Net, but did little to conceal the fact that Disney/ABC had dumped far more money into the site than they could ever see in returns. Disney's press-releases also made no acknowledgement that the company had recently paid $21.5 million to settle a legal suit charging that Disney had ripped off the proprietary name "Goto.com" from another company; or that Disney would lay off 400 programmers as it soon did. The old economic realities had, in effect, stepped forward to shut down the portal. In a way that suggested that new media could not be killed, however, Disney spokesmen surprised observers six weeks later in March, when they announced that the studio was going to revive Go.com but with a new business plan—one that did not depend on generating real revenues or profits. Their explanation "that the site can be operated with no staff, and that Disney can earn an undisclosed sum for directing its Go Traffic to partners" (Times 2001, C18) provided a more realistic version of how media/dot-com sites work – not by generating direct revenues, but by linking and referring users to the many other segments of the Disney conglomeration and its subsidiary and contract clients. This gambit and solution underscored the logic of something Hollywood had used since the early 90s to defend its costly investments into new media. That is, new media forms provided "value-added" entertainment to any brand as a whole. In this logic, media/dot-com sites would necessarily lose money as "loss-leaders" for the conglomeration, but would be justified nevertheless for using interactivity to keep users within a loop or constellation of sites and services that were either owned or contractually related to Disney/ABC/ESPN/etc.

Digital re-conglomeration/the digital entertainment studio

Semel's appointment (from Warner Bros) continues the Internet's love affair with Hollywood and comes as Yahoo! has aggressively spent the past year trying to expand its site beyond serving solely as a portal for news and information and grow into a major entertainment player of music, movies, and other original content.

> – *Marriage of new media and old media by Yahoo to*
> *prevent hostile take-over (Goldsmith and Graser 2001).*

Yahoo, Sony announce multi-year partnership ... 'If this isn't an outright marriage, it's least holding hands. Sony is also dating Yahoo's competitor AOL.com.

– Old Media/New Media courtship (Piller 2001: C5).

As I have suggested so far, it is difficult to talk about the aesthetic forms of TV/dot-com convergence and augmentation, without accounting for the cultural and economic context that informs and capitalizes such developments. Before Hollywood had to face the phalanx of new dot-com competitors in the 1990s, it had to confront broad-based changes that came with the advent of earlier digital technologies in the 1980s. In some ways the development of digital effects industry mirrors the trajectory of the television and cable industries in the past two decades, and establishes an economic context for better understanding old-media/new-media alliances. Both the TV and "f/x" (special effects) industries started the period with relatively few corporate players who dominted and controlled the market for effects and programming respectively. Both industries witnessed a rapid expansion of competitors in what came to be seen as the splintered but multi-channel (and multi-boutique) world of the 1980s. And both industries are now undergoing and feeling the effects of conglomeration. Ironically, although the digital boutiques gained advantage and market share early on – because of the cost-effectiveness of niche production and diversity of clientele – they are now being subsumed and re-aggregated under singular roofs. For example Sony – the heir of major studio Columbia – is currently making a vigorous attempt to rebuild the comprehensive studio model, but in the age of digital. Termed Sony Digital Entertainment, the company has built an "SPDE digital backbone" on the lot in Culver City to manage and support its "full-service" digital resources, including its F/X studio Sony Pictures Image works, Sony Online Entertainment, and its internet programming arm Soap City. As an integrated unit Sony now cross-collateralizes its many movie and television web-sites, its video-on-demand service "MovieFly," and its entertainment venture "ScreenBlast," which "distributes new content across Sony's digital platforms – computer and television screens, hand-held devices and vidgame consoles" (Graser 2001: 5). This is indeed

Hollywood, and the historic Columbia lot, but this is not the same restricted and inertial constellation of labor arrangements that maintained the studio's prominence in the past. Sony has reconfigured the studio system by exploiting all of the advantages of the digital boutique era—a flexible but high-skilled contract workforce, niche production specialties, high-end technologies, and implicit partnerships – all of which are now managed all under the same roof. Dreamworks, which started as a prestige motion-picture boutique when Spielberg moved beyond his Amblin Entertainment/Universal roots, now puts forward the same comprehensive posture that Sony does, as a full-service digital entertainment company.

The bankruptcies of Boss studios (in the digital f/x world) and DEN/the Digital Entertainment Network (in the media/dot-com world) underscored the precarious nature of technology-based niche markets in two very different digital industrial subcultures. In the aftermath of boutique studio obsolescence, Sony and Dreamworks now work to tame and bring "in-house" the skills of each subculture as part of each studio's stable, multi-media, transnational presence.

Innovation & technology discontinuities:
Fordism/modernism/post-fordism

Adequately theorizing about new media/old media practice, given the context I've outlined above, depends upon ones model of innovation and technological development. The impact of Fordism, modernism and Post-Fordism have made the search for innovation – as well as the quest for new technologies that are discontinuous – basic industrial goals at the newly allied studios. The current situation suggests that a re-thinking of aesthetic and academic theory is in order. In characterizing the logic of old media/new media, we would do well to make a clear distinction between an "aesthetic" or "semiotic economy" of new media on the one hand (Fiske 1987), and a "cultural" or "political economy" of new media on the other (Schiller 1999). The former approach helps explain the bias of a number of key publications on new media that have sought to "frame" new media in rather comprehensive ways (Hanhardt 1986, Hall and Fifer 1990, Druckery 1996). These critical works tend to reinscribe two intellectual ideologies as they organize and narrow the field. First, the vestiges of modernism continue to fuel critical theorization long after modernism gave way to its many "posts-". An obligatory and essential "new," that is, forms the basis for critical initiatives like these which attempt to map the field by focusing on experimental media works and artworld-like commentaries. Second, an avant-gardist predilection further demarcates the theoretical tradition, by inevitably looking for new media practices that pose as forms of resistance, deconstruction, or oppositionality. Yet few of the semioticians or aestheticians of artworld new media forms admit to the rather evident connection that exists between modernism and the Fordist economy. Historical hindsight shows a remarkable (but largely unacknowledged) congruence between modernism and Fordism. While much has been written about the Taylorist efficiencies used to engineer assembly-line mass production in the modern industrial age – tendencies that predisposed the system to redundancy and uniformity – less emphasis has been placed on Fordism's obligatory dependence on a successively manufactured "new." That is, *planned obsolescence* was an early and necessary lesson learned by industrialists.

As Lipsitz (1990) and Ewen (1997) demonstrate, without a clockwork-like invention and delivery of the "very latest" fashion or "cutting-edge" style, industrialism would simply grind to a halt precisely because of its success at market penetration (and thus over-saturation). A culture of consumerism-and-the-new emerged, which revealed advertising to be a far more vigorous and successful proponent of the modernist cutting edge than any academic or curatorial exercises might. As I have argued elsewhere (Caldwell 1995, 2001), electronic media and advertising survive only by scanning the horizon for semiotic uneven-ness (localism, marginalism, indigenism, etc.) and appropriating it as their own. A semiotic of oppositionality, that is, is the very basis for successful industrial marketing in the modern era. The glossy, knowing, minimalist ads of a hip (very) upscale publication like *Wired* demonstrate the perfect marriage between modernism and Fordism; between the semiotic imperative of oppositional marketing and the

Fordist industrial efficiencies that still drive the assembly lines of high-tech digital manufacturers world-wide that advertise in such venues. While much has changed (and accelerated) in corporate presence and pretense – for companies like NEC, Cisco, Intel, Nintendo, Yahoo, and Sony – much remains the same in both semiotic and industrial terms.

Flexible capital/flexible cultural labor

Failure of (negotiations) would raise serious questions about the credibility of the multinational corporations in managing creative content. The old-line studios and networks presided over generations of relatively peaceful relations with the artists and artisans in their employ. Will Hollywood's new rulers disrupt this tradition?

> – nostalgia for inflexible labor, Peter Bart (2001), editor, Daily Variety.

So if the industrial logic of contemporary hi-techs still depends in some ways upon Fordist and consumerist imperatives, how and why is the new media age of the dot-com so much more volatile and unsettled than the old media age of the industrialists, the Hollywood studio system, and network television? Post-Fordism emphasizes the economic importance of "flexible" manufacturing, flexible capital, and flexible labor. In contradistinction to earlier corporations that were defined by and anchored to heavy manufacturing plants, studio back-lots, or guaranteed network programming pipelines—typically protected by governmental regulations or sanctioned by nationalisms—the new economy rewards those companies adept at a range of new corporate competencies, able, that is: to quickly exploit R&D, to secure and make proprietary new intellectual properties, to mine (and then aggregate) niche demographics, to reconfigure corporate alliances, and to find and embrace "synergies" at almost every level (from workplace relations to transnational conglomeration).

In the 1990s Silicon Valley start-ups became the poster-boys of Post-Fordist glory in everything from *Wired* and *The Wall Street Journal* to books like *Nerds 2.01: A History of the Internet* (Segaller 1998). Unchained from the standard constraints of the business world, caricatured visionaries, geeks, and artists pursued their niches, venture capitalists, and IPOs with a range of unorthodox predilections. The dot-coms became exemplars of successful Post-Fordist management; lauded by many for the rapid flexibility they brought to any needed technical application or untapped market. The flaw of such paeans, of course, is that they assigned to the internet an undeserved agency and autonomy as the causal "force" that freed businesses to move and amass capital in the dizzying ways of the visionary dot-coms. The story of demise in 2000 that greeted this frenzy of over-valued speculation of the high-techs has been oft-told.

What has received less attention are the ways that digital technologies and digital business practices changed the value assigned new media forms, and changed and are changing the nature and culture of (old and new) media labor. Silicon Valley worked so well during the run-up because it altered the nature of the industrial work-force on at least two levels. First, the economic explosion left a short supply of qualified computer engineers and programmers. The hi-techs began to develop a talented but inexpensive computer work-force in Bangalore and other cities in India. This gambit, of course, lowered the R&D, manufacturing, and per unit costs of hi-tech products, even as it kept the peskier aspects involved in maintaining and developing an industrial work-force "off-shore" and out-of-sight of domestic and work-place laws. For the high-techs, Asia became a central region that manufactured products, while the Silicon Valley centers simply manufactured concepts and capital – great amounts of capital. While the dot-com run up was broadly praised as a needed and timely "economic engine" for California, fewer analysts noted the inflationary pressures had left the valley far too expensive for any of the the domestic service laborers as well. New media business practices worked so well, in part, because the companies kept any human downside at arms-length – either in programming and manufacturing plants in India, or in far cheaper apartments in bus-accessible cities like San Jose, Oakland, or Hayward. In this way, the dot-coms and old media/new media hi-techs learned well the lessons of Nike and others: Trans-nationalism is less about synergies and globalization, than about dispersing corporate responsibility into off-world re-positories.

Prospects/cultural impact

Regardless of the confident, new media make-overs unfolding in many old media companies after the dot-com crash, uncertainties about digital media still lurk as threats to the established media companies and studios. I would like to conclude by summarizing four areas in which digital technologies used in old media/new media alliances are forcing substantive changes in industrial practice. These include issues of: proprietary content and intellectual property; syndication and re-purposing; production culture labor relations in the context of digital; and industrial relations with the domestic and private spheres. All of these factors impact the institutional authoring of new media, and thus the cultural impact of those forms as well.

First, digital media technologies threaten to the centrality of proprietary content. The much reported legal soap-opera surrounding MP3 and Naptster downloading was but the tip of a very large and only partially submerged iceberg involving unauthorized duplication and piracy. "Meta-browsers" like Octopus.com, for example, allow users the ability not just to "copy" someone elses proprietary web content, but to strip such content of its original contractually based context (away from the ads of sponsors and licensors) – and to automate this process on a weekly basis – in order to re-configure it as ones own personal web publication. DVD distribution similarly raises the stakes considerably by circulating infinitely reproduce-able, high-quality "masters." While the studios labor endlessly to improve encryption schemes that technically block copiers, hackers are always but a few steps behind, and many boast that the coding protocols on DVDs can always be broken by anyone with even a rudimentary understanding of programming. The international situation creates even more anxieties. In countries like China, the technical possibilities of unauthorized duplication join with a broad range of cultural forces that sanction piracy. These sanctioning forces include the traditional Confucian notion of sharing knowledge as a moral posture; and the Marxist Chinese notion that the people own all state properties. In such a climate, guarding new media content to send revenues elsewhere makes little sense. As Michael Keane has shown (2001) Chinese television now institutionalizes what the West sees as piracy, by addressing it as "re-formatting"; essentially discounting proprietorship by explicating the shared nature of all genres. So the threat of digital culture is not one thing in all places. The CD-ripping assemblage of Napster and meta-browsing in the United States, is far different from the nationalized effort in China to find justifiable ways to extend media and develop creative industries nationwide.

Second, digital media has fundamentally altered the conditions under which the economies of film and television have traditionally been rationalized. That is, both box-office (in film) and ratings (in TV) are based on the consensus view that the economic value of any media property is determined by a snap-shot picture of its "market-share." By this, I mean that Nielson ratings and weekend box-office numbers create a static picture of how each competitor performed at a single point in time. Agreeing on who got what piece of the pie gives a market stability. Whether one wins or loses in the sweeps-week or weekend, this single-point analysis inherent in market-share models provides predictable rules that give the game stability. I would argue that digital media, by accelerating the shift to a multi-channel (rather than regulated or controlled) media marketplace has actually broken the market share benchmark by establishing performance over time as a far more important index of economic value. In the age of digital, that is, the economic value of any media content is determined by its temporal performance in syndication, and by its ability to be re-purposed or resurrected endlessly for subsequent releases, distribution windows, and ancillary markets known as well as not yet anticipated. The current, widespread success of syndicated *re-purposing* has in fact made *multi-purposing across media platforms* a starting point for many new media projects. Albie Hecht, president of Film and TV Entertainment at Nickelodeon/Nick at Nite/TNN explains the multimedia logic behind "Jimmy Neutron: Boy Genius":

Rather than merely re-purposing from one medium to another, Jimmy was created to exist in comic books, television, movies, video games, on the internet and other places right from the start. Jimmy is virtual. He's everywhere. When kid's are listening to music, playing games, watching TV, Jimmy will be there (Marlowe 2001).

Digital media projects like Nick's Jimmy Neutron ensures that front-end syndication deals (and content development based on a project's potential for reiteration across platforms) are as crucial today as initial air-dates were in electronic media's analog era. The kind of calculus needed for projecting and determining economic value in the new media era is, therefore, far less rational and predictable than old media corporations would like. This creates additional volatility and makes publicity, marketing, and spin even more crucial in fortifying media properties for the ancillary lives they aspire to in the long haul.

Third, digital media unsettles the social relations and communities at both the production and consumption ends of the media exchange. The much-noted WGA strike negotiations in Spring 2001 were widely feared as a momentous first step that might work to dismantle the tried and proven continuities that had somehow kept all of the craft unions and guilds profitably employed over time. Reactions critical of the writers came from all corners – including IATSE and the other unions – and not just from Wall Street or management's executive suites. While this hand-wringing was couched as a concern for the economic health of the region, much less concern was focused on the actual cause of the strike threats. Digital media technologies, that is, had out-paced the industry's ability to keep track of, to account for, and to reimburse – on a uniform contractual basis – revenues from the new ancillary markets. When the writers gave in, and management acquiesced, many observers realized that the agreement was only a very provisional and partial holding action. Development of digital technologies continues to threaten sweet-heart deals, union privilege, and network affiliation, even as it unsettled the willed affinity and public confidence of an extensive labor-corporate coalition that now teetered in the face of digital. This pushing-and-pulling, merging and jockeying for position in the face of digital has had a dramatic effect on the ground, and in the lived communities of the industry. That is, the studios, network control rooms, story sessions, and guild halls in Los Angeles and New York all began to evidence great anxieties and volatilities during this period. Members of the television and production communities arguably faced a far more uncertain future than those above them in the board rooms. For while Hollywood and television have jumped into digital with great public confidence, the lived communities that comprise those public fronts have had to navigate and negotiate change in ways that have substantively transformed what television and film look like and sound like in the age of digital.

Finally, digital technologies began to accelerate changes in the domestic and private spheres. While academic media and cultural studies have typically segregated research on the home (Morley and Silverstone 1990) from the production world (Gitlin 1983, Newcomb and Alley 1983), it is really no longer credible to imagine the domestic sphere as separated from the worlds of media production. Ien Ang's (1994) important research shows, in fact, how crucial an analysis and engagement with the home is for media industries, who are "desperately seeking an audience." Nick Couldry has further explicated the boundary zones that exist between producer and audience in his book *The Place of Media Power* (2000). What I am arguing is that fully understanding the new media production culture or digital economy is impossible without considering how crucial and complex audience usage and behavior has become to producers. While broadcasters in the analog era made token, obligatory efforts at understanding the audience (through ratings, diaries and questionnaires) the major Hollywood studios had settled lazily on the simply quantified bottom-lines of box-office numbers or home-video units sold. New media practice has made the traditional studio approach obsolete, and broadcaster "research" far from effective.

With the kinds of "flexible" media useage, ancillary applications, and multi-tasking in the home that I have referred to above, all of the players on the new media production end – producers, developers, investors, distributors – must have far more scientific understandings of users than they have had in the past. And this factor has exacerbated one of the internet's greatest ironies. Although the Net was predicated on de-centralized, democratic, useage for any and all unsanctioned activities, it has become the most efficient and comprehensive way yet of monitoring and surveilling viewer-user behaviors. Every line into the home, is a line out – and not necessarily for independently made digital movies or music, either. Net developers now even refer to such surveillance as "personal data mining" (Caldwell 2001). Network television was never about selling programs to audiences but about selling and delivering audiences to advertisers. When WWF Smackdown takes full-page ads in the trades to prove statistically that their "typical viewer is a computer savvy, college-educated professional" rather than working class trailer trash that concerned critics imagine (WWF 2001), they are actually escalating the financial value of the audience that they sell to advertisers. Cable, digital media and the internet – especially after the high-tech/venture capital collapse – continue the tradition of selling and packaging known audiences (no matter how splintered and narrow) to those, who for economic interests, need to make contact with them. With a "mass" market possible on the internet developers and producers almost inevitably need to do this by *aggregating* them with other niches. Search engines and Net travel have made the dynamic of "navigation" a central and compelling part of the new media experience. But any user's navigation or search on the Net also leaves documentable electronic traces of the real and material behaviors that surveys and ratings research could never approximate. Many new media/old media developers and investors, then, make the monitoring and collection of such user information an obligatory part of any business plan, start-up, and IPO.

In the early 90s "interactivity" was touted by academic theorists as the key to liberating the top-down, push media industries from their dominance over viewer/user/subordinates. Such theorists – betraying little apparent awareness for almost a century of electronic media history – ignored the fact that broadcasting and television had always necessarily been interactive in fundamental ways. For while television never had pull-down menus, it did have 800 numbers, sweepstakes, viewer editorial comments, telethons, public affairs and public service departments, FCC licensing reports on station responsivity to local communities, marketing research, and constantly articulated product consumption numbers (the advertising industry's Holy Grail). All of these provided important forms of audience data needed to keep the industrial engines of electronic media churning away. In the commercial sphere today – at least outside of academic research labs and new media galleries – the very same concern with quantifying and leveraging audience behavior informs almost any new media development. Multi-platforming, re-purposing, syndication, meta-browsing, bots, and multi-tasking all mean new media has to develop more sophisticated ways to rationalize the economies of digital. Fortunately for developers, the very network connections, portals, fiber-optic cables and broad-band lines that liberate digital users utilize, also enable new media producers to "lock-on" to viewer-user behaviors and tastes with great confidence. The flexible economies of new media/old media digital alliances require that responsiveness – not hegemony – must be a corporate house rule for digital developers as well. Less agents of hegemony, new media artists and developers at industry gatherings and mixers, obsess on questions about what users want or need. Their livelihoods depend upon it.

References

Bart, Peter. 2001. "Key Question: Is strike about ego or economics?" *Daily Variety*, April 16, 2001.

Caldwell, John T. 1995a. "Hybridity on the Media Superhighway: Techno-Futurism and Historical Agency". *Quarterly Review of Film and Video*, vol. 16, no.1.

Caldwell, John T. 1995b. *Televisuality: Style, Crisis, and Authority in American Television*. New Brunswick: Rutgers University Press.

Caldwell, John T. 2000b. "Theorizing the Digital Landrush". In *Electronic Media and Technoculture*, edited by John Caldwell. New Brunswick: Rutgers University Press.

Caldwell, John T. 2001. "Introduction: Cultural Studies in the Age of Digital". *Emergences: Journal for the Study of Media and Composite Cultures*. Special Issue on: "Globalization, Convergence, and Identity," vol 11, no. 1.

Couldry, Nick. 2001. *The Place of Media Power*. London: Routledge.

Ewen, Stuart. 1997. *P.R.*. New York: Basic Books.

Fiske, John. 1987. *Television Culture*. New York: Routledge.

Gitlin, Todd. 1983. *Inside Prime Time*. New York: Pantheon.

Goldsmith, Jill and Marc Graser. 2001. "Semel Ends Yahoo! Search: Hollywood Vet Tapped to Top Popular Portal as CEO". *Daily Variety*, April 18: 1.

Graser, Marc. 2001. "Sony Woos Z's Chey: Techno Veep to Ramp Up SPDE's Web Efforts". *Daily Variety*, April 23: 5.

Grotticelli, Michael and Ken Kerschbaum. 2001. "ITV: How We Define It". *Broadcasting and Cable*, July 9: 34.

Hall, Doug and Fifer, Sally. 1990. *Illuminating Video: An Essential Guide to Video Art*. San Francisco: Aperture Foundation/Bay Area Video Coalition.

Hanhardt, John. 1986. *Video Culture: A Critical Investigation*. Rochester: Visual Studies Workshop.

Keane, Michael. 2001. "Cultural Technology Transfer: Redefining Content in the Chinese Television Industry". *Emergences: Journal for the Study of Media and Composite Cultures*, vol. 11, no. 2.

Lipsitz, George. 1990. *Time Passages: Collective Memory and American Popular Culture*. Minneapolis: University of Minnesota Press.

Morley, David and Roger Silverstone. 1990. "Domestic Communications – Technologies and Meanings". *Media, Culture, and Society*, vol. 12, no. 1: 31-55.

Newcomb, Horace and Robert S. Alley. 1983. *The Producer's Medium*. New York: Oxford University Press.

Piller, Charles. 2001. "Yahoo, Sony Announce Multi-Year Partnership". *Los Angeles Times*, August 1: C5.

Segaller, Stephen. 1998. *Nerds 2.01: A History of the Internet*. New York: TV Books/L.L.C./ Oregon Public Broadcasting.

Schiller, Daniel. 1999. *Digital Capitalism*. Cambridge, MA: MIT Press.

Times. 2001. "Disney's Go.com Site Avoids Shutdown". *Los Angeles Times*, March 13: C18.

WWF. 2001. "Our Typical Viewer is a Computer-savvy, College Educated Professional ..." *Broadcasting and Cable*, April 30: 33.

Contributors

Ib Bondebjerg is Professor at the Department of Film and Media Studies, University of Copenhagen.

John Thornton Caldwell is Associate Professor at the Department of Film and Television, University of California at Los Angeles.

John Corner is Professor of Communication Studies at the School of Politics and Communication Studies, University of Liverpool.

John Ellis is Head of Research and Professor of Moving Image Studies at the Bournemouth Media School, Bournemouth University.

Mikkel Eskjær is Ph.D. student at the Department of Film and Media Studies, University of Copenhagen.

Torben Grodal is Professor at the Department of Film and Media Studies, University of Copenhagen.

Stig Hjarvard is Professor at the Department of Communication, Journalism and Computer Science, Roskilde University.

Anne Jerslev is Associate Professor at the Department of Film and Media Studies, University of Copenhagen.

Arine Kirstein is Ph.D. student at the Center for Cultural Studies, Roskilde University.

Birger Langkjær is Assistant Professor at the Department of Nordic Literature, University of Copenhagen.

Johannes Riis is Assistant Professor at the Department of Film and Media Studies, University of Copenhagen.